THE
Mediterranean
COOKBOOK

The Mediterranean Cookbook

Anna Macmiadhacháin   Mary Reynolds

Claudia Roden   Helge Rubinstein

Lyric

Contents

Foreword	6
Introduction	8
Appetizers, soups and salads	10
Fish dishes	42
Meat dishes	60
Poultry and game	92
Light meals, vegetables and sauces	108
Desserts	136

First published 1979 by
Lyric Books Limited
66b The Broadway
London NW7

© 1979 Lyric Books Limited

ISBN 0 7111 0009 8

Printed in Yugoslavia

Foreword

It is around the Mediterranean that some of the oldest and most refined civilizations were born, where the abundance of food and the ease with which fruit and vegetables could be cultivated enabled the Egyptians, Greeks and Romans to provide for their great armies and legions.

The Mediterranean is still a rich sea in the variety of the species of fish and shellfish it contains, and around its shores are some of the most fertile terrains.

It is also around the Mediterranean that many people spend their leisure and vacation time. These constant comings and goings have developed a special sense of hospitality and a desire to please; and how better to please than flattering the appetite of your guests by serving unusual, appetizing and colorful dishes consisting of the fishes from its sea, the vegetables from its land, and the herbs, fruits and spices that have ripened under its sun.

There is a lot here to inspire the housewife, or amateur chef, particularly in the realm of creativity. The reader will not be bored with lengthy recipes and descriptions or by complicated technical terms and jargon, which make certain cookery books sound to the novice like pure sorcery, and the work of the chef look like that of a conjuror. Rather, he or she will be impressed by the variety of recipes and the beauty of presentation.

Cooking itself is fun; so are the following pages which I find pleasurable and instructive. The recipes are simple but exotic and should help you to cook the dish that you enjoyed by the sea shore last summer, or by candlelight in a small restaurant in Spain, Provence or Greece. Only the guitars will be missing.

The ingredients are easy to obtain, and flexibility is given in their choice. Most of them are usually reasonably priced. The method and preparation processes are straightforward to understand, giving alternatives of both ingredients and utensils.

The result of the whole book is spectacular, and spectacular dishes will always have a role in emphasizing a celebration.

REMY FOUGÈRE
EXECUTIVE HEAD CHEF
ROYAL GARDEN HOTEL, LONDON

Introduction

There is no greater uplift for a jaded spirit than a visit to one or other of the sun- and sea-lapped countries or islands of the Mediterranean. These are lands richly endowed with natural resources where local products, rather than the studied art of chefs, form the basis of a marvellously colorful and flavorsome cuisine.

For the greater part of the year Mediterranean food markets are a technicolor world where succulent fruits are brilliantly hued, the vegetables shining with freshness and color, the herbs more aromatic and the spices spicier. The sea provides a treasure house of unfamiliar species – many of them delicious, some rubbery and disappointing, many destined to add character to the colorful fish soups which are such a feature of coastal restaurants all around the Mediterranean.

Poor grazing land may militate against the rearing of prime beef cattle (except in areas like Tuscany where the meat is renowned for its quality) but the ingenuity of various countries in producing original ragoûts and exquisitely spiced minced meat dishes is an inspiration. Sheep thrive on poor pasture, so lamb is the favorite meat of many Middle Eastern countries where it forms the basic ingredient of the kebabs which sizzle over charcoal braziers, as well as the richly flavored meat balls. Pork and pork products are popular too except, of course, in Jewish and Moslem countries where religious customs forbid the eating of pig meat.

Other ever recurring ingredients, indispensable to the flavor, savor and aroma of Mediterranean dishes, are green and black olives, with olive oil for cooking; garlic and onions; rough local wines; sheep and goats' milk cheeses; dried fruits and nuts, especially almonds, walnuts and pine nuts; shiny purple eggplants (aubergines), red and green peppers, zucchini (courgettes) and tasty tomatoes; lemons, oranges, limes, melons and peaches; herbs – especially basil, thyme, marjoram, mint and parsley; saffron, coriander, cumin, cinnamon, allspice and ginger.

When a visit to the Mediterranean is a physical impossibility this book can help you to conjure up the warm scents and flavors of authentic dishes without leaving your own kitchen. You can even take an extended vacation and visit each country in turn, savoring the individual character of its cuisine. For despite the interchange of trade and inevitable cross-fertilization of ideas, each Mediterranean country has retained a clearly recognizable national cuisine, even if this is often extended with 'borrowed' dishes that have crossed the frontier and been adopted at some time during the turbulent past history of the area.

For instance you might start off a Spanish evening by serving a selection of *tapas*, those hot and cold starters, such as Chicken Croquettes or Melon and Ham, which accompany a choice of sherries or wines and can sometimes be substantial enough to make a meal. On the French Riviera dinner might begin with the simple Tomato Salad, or with a plate of Crudités, and finish with goats' milk cheese and fresh fruit. If your meal started with a colorful *caponata* (or vegetable antipasto) and ended with Chilled Zabaione you would of course have traveled beyond the toe of Italy to Sicily, where both ancient Greek and Roman influences can still be found in the local dishes. An entire Greek evening can be prepared ahead: this might consist of Taramosalata served with hunks of bread and olives, or Stuffed Vine Leaves, followed by a large dish of Mousaka combining minced meat and vegetables in one richly flavored casserole. Sweet-toothed friends will welcome one or other of the syrup-drenched confections, such as Nut Stuffed Pastry Rolls, to end a Greek, Turkish or Middle Eastern meal. These are easy and inexpensive to make using *phyllo* pastry bought ready made from a delicatessen. A modern Israeli meal must include traditional Jewish dishes as well as some of the excellent vegetables and fruit which that country produces so prolifically.

Hospitality in the Arab countries is legendary, as are the many highly original salads and delicious dips, all of them served as meal starters with flat Arab bread. As you travel with this book through Syria, Lebanon and across North Africa pause awhile to try an Egyptian party piece, such as Rice with Meat and Nuts made in an attractive ring mould, the traditional Tunisian Meat Pie, or the Moroccan Couscous.

It is not nearly as difficult as you might think to bring the colorful scents and flavors of these sunny lands to our Western kitchens.

Appetizers, soups and salads

Piquant Artichokes

Les Artichauts avec Sauce Ravigotte

The large globe artichokes which grow plentifully in Provence are usually served cold as an appetizer, with a piquant sauce which combines some of the characteristic flavourings of the area.

Preparation time: 10 minutes (plus chilling)
Cooking time: 20 to 40 minutes
To serve: 6

Metric/Imperial
6 *large globe artichokes*
Sauce:
½ *teaspoon salt*
½ *teaspoon freshly ground black pepper*
¼ *teaspoon sugar*
½ *teaspoon French mustard*
2 *tablespoons wine vinegar*
6 *tablespoons olive oil*
1 *clove garlic, peeled and finely chopped*
2 *teaspoons capers, finely chopped*
1 *gherkin, finely chopped*
2 *shallots, finely chopped*
small bunch of fresh parsley, finely chopped
4 *green olives, stoned and finely chopped*

American
6 *large globe artichokes*
Sauce:
½ *teaspoon salt*
½ *teaspoon freshly ground black pepper*
¼ *teaspoon sugar*
½ *teaspoon French mustard*
2 *tablespoons wine vinegar*
6 *tablespoons olive oil*
1 *clove garlic, peeled and finely chopped*
2 *teaspoons capers, finely chopped*
1 *small pickle, finely chopped*
2 *shallots, finely chopped*
small bunch of fresh parsley, finely chopped
4 *green olives, pitted and finely chopped*

Trim the stalks off the artichokes. Cook in boiling salted water until a leaf can be pulled out easily and each artichoke is tender at its base. Leave the artichokes upside down to drain and cool. When cool enough to handle, remove the chokes by gently opening out the leaves and scooping out the hairy choke with a teaspoon. Then close the artichoke up again.

Make the sauce by combining the salt, pepper, sugar and mustard to a smooth paste. Add the vinegar and then the oil, slowly, stirring well so that all the ingredients become amalgamated. Stir in the garlic, capers, gherkin (pickle), shallots, parsley and olives.

Serve the sauce in small dishes, one for each person, so that everyone can dip their artichoke leaves in one by one, before eating the tender base of each leaf, and then the heart.

Left: Piquant Artichokes
Centre: Lemon Mushroom Hors d'Oeuvre
Right: Les Crudités

Lemon Mushroom Hors d'Oeuvre

Champignons en Marinade

These mushrooms are served in Nice either alone or as part of a mixed hors d'oeuvre. Small button or pickling (pearl) onions can be cooked and served in the same way, together with the mushrooms or separately.

Preparation time: 5 minutes
Cooking time: 15 to 20 minutes
To serve: 6

Metric/Imperial
150 ml/¼ pint water
150 ml/¼ pint white wine
150 ml/¼ pint olive oil
juice of 1 lemon
6 peppercorns, lightly crushed
6 juniper berries, lightly crushed
2 cloves garlic, peeled and halved
2 bay leaves
1 sprig of fresh thyme
1 teaspoon salt
0.5 kg/1 lb white, unopened button mushrooms, trimmed
1 tablespoon finely chopped fresh parsley

American
⅔ cup water
⅔ cup white wine
⅔ cup olive oil
juice of 1 lemon
6 peppercorns, lightly crushed
6 juniper berries, lightly crushed
2 cloves garlic, peeled and halved
2 bay leaves
1 sprig of fresh thyme
1 teaspoon salt
1 lb white, unopened button mushrooms, trimmed
1 tablespoon finely chopped fresh parsley

Put all the ingredients except the mushrooms and parsley into a heavy saucepan and bring to the boil. Boil for 2 minutes, then simmer for 10 minutes and strain. Return to the pan.

Put the mushrooms into the strained marinade and simmer for 5 minutes, until they are just tender. Pour into a serving dish and leave to cool. Sprinkle on the parsley just before serving.

Les Crudités

Raw Vegetable Hors d'Oeuvre

A simple but delicious hors d'oeuvre, *crudités* are excellent for long, desultory conversations in the sun. The selection of vegetables can be varied according to what is in season. Sometimes a plate of coarse country salami is also served at the same time.

Preparation time: 10 to 15 minutes
Cooking time: nil
To serve: 6

Metric/Imperial/American
0.5 kg/1 lb mixed fresh young vegetables
 – carrots, beans, very young peas in the pod, radishes, strips of (Florence) fennel, florets of cauliflower, peppers seeded and cut into strips, small firm tomatoes, sticks of celery, slices of cucumber
bowls of sauce: mayonnaise, aioli (see page 46), rouille (see page 132), tapenade (see page 14), or caviar Provençal (see page 14)
bowl of sea (coarse) salt
plate of olives, green or black

Arrange the vegetables attractively on a platter, leaving small ones whole, cutting larger ones into strips or slices.

Serve with either one or a selection of sauces.

Caper and Olive Dip

Tapenade

A typical Provençal dip, this can be served with toast, croûtons or biscuits (crackers), or with crudités (see page 13) or hard-boiled (hard-cooked) eggs, or with French bread.

Preparation time: 10 to 15 minutes
Cooking time: nil
To serve: 4 to 6

Metric/Imperial/American
100 g/4 oz (¾ cup pitted) black olives, stoned
2 tablespoons capers
8 anchovy fillets
2 tablespoons olive oil
squeeze of lemon juice
freshly ground black pepper

Put the olives, capers and anchovies into a mortar or blender and pound or blend to a fine paste. Blend in the olive oil drop by drop, using the same method as for making mayonnaise. You should end up with a thick paste, somewhat the same consistency as mayonnaise. Add lemon juice and pepper to taste.

Anchovy Spread

Anchoiade

Serve this Provençal appetizer with drinks.

Preparation time: 15 minutes
Cooking time: nil
To serve: 6

Metric/Imperial/American
2 x 50 g/1¾ oz cans anchovy fillets, drained
2 cloves garlic, peeled and crushed
1 tablespoon wine vinegar
3 tablespoons olive oil (including, if you like, the oil from the cans)
good (large) squeeze of lemon juice
freshly ground black pepper
1 to 2 thin slices of bread per person

Put the anchovies and garlic in a mortar or blender and mash or blend to a fine paste. Slowly add the vinegar and then the oil, drop by drop, as you would for making mayonnaise. Season to taste with lemon juice and pepper.
Grill (broil) the slices of bread on one side. Spread the *anchoiade* on the other side and flash briefly under the very hot grill (broiler). Cut into squares or triangles and serve hot.

14

Countryman's Caviare

Caviar Provençal

Serve this dip with toast, croûtons or biscuits (crackers), or with crudités (see page 13) or hard-boiled (hard-cooked) eggs.

Preparation time: 45 minutes to 1¼ hours
Cooking time: nil
To serve: 6

Metric/Imperial/American
1 kg/2 lb aubergines (eggplants)
3 cloves garlic, peeled and crushed
4 tablespoons (¼ cup) olive oil
juice of ½ lemon
salt
freshly ground black pepper
Garnish:
chopped fresh parsley or 1 anchovy fillet

Slice the aubergines (eggplants) in half lengthways and grill (broil) very gently on both sides until very soft – this may take up to 1 hour, and you must be careful not to let the skin burn. Scoop out the flesh and place in a blender or mortar, together with the garlic. Blend together, then slowly add the oil, drop by drop, as for making mayonnaise. Add the lemon juice and season to taste.
Serve in a bowl, garnished with parsley or a rolled anchovy fillet.

The twisted trunks of olive trees

Provençal Sandwich

Pan Bania

A substantial snack, *Pan Bania* is sold in the streets or served in cafés, with a glass of wine. The exact proportion or combination of ingredients is not important, and varies according to what happens to be available.

Preparation time: 5 minutes (plus 30 minutes pressing)
Cooking time: nil
To serve: 4 to 6

Metric/Imperial/American
1 French loaf
1 clove garlic, peeled and halved
1 tablespoon olive oil
1 onion, peeled and thinly sliced
2 tomatoes, sliced across
anchovy fillets
stoned (pitted) olives
gherkins (pickles), sliced
capers

Slice the bread in half lengthways and rub both cut surfaces with the cut side of the garlic. Dribble on the olive oil. Then distribute whatever filling you wish to use evenly over one side. Cover with the other half of the bread and press together with a heavy weight for about 30 minutes. The flavour of the filling will permeate the entire sandwich, which will also become pleasantly soggy.

Above left: Caper and Olive Dip
Above right: Countryman's Caviare
Below left: Anchovy Spread
Below right: Provençal Sandwich

Left: Neapolitan Cheese and Anchovy Toasts. Right: Eggs with Tuna Fish Mayonnaise

Neapolitan Cheese and Anchovy Toasts

Crostini alla Napoletana

The flavours of anchovies and oregano give these quickly made cheese savouries a typically Italian taste. They can be prepared ahead of time and slipped into the oven to serve as appetizers or hot snacks. If Bel Paese is not available try using a well-flavoured processed cheese instead.

Preparation time: 10 minutes
Cooking time: 15 minutes
Oven temperature: 180°C/350°F, Gas Mark 4
To serve: 4

Metric/Imperial
4 slices of bread, cut 5 mm/¼ inch thick, crusts removed

100 g/4 oz Bel Paese cheese, thinly sliced
8 anchovy fillets
freshly ground black pepper
a little dried oregano
8 thin slices of tomato
8 teaspoons olive oil

American
4 slices of bread, cut ¼ inch thick, crusts removed
¼ lb Bel Paese cheese, thinly sliced
8 anchovy fillets
freshly ground black pepper
a little dried oregano
8 thin slices of tomato
8 teaspoons olive oil

Cut each slice of bread diagonally in half. Arrange in a single layer on a well-oiled baking sheet. Cover each piece of bread completely with cheese. Cut the anchovy fillets lengthways in two and criss-cross the pieces over the cheese. Grind a little pepper over each of the *crostini*, sprinkle with oregano and

top with a slice of tomato.

Just before baking dribble a teaspoon of olive oil over each of the *crostini*. Bake for about 15 minutes, or until the cheese has melted and the bread is crisp. Serve hot.

Eggs with Tuna Fish Mayonnaise

Uova Sode Tonnata

A delicious appetizer, this can be prepared several hours in advance of serving time. The same sauce, but without the cream, can be used to fill scooped-out ripe tomatoes to make yet another attractive Italian appetizer.

Preparation time: 20 minutes
Cooking time: nil
To serve: 4

Metric/Imperial
4 large hard-boiled eggs
8 anchovy fillets
Tuna fish mayonnaise:
75 g/3 oz canned tuna fish
200 ml/⅓ pint thick home made
  mayonnaise
few drops of lemon juice
white pepper
1 to 2 tablespoons thin cream
Garnish:
8 small gherkins
sprigs of fresh parsley

American
4 large hard-cooked eggs
8 anchovy fillets
Tuna fish mayonnaise:
3 oz canned tuna fish
1 cup thick home made mayonnaise
few drops of lemon juice
white pepper
1 to 2 tablespoons light cream
Garnish:
8 small pickles
sprigs of fresh parsley

Pork Terrine

Press the tuna fish through a sieve, then beat it, a little at a time, into the mayonnaise. Season to taste with lemon juice and pepper and stir in enough cream to thin the sauce to a thick coating consistency.

Shell the eggs and halve them lengthways. Arrange in a circle, cut sides down, on a flat serving dish and coat each egg with tuna mayonnaise. Cut the anchovy fillets in half lengthways and make a cross on each egg. Cut the gherkins (pickles) into fan shapes and arrange between the eggs around the edge of the dish. Just before serving put parsley sprigs in the centre of the dish.

Pork Terrine

Terrine de Campagne

The pâtés of the south of France are distinguished by a strong flavouring of herbs and often the addition of juniper berries. Serve this pork terrine as a first course, or as the main dish for a summer lunch, accompanied by some gherkins (pickles) and capers.

Preparation time: 30 minutes (plus overnight chilling)
Cooking time: 1½ to 2 hours
Oven temperature: 220°C, 425°F, Gas Mark 7, reduced to 190°C, 375°F, Gas Mark 5
To serve: 6 or 12 (see above)

Metric/Imperial
1 kg/2 lb belly of pork, skinned and
  boned
225 g/8 oz pig's liver
1 onion, peeled and finely chopped
2 cloves garlic, peeled and finely
  chopped
1 tablespoon chopped fresh rosemary
1 teaspoon chopped fresh thyme
salt
12 peppercorns, roughly crushed
12 juniper berries, roughly crushed
2 tablespoons brandy
1 egg
100 g/4 oz streaky bacon or pork fat,
  sliced
1 sprig of fresh rosemary
1 bay leaf

American
2 lb fresh pork sides, skinned and boned
½ lb pork liver
1 onion, peeled and finely chopped
2 cloves garlic, peeled and finely
  chopped
1 tablespoon chopped fresh rosemary
1 teaspoon chopped fresh thyme
salt
12 peppercorns, roughly crushed
12 juniper berries, roughly crushed
2 tablespoons brandy
1 egg
¼ lb bacon slices or pork fat back, sliced
1 sprig of fresh rosemary
1 bay leaf

Mince (grind) the belly of pork and the liver together. Put into a large bowl and add the onion, garlic, chopped rosemary, thyme, salt, peppercorns and juniper berries. Beat the brandy into the egg, then add to the bowl and mix everything well together. Fry a small pat of the mixture in a little butter to taste for seasoning.

Line a 1 litre/2 pint terrine or loaf pan with the bacon or pork fat and spoon in the meat mixture. Lay the sprig of rosemary and the bay leaf on top. Place the terrine in a roasting pan, add water to come halfway up the sides and put into the hot oven. Bake for 20 minutes, then reduce the temperature and cook for a further 1 to 1½ hours, or until the pâté has shrunk away from the sides of the dish, and the juice is clear. Leave to cool. If possible place a weight on top before the fat sets. Refrigerate at least overnight before serving, to allow the flavour to mature.

Pork Terrine

Jumbo Shrimp Fries

Gambas al Ajillo

For this delicious start to a meal you can use the prawns (shrimp) either beheaded and shelled or in their whole state. The latter are messier to eat but more authentically Spanish.

Preparation time: 10 minutes
Cooking time: about 4 minutes
To serve: 4

Metric/Imperial
24 cooked large prawns
150 ml /¼ pint olive oil (or groundnut or
*   soya bean oil)*
4 cloves garlic, peeled and roughly
*   chopped*
pinch of cayenne pepper

American
24 cooked jumbo shrimp
⅔ cup olive oil (or groundnut or soya
*   bean oil)*
4 cloves garlic, peeled and roughly
*   chopped*
pinch of cayenne pepper

Remove the heads and shells of the prawns (shrimp), if preferred. Have ready four individual earthenware bowls or dishes, thoroughly heated.

Heat the olive oil in a frying pan (skillet) and toss in the garlic. Turn it around in the oil. Just as it begins to colour, add the prawns (shrimp) and cook for 2 to 3 minutes in the sizzling hot oil, turning once. Add the cayenne. Turn immediately into the hot dishes, with all the oil. Serve with plenty of crusty bread, and paper napkins.

Chicken Croquettes

Croquetas de Pollo

Croquettes of all kinds are popular in Spain. Usually about the size of half a chipolata (link) sausage, they are crisp on the outside and delightfully smooth and soft inside.

Preparation time: 20 minutes
Cooking time: about 8 minutes
To serve: 4

Metric /Imperial
50 g /2 oz butter
2 tablespoons flour
300 ml /½ pint mixed milk and chicken
*   stock (or milk only if stock is not*
*   available)*
0.5 kg /1 lb minced cooked chicken

salt
freshly ground black pepper
1 egg, beaten
2 tablespoons dry breadcrumbs
oil for frying

American
¼ cup butter
2 tablespoons flour
1¼ cups mixed milk and chicken stock
*   (or milk only if stock is not available)*
2 cups ground cooked chicken
salt
freshly ground black pepper
1 egg, beaten
2 tablespoons dry breadcrumbs
oil for frying

Melt the butter in a saucepan and stir in the flour. Gradually stir in the liquid and cook, stirring, until the sauce is thick and smooth. Stir in the minced (ground) chicken and season well. Continue cooking for about 1 minute, on a low heat, until the mixture is firm enough to hold together in a mass. Remove from the heat and allow to cool slightly, then, with floured hands, form the mixture into little sausage shapes. Brush these with beaten egg and coat with breadcrumbs. Shallow fry in hot oil until golden brown. Serve hot or cold.

Fried Whitebait

Chanquetes Fritos

Whitebait, crisply fried, has a unique and delicate flavour.

Preparation time: 5 to 10 minutes
Cooking time: 3 to 4 minutes
To serve: 4

Metric/Imperial
0.5 kg /1 lb fresh whitebait
50 g /2 oz flour
1 teaspoon salt
150 ml /¼ pint olive oil (or groundnut or
*   soya bean oil) for frying*
1 lemon, cut into quarters

American
1 lb fresh whitebait
½ cup flour
1 teaspoon salt
⅔ cup olive oil (or groundnut or soya
*   bean oil) for frying*
1 lemon, cut into quarters

A fish market in Calpe, Southern Spain

Put the whitebait in a colander and rinse briefly with cold water. Spread them out on a cloth or paper towels and pat dry. Dust lightly with salted flour. The fish should be left whole. Heat some oil in a frying pan (skillet) and quickly fry the whitebait, a few at a time, turning once. Drain on paper towels and serve as soon as possible on small heated plates, garnished with wedges of lemon.

Above right: Chicken Croquettes
Centre: Fried Whitebait
Below: Jumbo Shrimp Fries

Melon and Ham

Melon y Jamón

This pleasant and unusual hors d'oeuvre comes from Andalucia. In Spain serrano ham, a fine raw cured ham rather similar to Parma ham, would be used. If this is not available you could use a good smoked ham, but of course it would change the character of the dish.

Preparation time: 2 to 3 minutes
Cooking time: nil
To serve: 4

Metric/Imperial
½ ripe melon, chilled
8 thin slices of serrano ham

American
½ ripe melon, chilled
8 thin slices of serrano ham

Slice the melon into four, remove the seeds and serve on small plates with two slices of ham per person.

Left: Melon and Ham
Centre: Toasted Almonds
Right: Egg Nests

Toasted Almonds

Almendras al Parrilla

A very simple alternative to the usual peanuts to serve with pre-dinner drinks, these are popular in the south of Spain, and go very well with a glass of sherry.

Preparation time: 5 minutes
Cooking time: 4 to 5 minutes
To serve: 4

Metric/Imperial
225 g/8 oz blanched almonds, split in
    half
50 g/2 oz butter

American
½ lb (2 cups) blanched almonds, split in
    half
¼ cup butter

Arrange the almonds in a single layer in the grill (broiler) pan with a few pieces of butter dotted about. Toast under the preheated grill (broiler) for a few minutes, watching the nuts carefully, and turning them once. When they are golden brown drain off any surplus butter and serve the nuts in small dishes.

Egg Nests

Huevos al Nido

This is a Spanish way of using up left-over mashed potatoes.

Preparation time: 30 minutes
Cooking time: 8 to 10 minutes
To serve: 4

Metric/Imperial
0.5 kg/1 lb mashed potatoes
2 tablespoons milk
25 g/1 oz butter
½ teaspoon salt
2 spring onions or shallots, finely
    chopped or 2 tablespoons chopped
    fresh chives
4 eggs, separated
olive oil (or vegetable oil) for frying

20

American

2 cups mashed potatoes
2 tablespoons milk
2 tablespoons butter
½ teaspoon salt
2 *scallions* or *shallots, finely chopped,* or
   2 tablespoons chopped fresh chives
4 eggs, separated
olive oil (or *vegetable oil) for frying*

If the potatoes are cold, warm the milk and melt the butter in it. (If the potatoes are still warm, this will not be necessary.) Mix thoroughly with the potatoes. Add the salt and finely chopped onions (scallions), shallots or chives and mix thoroughly into the potatoes, creaming with a fork.

Divide into four and form into balls. This is easier if the potato mixture is allowed to cool. Make a hollow on the top of each ball and carefully put an egg yolk into each. Whisk the whites until fairly firm. Brush each ball of potato with egg white.

Heat some oil (about 2.5 cm/1 in) in a frying pan (skillet) until a light haze forms above it, then carefully fry each potato nest, basting with the hot oil until golden, and the egg yolk just set. Remove on to hot plates and serve at once.

21

Avocado Purée

This dip has made a recent appearance on Middle Eastern soil since the introduction of the avocado by Israel. It may be varied by stirring in a little mayonnaise and some flaked tuna or some cream cheese. Serve with very thin slices of toast or biscuits (crackers) as an appetizer or as an accompanying cream sauce for grilled (broiled) chicken or fish.

Preparation time: about 15 minutes
Cooking time: nil
To serve: 6

Metric/Imperial/American
3 ripe avocados
juice of 1 lemon
1 to 2 cloves garlic, peeled and crushed
 (optional)
salt
freshly ground black pepper
½ mild Spanish onion, peeled and grated
4 tablespoons (¼ cup) olive oil
3 tablespoons finely chopped fresh
 parsley
pinch of sugar

Peel the avocados and remove the stones (seeds). Mash the flesh. Add the rest of the ingredients and mix well.

Humus bi Tahina

Chick Pea and Sesame Meal Salad

This thick creamy paste, together with *falafel* (page 23) in half a pouch of *pitta* bread, has become the Israeli national meal-in-the-street.

It makes a tasty appetizer, served with bread to dip in, as well as a side dish for kebabs and all types of grilled (broiled) meats and fish. It is the kind of food which is made by tasting constantly and gradually adding whatever seems to be lacking. Although in the past chick peas had to be soaked overnight, then boiled with soda before they could become tender, the quality available today is more easily softened and needs only about 4 hours soaking.

Preparation time: 20 minutes
Cooking time: 1½ to 2 hours
To serve: about 6

Metric/Imperial
175 g/6 oz chick peas, soaked for 4
 hours or overnight
salt
150 ml/¼ pint jar tahina paste (sesame
 meal)

juice of 2 lemons
2 cloves garlic, peeled and crushed
freshly ground black pepper
Garnish:
finely chopped fresh parsley
a sprinkling of cayenne or paprika
a few black olives (optional)

American
1 cup chick peas, soaked for 4 hours or
 overnight
salt
5 fl oz jar tahina paste (sesame meal)
 (about ⅔ cup)
juice of 2 lemons
2 cloves garlic, peeled and crushed
freshly ground black pepper
Garnish:
finely chopped fresh parsley
a sprinkling of cayenne or paprika
a few black olives (optional)

Drain the chick peas and put them in a saucepan. Cover with fresh water, bring to the boil and simmer for about 2 hours or until they are soft, adding salt when they are tender. Drain, reserving the cooking water. Keep a few chick peas whole for decoration, and put the rest through a food mill or blender with as much of the cooking water as is necessary to achieve a thick cream. Add

the tahina, lemon juice, garlic and salt and pepper to taste. Beat or blend to a smooth creamy consistency. It is often easier to blend the mixture in smaller batches.

Serve on shallow plates garnished with chopped parsley, cayenne or paprika and the whole chick peas or, if you like, black olives.

Falafel

Chick Pea Patties

This is a national dish shared by Israelis and Egyptians. Both never seem to tire of the little patties which are fried by street vendors at all times of the day. The Egyptians have been making them at home reputedly since pharaohic times with dried white broad (lima) beans. The Israelis have adopted a chick pea version with undisguised delight. Serve as an appetizer with drinks or as part of a buffet meal.

Preparation time: about 1 hour
Cooking time: 30 minutes
To serve: 6 to 8

Metric/Imperial
0.5 kg/1 lb chick peas, soaked in water
* for at least 24 hours*
225 g/8 oz Spanish onion, peeled and
* grated, or a mixture of this with*
* spring onions, finely chopped*
finely chopped fresh parsley
finely chopped fresh coriander leaves
* (optional)*
2 cloves garlic, peeled and crushed
1 teaspoon cayenne pepper
1 teaspoon ground cumin
salt
25 g/1 oz flour
oil for deep frying
a few sprigs of fresh parsley to garnish

American
1 lb (about 2 cups) chick peas, soaked in
* water for at least 24 hours*
½ lb Spanish onion, peeled and grated, or
* a mixture of this with scallions, finely*
* chopped*
finely chopped fresh parsley
finely chopped fresh coriander leaves
* (optional)*
2 cloves garlic, peeled and crushed
1 teaspoon cayenne pepper
1 teaspoon ground cumin
salt
¼ cup flour
oil for deep frying
a few sprigs of fresh parsley to garnish

Left: Avocado Purée
Centre: Humus bi Tahina
Right: Falafel

Drain the chick peas and mince or pound them to a pulp. A food processor will do this very well.

Put the onions, parsley and coriander through the mincer (grinder) or food processor, too, if you have one. Add garlic, cayenne pepper, cumin and salt to taste, then the chick peas and flour. Mix and work all the ingredients together until well blended. The flour helps to bind the paste.

Roll into small balls about 2.5 cm/1 inch in diameter and flatten into patties. Let them rest for 15 minutes, then deep fry in hot oil in batches, turning them over once until they are a rich brown. Drain on paper towels.

Serve hot garnished with a little parsley, and accompanied by a chopped mixed salad of lettuce, cucumber and tomatoes and Humus bi Tahina. It is also nice to drop the falafel into the pouch of pitta bread.

Miniature Meat Balls

Keftethakia

Meat balls are popular throughout Greece, where miniature ones are offered as appetizers or larger ones as a main course. They can be made from either lamb or beef provided the meat is lean and very finely minced (ground). They must always be tasty and well seasoned; popular flavourings include chopped fresh mint, grated cheese or marjoram.

Preparation time: 30 minutes, plus 1 hour for chilling
Cooking time: 7 to 10 minutes
To serve: 4 as a main course, 6 to 8 as appetizers

Metric/Imperial
50g/2 oz firm white crustless bread
3 tablespoons water or *wine*
2 tablespoons olive oil
50 g/2 oz peeled and very finely chopped onion
450 g/1 lb finely minced lean beef or *lamb*
1 egg, beaten
2 tablespoons finely grated dry cheese
1 tablespoon finely chopped fresh mint or parsley
¼ teaspoon dried marjoram
salt
freshly ground black pepper
flour for coating
oil for frying

American
2 slices firm white crustless bread
3 tablespoons water or *wine*
2 tablespoons olive oil
½ cup peeled and very finely chopped onion
1 lb finely ground lean beef or *lamb*
1 egg, beaten
2 tablespoons finely grated dry cheese
1 tablespoon finely chopped fresh mint or parsley
¼ teaspoon dried marjoram
salt
freshly ground black pepper
flour for coating
oil for frying

Soak the bread in the water or wine. Meanwhile heat the olive oil in a heavy based saucepan and fry the onion very gently until soft but not coloured, about 6 to 8 minutes. Remove from the heat.

Squeeze the bread dry and add to the onion with the minced (ground) meat, egg, cheese, mint or parsley, marjoram and salt and pepper to taste. Beat the mixture thoroughly with a wooden spoon, or knead with your hands, until very well mixed and smooth.

Depending on the size of balls required, take a small or large spoonful of the mixture at a time and roll into a ball between well floured hands. Cover and chill for at least 1 hour, until firm.

When ready to cook heat 3 to 4 tablespoons of oil in a large frying pan (skillet). When hot, fry the meat balls in several batches over moderate heat for 6 to 10 minutes according to size, shaking the pan frequently to brown them evenly. Lift the meat balls out of the pan with a perforated spoon, drain on crumpled kitchen paper and keep warm in the oven until all are ready to serve.

Cheese Triangles

Tiropitakia

These crisp, flaky, bite-size cheese nibbles are a delicious form of *mezze* and are often served with drinks in the Greek islands as well as on the mainland. Once you get the hang of folding the narrow strips of pastry to form triangles around the filling they are simple to make and bake. Crumble or mash the Feta cheese with a fork before using; if using curd (cottage) cheese instead, remember that additional salt will be needed.

Preparation time: about 40 minutes
Cooking time: 15 to 20 minutes
Oven temperature: 180°C/350°F, Gas Mark 4
To serve: makes about 4 dozen

Metric/Imperial

225 g/8 oz Feta or *curd cheese*
100 g/4 oz finely grated tasty dry cheese,
    e.g. kefalotiri, Parmesan or Cheddar
2 tablespoons chopped fresh parsley
2 medium eggs, lightly beaten
freshly ground black pepper
salt if necessary
225 g/8 oz (about 12 sheets) phyllo
    pastry (see note on page 148)
100 g/4 oz butter, melted

American

1 cup crumbled or mashed Feta or *small
    curd cottage cheese*
1 cup finely grated tasty dry cheese, e.g.
    kefalotiri, Parmesan or Cheddar
2 tablespoons chopped fresh parsley
2 eggs, lightly beaten
freshly ground black pepper
salt if necessary
½ lb (about 12 sheets) phyllo pastry
    (see note on page 148)
½ cup butter, melted

Put both the cheeses into a bowl, add the parsley and eggs and beat to a soft-ish paste. Taste, and season generously.

Heat the oven and oil two or three flat baking sheets.

Lay the sheets of phyllo pastry flat. Mark the longer side into 5 cm/2 inch wide strips and cut through. Cover to prevent the strips drying out.

Take two strips of pastry at a time and put one on top of the other. Brush the top one lightly with melted butter. Place a small teaspoon of the cheese mixture about 2.5 cm/1 inch from one end of the strip. Fold the end over to form a small triangle, then continue folding over and over, always forming a triangle, to the end of the strip. Place on an oiled baking sheet. When all the triangles are pre-pared brush the tops with the remaining melted butter.

Bake in the hottest part of the oven for 15 to 20 minutes, until the little triangles are golden.

Note: Some Greek cooks like to deep fry the cheese triangles for 3 to 5 minutes until golden, instead of baking them, in which case they do not require brushing with butter.

Left: Miniature Meat Balls
Centre: Cheese Triangles
Right: Cucumber in Yogurt

Cucumber in Yogurt

Anguri me Yaóurti

Fresh, crisp cucumbers should be used for this very popular refreshing and ver-satile mixture. In Greece it is served in small bowls as a first course or as a side salad with a main dish. It also provides an unusual and delicious sauce when served with grilled (broiled) fish or chicken.

Preparation time: 15 minutes
Cooking time: nil
To serve: 3 to 4 as a first course or salad, 6 as a sauce

Metric/Imperial

1 medium cucumber, peeled and finely
    chopped or diced
salt
300 ml/½ pint plain yogurt
1 clove garlic, peeled and finely crushed
1 tablespoon olive oil
1 to 2 teaspoons white wine vinegar
white pepper
chopped fresh parsley or *mint to garnish*

American

2 cucumbers, peeled and finely chopped
    or diced
salt
1¼ cups plain yogurt
1 clove garlic, peeled and finely crushed
1 tablespoon olive oil
1 to 2 teaspoons white wine vinegar
white pepper
chopped fresh parsley or *mint to garnish*

Put the cucumber into a bowl and stir in 1 teaspoon salt. Leave for 15 minutes. In another bowl mix together the yogurt, garlic, oil and vinegar.

Drain as much liquid from the cucumber as possible, then fold the cucumber into the yogurt mixture. Sea-son to taste with salt and pepper. Cover and chill. Sprinkle with parsley or mint before serving.

25

Poached Eggs with Yogurt

Çilbir

A very pleasant way of making an unusual dish out of ordinary poached eggs reflects Turkey's special fondness for yogurt. In a country where the secret of longevity is attributed to it, yogurt is often present at meal time. This makes a good snack meal served with bread, but can also be an appetizer or a breakfast dish.

Preparation time: 5 minutes
Cooking time: 15 minutes
To serve: 6

Metric/Imperial
6 eggs
vinegar
600 ml/1 pint plain yogurt, at room
   temperature
1 to 2 cloves garlic, peeled and crushed
   (optional)
salt
freshly ground black pepper
Garnish:
40 g/1½ oz butter
1 tablespoon paprika

American
6 eggs
vinegar
2½ cups plain yogurt at room
   temperature
1 to 2 cloves garlic, peeled and crushed
   (optional)
salt
freshly ground black pepper
Garnish:
3 tablespoons butter
1 tablespoon paprika

Poach the eggs in the usual way by sliding them, not more than two at a time, into barely trembling water with a little vinegar, and cooking them for 3 to 5 minutes or until the white is firm. Remove carefully with a slotted spoon and drain well.

Beat the yogurt with garlic, salt and pepper.

Melt the butter and stir in the paprika.

Serve each egg covered with yogurt and garnished with a dribble of melted paprika butter.

Yogurt Cream Cheese

Labna

The health-giving qualities of yogurt have always been appreciated East of the Mediterranean where it is usually made at home. Thickened by straining and well flavoured, this Arab favourite makes a refreshing appetizer to be dipped into and eaten with bread, as well as a side dish for a light meal. It is very nice with olives.

Preparation time: 10 minutes (plus 8
   hours draining)
Cooking time: nil
To serve: 4 to 6

Metric/Imperial/American
600 ml/1 pint (2½ cups) plain yogurt
½ to 1 teaspoon salt
white pepper
2 tablespoons finely chopped fresh mint
   or 1 tablespoon crushed dried mint
   leaves (optional)
1 clove garlic, peeled and crushed
   (optional)
Garnish:
a dribble of olive oil
a sprinkling of paprika
a few fresh mint leaves

Beat the yogurt with salt to taste. Pour into a fine dampened cheesecloth or muslin in a large sieve. Or tie the corners of the cloth together and suspend the bundle over a bowl or the sink. Let the whey drip for 8 hours or overnight. Transfer the resulting thick cream cheese to a serving bowl. Add pepper to taste, and mint or garlic, if liked. Stir well and garnish with olive oil, paprika and mint leaves.

Alternatively, you may serve the cream cheese rolled into little balls in the oiled palm of your hand.

Egg and Lemon Soup

Soupa Avgolemono

Rich homemade chicken stock is the usual basis of this refreshing soup which acquires its lemony flavour and velvety

Above: Yogurt Cream Cheese. Below: Poached Eggs with Yogurt

texture from the addition of lemon juice and eggs. In Greece homemade meat or fish stock is sometimes used instead of chicken stock.

Preparation time: 10 minutes, asuming the stock is available
Cooking time: about 25 minutes
To serve: 5 to 6

Metric/Imperial
1.5 litres/2½ pints chicken stock
1 to 2 stock cubes if necessary
50 g/2 oz rice
2 large eggs
2½ tablespoons lemon juice
salt
freshly ground black pepper
1 tablespoon finely chopped fresh
parsley

American
1½ quarts chicken stock
1 to 2 bouillon cubes if necessary
¼ cup rice
2 large eggs
2½ tablespoons lemon juice
salt
freshly ground black pepper
1 tablespoon finely chopped fresh
parsley

Bring the stock to the boil in a large saucepan, then taste it and if necessary add stock cubes to strengthen the flavour. Throw in the rice and simmer gently until the grains are just tender, about 12 to 15 minutes.

Beat the eggs with a whisk until well mixed and frothy and add the lemon juice. Stir in about 4 tablespoons of the simmering stock, then pour slowly back into the saucepan, stirring constantly. Over very low heat continue cooking and stirring for a few minutes, just until the soup thickens enough to coat the back of the spoon lightly. On no account allow to boil or curdling may result.

Add salt and pepper to taste, sprinkle with parsley and serve at once.

Taramosalata

Smoked Fish Roe Dip

Tarama is the salted roe of grey mullet and is used by the Greeks as the basis for a deliciously zesty, creamy pink 'dip'. It is served as a *mezze* (appetizer), piled in a bowl, garnished with black olives and accompanied by crusty bread or dry toast. It can also form part of a platter of mixed appetizers. A soft piece of freshly smoked cod's roe is an excellent substitute for *tarama*, and the dip is quickly made with the help of an electric blender. Without a blender vigorous pounding is necessary, preferably with the aid of a pestle and mortar, to achieve a smooth dip.

Preparation time: 25 minutes by hand, 10 minutes in a blender
Cooking time: nil
To serve: 4 to 6

Metric/Imperial
50 g/2 oz firm white crustless bread
4 tablespoons cold water
150 g/5 oz smoked cod's roe
1 clove garlic, peeled and finely crushed, or 1 tablespoon finely grated onion
2 tablespoons lemon juice
150 ml/¼ pint olive oil
freshly ground black pepper
black olives to garnish

American
2 slices firm white crustless bread
¼ cup cold water
5 oz smoked cod's roe
1 clove garlic, peeled and finely crushed, or 1 tablespoon finely grated onion
2 tablespoons lemon juice
⅔ cup olive oil
freshly ground black pepper
black olives to garnish

Soak the bread in the water for several minutes, then squeeze as dry as possible with your hands. Put the squeezed bread into a mortar or bowl and crush and beat it with a pestle or wooden spoon until smooth.

Scrape the soft cod's roe off the skin and add, little by little, to the bread, mashing and beating well after each addition. When all the roe has been incorporated work in the garlic or onion and 1½ tablespoons of the lemon juice, beating until the mixture is very smooth.

Using a whisk, beat in the oil a spoonful at a time, checking that each addition is absorbed before adding the next. When half of the oil has been added and absorbed add the rest in a thin stream, beating continuously, as if making mayonnaise. Season to taste with pepper and the remaining lemon juice, then cover and refrigerate until required. Serve garnished with black olives.

Note: If using an electric blender add the roe, lemon juice and oil alternately to the squeezed bread, adding a very little water if the mixture should become too stiff to work.

Above: Taramosalata
Below: Egg and Lemon Soup

Courgette (Zucchini) Soup

Zuppa di Zucchini

In Italy, a land which grows such luscious vegetables, it is not surprising to find some delicious soups. This is a pale green, delicately-flavoured yet very nourishing soup. If no stock is available use water with chicken stock cubes.

Preparation time: 15 minutes
Cooking time: 35 to 40 minutes
To serve: 6

Metric/Imperial
50 g/2 oz butter
100 g/4 oz onion, peeled and sliced
0.75 kg/1½ lb courgettes, thinly sliced
1.5 litres/2½ pints chicken stock
2 eggs
3 tablespoons finely grated Parmesan cheese
1 tablespoon chopped fresh basil, or 2 tablespoons chopped fresh parsley
salt
freshly ground black pepper
For serving:
small crustless slices of freshly toasted bread
grated Parmesan cheese

American
¼ cup butter
¼ lb onion, peeled and sliced
1½ lb zucchini, thinly sliced
3 pints chicken stock
2 eggs
3 tablespoons finely grated Parmesan cheese
1 tablespoon chopped fresh basil, or 2 tablespoons chopped fresh parsley
salt
freshly ground black pepper
For serving:
small crustless slices of freshly toasted bread
grated Parmesan cheese

Melt the butter in a large pan, add the onion and fry gently for 5 minutes. Add the sliced courgettes (zucchini), stir well to mix with the butter and cook over low heat for 7 or 8 minutes, stirring frequently. Add the stock and bring to the boil, then cover and simmer gently until soft, about 20 minutes. Purée the soup in an electric blender or pass through a sieve, then return to the pan.

Bring the soup back to boiling point. Beat the eggs, cheese and herbs together thoroughly in a bowl and beat in a few tablespoons of the hot soup. Pour all into the saucepan and stir continuously over low heat for 2 to 3 minutes, until the soup thickens slightly; do not allow to boil or it may curdle. Check the seasoning.

Put a slice of toast in each soup plate, pour the soup over it and serve immediately. Hand the cheese separately.

Mussels Taranto-Style

Zuppa di Cozze alla Tarantina

Taranto is famous for its fine mussel beds. Although this recipe sounds like a soup there is only a small amount of liquid so it is more like a dish of mussels cooked in wine. Serve it as a first course with some crusty bread.

Preparation time: 20 minutes
Cooking time: 25 minutes
To serve: 4

Metric/Imperial
2.75 litres/5 pints large fresh mussels
4 tablespoons olive oil
1 onion, peeled and finely chopped
3 cloves garlic, peeled
2 tablespoons chopped fresh parsley
300 ml/½ pint dry white wine
freshly ground black pepper
4 slices of bread, 5 mm/¼ inch thick

American
3 quarts large fresh mussels
¼ cup olive oil
1 onion, peeled and finely chopped
3 cloves garlic, peeled
2 tablespoons chopped fresh parsley
1¼ cups dry white wine
freshly ground black pepper
4 slices of bread, ¼ inch thick

Scrub and scrape the mussels to remove the beards and then wash in several changes of cold water until free from sand. Discard any mussels that fail to shut when given a sharp tap. Cover with fresh cold water and leave in a cool place until ready to cook.

Heat the oil in a wide saucepan, add the onion and 2 of the garlic cloves and cook gently for about 10 minutes or until the onion is soft; discard the garlic. Stir in the parsley, wine and a generous seasoning of pepper, but no salt. Leave to simmer gently for about 5 minutes.

Meanwhile, toast the slices of bread and rub them with the remaining clove of garlic cut in half. Put one slice in each soup plate.

Add the mussels to the wine mixture in the saucepan and cook over high heat, shaking the pan frequently so that they all come in contact with the heat. In about 10 minutes, as soon as all the mussels open (discard any that fail to open), ladle them into the soup bowls on top of the toast. Carefully pour the liquid over the mussels, making sure that any sand or sediment is left behind in the pan. Serve immediately.

'Ragged Egg' Chicken Soup

Stracciatella

The word *stracciatella* means 'little rags', and you cook this soup only until the eggs break up into flakes or rags. It is a very nourishing soup from Lazio and very quickly made whenever some good homemade chicken stock is available.

Preparation time: 10 minutes
Cooking time: 5 minutes
To serve: 4 to 6

Metric/Imperial
2 eggs
2 tablespoons fine semolina
3 tablespoons grated Parmesan cheese
salt
freshly ground black pepper
grated nutmeg
1.2 litres/2 pints chicken stock

American
2 eggs
2 tablespoons cream of wheat
3 tablespoons grated Parmesan cheese
salt
freshly ground black pepper
grated nutmeg
2½ pints chicken stock

Beat the eggs, semolina (cream of wheat) and cheese together in a bowl. Add seasonings of salt, pepper and nutmeg and beat in about 150 ml/¼ pint (⅔ cup) of the chicken stock.

Heat the rest of the stock in a saucepan. When almost but not quite boiling, beat in the egg mixture. Cook the soup over low heat for 2 to 3 minutes, beating frequently, and as soon as the eggs break up into flakes serve it.

Left: Courgette (Zucchini) Soup
Centre: Mussels Taranto-Style
Right: 'Ragged Egg' Chicken Soup

Mallorcan Fish Soup

Sopa de Pescado Mallorquin

Most coastal regions of Spain have a version of fish soup, usually a thick *bouillabaisse* type, containing a mixture of fish and several vegetables including potatoes. This one from Mallorca is flavoured with fennel and thyme, which grow prolifically on the island and give the soup a special flavour. If fresh herbs are not available, use a pinch each of dried.

Preparation time: 30 minutes
Cooking time: 40 minutes
To serve: 4 to 6

Metric/Imperial
1 kg/2 lb assorted fish, including hake, halibut, whiting, bass, bream, or any white fish, cleaned
salt
1 bay leaf
4 tablespoons olive oil
4 onions, peeled and sliced
4 tomatoes, skinned and chopped
1 green pepper, cored, seeded and sliced
2 cloves garlic, peeled and chopped
4 small or 2 large potatoes, peeled and cut into chunks
1 tablespoon chopped fresh parsley
1 sprig of fresh fennel, chopped
1 sprig of fresh thyme, chopped
1 sprig of fresh marjoram, chopped
a few saffron threads or ½ teaspoon saffron powder
4 slices of brown bread (optional)

American
2 lb assorted fish, including hake, halibut, whiting, bass, porgy, or any white fish, cleaned
salt
1 bay leaf
¼ cup olive oil
4 onions, peeled and sliced
4 tomatoes, skinned and chopped
1 green pepper, cored, seeded and sliced
2 cloves garlic, peeled and chopped
4 small or 2 large potatoes, peeled and cut into chunks
1 tablespoon chopped fresh parsley
1 sprig of fresh fennel, chopped
1 sprig of fresh thyme, chopped
1 sprig of fresh marjoram, chopped
a few saffron threads or ½ teaspoon saffron powder
4 slices of brown bread (optional)

Put the fish in a large saucepan of water with salt and the bay leaf. Bring to the boil and simmer for about 15 minutes, or until the fish is just tender. Remove the skin and bones, then flake the fish.

Reserve it and 1 litre/2 pints (2½ US pints) of the strained stock.

Heat the olive oil in a large flameproof casserole, add the onions, tomatoes, green pepper, garlic and potatoes, cover and cook gently for 15 minutes. Stir in the parsley, the reserved fish stock, the herbs and saffron. (If you use saffron threads infuse them in a very little boiling water first, as this will draw out the colour and flavour.) Carefully check the fish again for bones and add it to the pot. Stir gently and simmer, partially covered, for 15 to 20 minutes, or until the potatoes are soft and the pieces of fish thoroughly cooked. Take the pot to the table and serve hot. In Mallorca a thin slice of brown bread is placed in each person's bowl before the soup is ladled in.

Catalan Vegetable Soup

Sopa de Legumbres Catalan

Cooking in Catalonia is probably the best in Spain because it is both light and subtle, yet satisfying. It is also very 'seasonal' by nature, and this is a springtime soup, when the vegetables are at their best. Another characteristic of Catalan soups is the *pelota*, a ball of mixed meat, nuts and herbs added to give extra flavour.

Preparation time: 30 minutes
Cooking time: about 40 minutes
To serve: 4 to 6

Metric/Imperial
a few each of as many young fresh vegetables as available— carrots, onions, broad beans, peas, celery, tomatoes and potatoes, peeled and chopped as necessary
1 litre/2 pints good stock, preferably chicken
salt
freshly ground black pepper
50 g/2 oz sobresada, if possible (this is a special Catalan sausage) or chorizo, sliced
Pelotas:
100 g/4 oz minced beef
2 cloves garlic, peeled and crushed
100 g/4 oz pine nuts or blanched almonds, crushed
1 tablespoon chopped fresh parsley
a little sherry
1 tablespoon flour
salt
freshly ground black pepper
oil or lard for frying

American
a few each of as many young fresh vegetables as available—carrots, onions, lima beans, peas, celery, tomatoes and potatoes, peeled and chopped as necessary
2½ pints stock, preferably chicken
salt
freshly ground black pepper
2 oz sobresada, if possible (this is a special Catalan sausage) or chorizo, sliced
Pelotas:
¼ lb ground beef
2 cloves garlic, peeled and crushed
1 cup pine nuts or blanched almonds, crushed
1 tablespoon chopped fresh parsley
a little sherry
1 tablespoon flour
salt
freshly ground black pepper
oil or lard for frying

Make the *pelotas* first. In a small bowl mix together the beef, garlic, nuts and parsley thoroughly, using just enough sherry to bind the mixture. Form it into small balls. Mix the flour with salt and pepper and use to coat the balls. Fry in shallow oil or lard until evenly browned. Drain on paper towels.

Put the prepared vegetables into a large saucepan or flameproof earthenware casserole with the stock and bring to the boil. Season to taste, then add the sausage and the *pelotas*. Simmer very gently until all the vegetables are tender and the liquid has reduced slightly, about 20 to 30 minutes. Serve with croûtons.

Above and right: Catalan Vegetable Soup
Left: Mallorcan Fish Soup

Left: Gazpacho. Right: Cold Almond and Grape Soup

Gazpacho

Chilled Soup from Andalucia

Gazpacho is known to most people, as it is one of Spain's major contributions to international cuisine. But it is strange to think that this cold soup originated as a humble peasant concoction, made to sustain and refresh those who could afford no better. Traditionally the ingredients were pounded together in a large mortar and left in a cool shadowed place to be consumed in the fields as a midday meal. Nowadays almost everyone uses an electric blender and refrigerator to make the preparation easy. There are many variations of this ancient dish. This one is from Andalucia.

Preparation time: 30 minutes (plus 1 hour chilling)
Cooking time: nil
To serve: 4

Metric/Imperial/American
4 ripe tomatoes, skinned and chopped
2 green peppers, cored, seeded and chopped
½ (1) cucumber, peeled and sliced
1 to 2 cloves garlic, peeled and chopped
1 thick slice of white bread, crusts removed, soaked in water and squeezed dry
4 tablespoons (¼ cup) olive oil
2 tablespoons wine vinegar

600 ml/1 pint (2½ cups) cold water
a few fresh mint leaves, chopped (optional)
salt
Garnish:
2 hard-boiled eggs, shelled and diced
½ (1) cucumber, peeled and diced
1 red pepper, cored, seeded and diced
1 sweet onion or 2 shallots, peeled and finely chopped

Put the prepared vegetables, garlic and bread into the blender and work to a purée (or pound in a mortar). Add the oil and vinegar. Blend for a few seconds longer and pour into a bowl. Dilute with the cold water, add the mint if using and salt to taste and stir well. Chill for at least 1 hour. Serve with ice cubes added at the last minute. The ingredients for the garnish should be served in separate small bowls and handed around to sprinkle on the soup.

Cold Almond and Grape Soup

Sopa Blanca al Uvas

A deliciously refreshing cold soup from the Southern coast of Spain, this has a garlic flavour that may surprise you.

Preparation time: 30 minutes (plus 1 hour chilling)
Cooking time: nil
To serve: 4

Metric/Imperial
100 g/4 oz blanched almonds
2 cloves garlic (or more to taste), peeled
½ teaspoon salt
1 tablespoon olive oil
1 tablespoon wine vinegar
600 ml/1 pint water
225 g/8 oz white grapes, skinned, pips removed and cut in half
8 ice cubes

American
1 cup blanched almonds
2 cloves garlic (or more to taste), peeled
½ teaspoon salt
1 tablespoon olive oil
1 tablespoon wine vinegar
2½ cups water
½ lb white grapes, skinned, seeds removed and cut in half
8 ice cubes

Thoroughly pound the almonds and garlic with the salt in a mortar, or use an electric blender.

Add the oil gradually, then the vinegar until a smooth consistency is achieved.

Transfer to the bowl in which you will serve the soup and stir in the water and the prepared grapes. Add the ice cubes and chill for 1 hour, or more if possible. Stir before serving.

Garlic Soup

Sopa de Ajo

Spanish garlic soup is an ancient peasant soup which is so simple that foreigners may scorn it. It is surprisingly good, however.

Preparation time: 10 minutes
Cooking time: 20 minutes
To serve: 4

Metric/Imperial/American
4 tablespoons ($\frac{1}{4}$ cup) olive oil
4 large cloves garlic, peeled and roughly chopped
$\frac{1}{2}$ stale white loaf, broken into walnut-sized pieces
1 litre/2 pints (1 quart) water
salt
2 eggs, beaten

Heat the oil in a large saucepan and gently fry the garlic until softened. Gradually add the bread pieces, turning them in the hot oil without browning them. Remove from the heat when all the bread is in the pan and carefully stir in the water. Add salt to taste and bring to the boil. Simmer for about 15 minutes or until the bread has become swollen and soft. Just before serving, stir in the beaten eggs (may be omitted if preferred). Serve very hot.

Lentil Soup with Vermicelli

Shorbat el Ads

All types of lentils are used to make a variety of soups dearly loved throughout the Middle East. The tiny red ones widely available here are best as they disintegrate very quickly. A sustaining first course, this is especially welcome in cold weather months.

Preparation time: 10 minutes
Cooking time: 50 minutes
To serve: about 6

Metric/Imperial
2 tablespoons oil
1 large onion, peeled and chopped
1 clove garlic, peeled and crushed
350 g/12 oz red lentils, washed if necessary
1.5 litres/2$\frac{1}{2}$ pints chicken stock
salt
freshly ground black pepper
1 teaspoon ground cumin
$\frac{1}{2}$ teaspoon ground coriander
juice of $\frac{1}{2}$ lemon
75 g/3 oz vermicelli, crushed

American
2 tablespoons oil
1 large onion, peeled and chopped
1 clove garlic, peeled and crushed
1$\frac{1}{2}$ cups red lentils, washed if necessary
3 pints chicken stock
salt
freshly ground black pepper
1 teaspoon ground cumin
$\frac{1}{2}$ teaspoon ground coriander
juice of $\frac{1}{2}$ lemon
1 cup crushed vermicelli

Heat the oil in a saucepan, add the onion and fry until lightly coloured. Add the garlic and stir until golden and sweet smelling. Stir in the lentils, 1 litre/1$\frac{3}{4}$ pints (1 quart) of the stock, salt and pepper to taste, the cumin, coriander and lemon juice. Bring to the boil and simmer gently until the lentils have disintegrated, usually about 40 minutes. The time varies according to their quality.

Add the vermicelli and remaining stock, if necessary, for a light consistency. Continue simmering until the vermicelli are tender.

Left: Garlic Soup
Right: Lentil Soup with Vermicelli

Stuffed Vine Leaves

Dolmathes

In spring and early summer the young fresh leaves are gathered from the vines to make these popular Greek appetizers. Later, when the leaves become tough or are not available, leaves preserved in brine, or canned leaves, are used instead. The rice-stuffed *dolmathes* given here can be served hot or cold. If the minced (ground) meat and rice stuffing (see page 122) is used instead, the rolls are usually served hot. Five to six hot *dolmathes* each make an unusual first course, especially when moistened with the remaining cooking liquid mixed with yogurt.

Preparation time: about 1 hour
Cooking time: 1½ hours
To serve: 7 to 8 (makes about 40 rolls)

Metric/Imperial
6 tablespoons olive oil
175 g/6 oz onion, peeled and very finely chopped
175 g/6 oz long-grain rice
300 ml/½ pint water
1 tablespoon tomato purée
salt
freshly ground black pepper
50 g/2 oz currants
25 g/1 oz pine nuts
1 tablespoon finely chopped fresh mint or parsley
1 x 300 g/11 oz can vine leaves (about 50 leaves)
juice of 1 lemon, made up to 150 ml/ ¼ pint with water

American
6 tablespoons olive oil
1½ cups peeled and very finely chopped onion
1 cup long-grain rice
1½ cups water
1 tablespoon tomato paste
salt
freshly ground black pepper
⅓ cup currants
¼ cup pine nuts
1 tablespoon finely chopped fresh mint or parsley
1 x 11 oz can vine leaves (about 50 leaves)
juice of 1 lemon, made up to ⅔ cup with water

Heat 4 tablespoons of the oil in a heavy based saucepan and fry the onion gently until soft and golden, about 10 minutes. Add the rice and stir for several minutes until all the grains are glistening with oil. Add the water, tomato purée (paste) and salt and pepper to taste. Bring to the boil, stir, cover tightly and simmer over very low heat until all the liquid has been absorbed, about 15 to 20 minutes. Stir in the currants, pine nuts and mint or parsley and check the seasoning. Leave to cool.

Meanwhile turn the canned vine leaves into a colander to drain. Stand the colander in a large bowl, cover the leaves with boiling water and leave for a few minutes, shaking the colander gently to help separate the layers of leaves. Drain, cover with cold water and drain again. This should remove all excess salt. Separate the leaves carefully and spread them flat, dull or vein side uppermost. Use about 10 broken or small leaves to line the bottom of a medium flameproof casserole.

Place a heaped teaspoon of stuffing in the centre of each leaf (varying the amount of stuffing to suit the size of the leaves). Fold the stem end, then the two sides, over the stuffing, and roll up firmly.

Place the rolls, seams downwards, side by side in layers in the casserole, packing them tightly to prevent movement while cooking. Sprinkle them with the remaining oil and pour in the lemon juice mixture. Bring the liquid to simmering point, cover the pan tightly and simmer very gently for about 1 hour until tender. If serving cold leave in the pan until quite cold, then arrange the rolls on a serving dish.

Stuffed Vine Leaves

A vine leaf in the sun

Greek Summer Salad

Greek Summer Salad

Salata Therini

Individual side salads dressed with olive oil and lemon juice are popular throughout Greece. The salad may consist of a single vegetable, such as cooked broccoli or cauliflower, or it may be almost a meal in itself like this mixed salad topped with cubes of white Feta cheese, black olives and herbs.

Preparation time: 20 minutes
To serve: 4

Metric/Imperial
8 to 12 crisp lettuce leaves
4 firm ripe tomatoes, skinned and
   quartered
½ cucumber, peeled and thickly sliced
1 mild onion, peeled, thinly sliced and
   pushed into rings

2 green peppers, cored, seeded and thinly
   sliced in rings
175 to 225 g/6 to 8 oz Feta cheese, cubed
24 large black olives
2 tablespoons chopped fresh parsley or
   mint
½ teaspoon dried marjoram
Dressing:
6 tablespoons olive oil
2 tablespoons lemon juice
salt
freshly ground black pepper

American
8 to 12 crisp lettuce leaves
4 firm ripe tomatoes, skinned and
   quartered
1 cucumber, peeled and thickly sliced
1 mild onion, peeled, thinly sliced and
   pushed into rings
2 green peppers, cored, seeded and thinly
   sliced in rings
about ½ lb Feta cheese, cubed
24 large black olives

2 tablespoons chopped fresh parsley or
   mint
½ teaspoon dried marjoram
Dressing:
6 tablespoons olive oil
2 tablespoons lemon juice
salt
freshly ground black pepper

Tear the lettuce leaves into pieces and arrange on four side plates to form a base for the salads.

Build up the ingredients in layers with pieces of tomato, cucumber, onion and green pepper. Arrange the cheese cubes on the top. Surround with the olives and sprinkle with the herbs.

Whisk the ingredients for the dressing together until well mixed, and serve separately.

35

Salad with Croûtons and Walnut Oil

Salade aux Chapons

For garlic lovers only.

Preparation time: 10 minutes
Cooking time: nil
To serve: 6

Metric/Imperial/American
4 tablespoons (¼ cup) walnut oil
4 thin slices of French bread
1 clove garlic, peeled and halved
salt
freshly ground black pepper
pinch of sugar
1 tablespoon wine vinegar
1 crisp green lettuce, torn into pieces

Heat 2 tablespoons of the oil in a frying pan (skillet), add the bread slices and fry quickly on both sides until they are golden brown and crisp. Leave to cool, then rub on both sides with the cut surface of the clove of garlic. Cut the bread into small cubes.

Crush the remaining garlic in a salad bowl, add salt, pepper and sugar and stir in the vinegar. Blend in the remaining oil and adjust the seasoning.

When you are ready to serve, mix the lettuce into the dressing, and sprinkle on the *chapons* of bread.

Fennel, Orange and Walnut Salad

Salade de Fenouil aux Oranges et aux Noix

This is a particularly refreshing salad.

Preparation time: 15 minutes
Cooking time: nil
To serve: 6

Metric/Imperial/American
3 to 6 heads of (Florence) fennel,
  depending on size
2 oranges, peeled and segmented
juice of ½ lemon
salt
freshly ground black pepper
1 tablespoon olive or walnut oil
10 fresh walnuts, shelled and chopped

Trim off the stalks, the coarse outer leaves and the base of the fennel (keep for flavouring stocks). Cut in half downwards, then slice across into thin strips. Mix with the orange segments in a salad bowl.

Squeeze out the orange juice remaining in the orange skin case, add lemon juice and seasoning and mix gently. Pour over the salad. Dribble on the olive or walnut oil, sprinkle on the walnuts, and chill for 10 minutes before serving.

Salade Niçoise

Tuna, Egg and Anchovy Salad

One of the classic dishes of Nice. Eat this as an appetizer, or as the main dish for a summer lunch.

Preparation time: 15 minutes
Cooking time: 5 minutes
To serve: 4 to 6

Metric/Imperial/American
0.5 kg/1 lb French (green) beans, topped
* and tailed*
1 Cos or round (romaine or iceberg)
* lettuce*
1 x 198 g/7 oz can tuna fish, drained and
* flaked*
4 to 6 hard-boiled (hard-cooked) eggs,
* quartered lengthwise*
4 to 6 tomatoes, quartered
¼ clove garlic, peeled
½ teaspoon salt
freshly ground black pepper
¼ teaspoon sugar
½ teaspoon French mustard
1 teaspoon lemon juice

1 tablespoon wine vinegar
3 tablespoons oil
Garnish:
1 x 50 g/1¾ oz can anchovy fillets,
* drained*
50 g/2 oz (⅓ cup) black olives, stoned
* (pitted)*

Cook the beans in boiling salted water for 5 minutes or until just tender. Drain and leave to cool.

Line a large salad bowl with the lettuce leaves. Pile the tuna fish in the centre of the bowl. Surround with the beans, and make an outer ring of the eggs alternating with the tomatoes.

Make the dressing by crushing the garlic with the salt. Mix to a smooth paste with the pepper, sugar and mustard, then add the lemon juice and vinegar and blend in the oil. Dribble evenly over the salad and garnish with the anchovy fillets and olives.

Left to right: Salad with Croûtons and Walnut Oil; Fennel, Orange and Walnut Salad; Tuna, Egg and Anchovy Salad; Tomato Salad

Tomato Salad

Salade de Tomates

Serve alone or as part of mixed hors d'oeuvre, or after fish or meat.

Preparation time: 10 minutes (plus 30 minutes marinating)
Cooking time: nil
To serve: 4 to 6

Metric/Imperial/American
0.5 kg/1 lb tomatoes, sliced
salt
freshly ground black pepper
½ teaspoon sugar
1 tablespoon olive oil
2 shallots or 1 small onion, peeled and
* finely chopped*
½ clove garlic, peeled and finely chopped
1 tablespoon finely chopped fresh basil
* or parsley*

Arrange the tomatoes in a shallow dish or bowl (preferably one whose colour sets off the tomatoes). Sprinkle generously with salt, pepper and the sugar. Dribble on the olive oil and turn once. Sprinkle over the shallot or onion, garlic and basil or parsley, and leave in a cool place for about 30 minutes before serving.

Neapolitan Cauliflower Salad

Insalata di Rinforzo

Traditionally this 'reinforcement' salad was eaten at the midnight supper on Christmas Eve in Naples. The rich contrasts in colour and flavour make it a good appetizer for any meal, but take care not to overcook the cauliflower which must retain a firm texture.

Preparation time: 15 minutes
Cooking time: 10 minutes
To serve: 4 to 6

Metric/Imperial/American
1 large cauliflower, broken into florets
8 anchovy fillets
2 tablespoons capers
12 black olives, stoned (pitted)
3 hard-boiled (hard-cooked) eggs, quartered
Dressing:
5 tablespoons olive oil
2 tablespoons lemon juice or wine vinegar
1 teaspoon salt
¼ teaspoon freshly ground black pepper

Cook the cauliflower florets in boiling salted water until just tender, from 5 to 8 minutes. Drain, rinse with cold water to stop further cooking, and drain thoroughly.

Mix all the dressing ingredients together in a salad bowl. Add the cauliflower florets and toss lightly to mix with the dressing. Cut the anchovy fillets into thin strips and arrange in criss-cross fashion over the cauliflower. Sprinkle with the capers and garnish with the olives and eggs.

Stuffed Tomato Salad

Insalata di Pomodori e Riso

The contrasting colours of this attractive Italian dish make it an ideal first course for a summer luncheon. If fresh basil is not available use fresh dill or fennel instead, and use feathery fronds of these herbs to decorate the serving dish.

Preparation time: 20 minutes
Cooking time: 20 minutes
To serve: 6

Metric/Imperial/American
175 g/6 oz (1 cup) long-grain rice
salt
4 tablespoons (¼ cup) olive oil
1 tablespoon wine vinegar
1 tablespoon chopped fresh basil
1 tablespoon chopped fresh parsley
freshly ground black pepper
6 large, firm, ripe tomatoes
½ (1) small cucumber, finely diced
6 small sprigs of fresh parsley

Cook the rice in boiling salted water until just tender, from 14 to 18 minutes depending on the type of rice. Drain, and while still hot dress with the oil, vinegar, basil, chopped parsley and salt and pepper to taste. Mix well and leave to become cold.

Meanwhile, cut the tops off the tomatoes, and with a teaspoon scoop out the flesh. Reserve this for use in a soup or sauce. Sprinkle the insides of the tomatoes with salt and leave upside down to drain.

Mix the cucumber into the cold rice. Fill the tomato cases with the rice mixture, replace the tops and garnish each with a sprig of parsley.

Left to right: Neapolitan Cauliflower Salad;
Stuffed Tomato Salad;
Anchovy and Potato Salad;
Fennel Salad

Anchovy and Potato Salad

Antipasto di Acciughe e Patate

In Southern Italy the anchovies used for this dish would be salted ones, soaked and filleted before use. Canned fillets may be used, but if a milder flavour is preferred wash them first in warm water and pat dry. Use new, or a firm 'waxy' type of potato for the salad.

Preparation time: 20 minutes
Cooking time: 20 minutes
To serve: 6

Metric/Imperial/American
0.75 kg/1½ lb potatoes, scrubbed
salt
1 tablespoon lemon juice
freshly ground black pepper
6 tablespoons olive oil
1 clove garlic, peeled and crushed
1 small onion, peeled and very thinly sliced
1 can anchovy fillets, drained
1 tablespoon chopped fresh parsley
4 hard-boiled (hard-cooked) eggs, quartered
about 75 g/3 oz (½ cup) large black olives, stoned (pitted)

Cook the potatoes in lightly salted boiling water for about 20 minutes, until just tender. Drain, and when cool enough to handle, peel and cut into 5 mm/¼ inch dice. In a large bowl, mix the lemon juice with a little salt and pepper, the oil and the garlic. Add the hot potato dice, toss gently together, then cover and leave until cold.

Shortly before serving, spread the potato salad over a flat serving dish and scatter over the onion rings. Cut the anchovy fillets in half lengthways and arrange in a criss-cross pattern over the salad. Sprinkle lightly with chopped parsley and arrange the quarters of hard-boiled egg and olives alternately all around the edge.

Fennel Salad

Insalata di Finocchi

The crisp texture and mild anise flavour of fennel root makes it a popular salad vegetable, either on its own or as part of a mixed salad. This composite salad from Southern Italy is particularly good with rich meats such as pork, duck or Mortadella sausage.

Preparation time: 20 minutes
Cooking time: nil
To serve: 4

Metric/Imperial/American
2 bulbs (Florence) fennel, cut into fine strips
2 heads chicory (Belgian endive), cut into 2.5 cm/1 inch pieces
½ (1) small cucumber, thinly sliced
4 radishes, thinly sliced
Dressing:
1 tablespoon lemon juice
salt
freshly ground black pepper
1 clove garlic, peeled and finely crushed
3 tablespoons olive oil

Put the vegetables in a salad bowl. Mix all the dressing ingredients together thoroughly. Just before serving pour the dressing over the salad, toss carefully and serve.

Sweet and Sour Salad

Salata Betingan

This salad is one of many versions of a Middle Eastern dish which can be served as an appetizer or a side dish. Broken pieces of toasted bread are sometimes placed at the bottom of the serving dish to become well moistened with the juice of the vegetables.

Preparation time: 15 minutes (plus 1 hour draining aubergines/eggplants)
Cooking time: about 30 minutes
To serve: 6

Metric/Imperial
0.75 kg/1½ lb aubergines, peeled and cubed
salt
olive oil
1 large Spanish onion, peeled and coarsely chopped
2 cloves garlic, peeled and crushed
1 x 400 g/14 oz can peeled tomatoes
4 tablespoons finely chopped fresh parsley
3 tablespoons wine vinegar
1 tablespoon sugar
freshly ground black pepper

American
1½ lb eggplants, peeled and cubed
salt
olive oil
1 large Spanish onion, peeled and coarsely chopped
2 cloves garlic, peeled and crushed
1 x 14 oz can peeled tomatoes
¼ cup finely chopped fresh parsley
3 tablespoons wine vinegar
1 tablespoon sugar
freshly ground black pepper

Sprinkle the aubergine (eggplant) cubes with salt and leave in a colander for about 1 hour for the juices to drain away. Rinse and squeeze out the water.

Cover the bottom of a heavy pan with olive oil. Heat, then add the onion and fry until it is soft and golden. Add the garlic and fry, stirring, until it begins to colour. Add the aubergines (eggplants) and fry, turning them, for about 5 minutes. Stir in the tomatoes, cut into small pieces, with their juice, the parsley, vinegar, sugar and pepper. Cook over very low heat for about 20 minutes, or until the aubergines (eggplants) are tender.

Above left: Sweet and Sour Salad
Below left: Tomato and Pepper Salad

Orange Salad

Shlada Dyal Laimoune

This refreshing salad from Morocco adds a delicious and unusual note to both hot and cold meals.

Preparation time: about 15 minutes
Cooking time: nil
To serve: 6

Metric/Imperial/American
3 large oranges
1 teaspoon ground cinnamon, or more
12 black olives and/or 6 radishes, thinly sliced to garnish

Peel the oranges, removing all the white pith. Slice very thinly. Arrange on a shallow serving plate, sprinkle with cinnamon and garnish with shiny black olives and radishes.

Tomato and Pepper Salad

Salata Filfil bi Outa

Use firm tomatoes, preferably large ones. This salad from the Middle East makes a good accompaniment to most dishes and can also be served as an appetizer. Though peppers may be left raw, it is felt they are rendered more digestible and certainly deliciously soft and mellow by grilling (broiling).

Cracked Wheat Salad

Tabbouleh

This is one of the national dishes of Syria and Lebanon. Sometimes called 'parsley salad' because so much of that herb is used, it is also refreshingly minty and very lemony. May be served as an appetizer or a side salad.

Preparation time: 15 minutes (plus 1 hour marinating)
Cooking time: nil
To serve: 6 to 8

Metric/Imperial
225 g/8 oz burghul (cracked wheat)
175 g/6 oz spring onions or mild Spanish onion, peeled and finely chopped
3 to 4 tomatoes, chopped
100 g/4 oz fresh parsley, finely chopped
a few sprigs of fresh mint, finely chopped, or 2 tablespoons dried mint
6 to 8 tablespoons olive oil
juice of 2 lemons, or more to taste
salt
freshly ground black pepper
vine leaves, lightly poached, or fresh Cos lettuce leaves to serve
a few black olives to garnish (optional)

American
1¾ cups burghul (cracked wheat)
6 oz scallions or mild Spanish onion, peeled and finely chopped
3 to 4 tomatoes, chopped
3 cups finely chopped fresh parsley
a few sprigs of fresh mint, finely chopped, or 2 tablespoons dried mint
6 to 8 tablespoons olive oil
juice of 2 lemons, or more to taste
salt
freshly ground black pepper
vine leaves, lightly poached, or fresh romaine lettuce leaves to serve
a few black olives to garnish (optional)

Soak the *burghul* (also called *bulgur* by Turks and Cypriots) in cold water for 10 minutes. Drain well and put in a large bowl with the other ingredients. Mix together, then leave for at least 1 hour before serving to allow the wheat to absorb the dressing and become plump and tender.

Serve in individual plates lined with vine leaves or lettuce leaves. Place a bowl of firm young lettuce leaves to use as scoops for the salad on the table.

Alternatively, pile all the salad in a pyramid and garnish with stoned (pitted) black olive halves.

Above right: Orange Salad
Below right: Cracked Wheat Salad

Preparation time: about 10 minutes
Cooking time for the peppers: 15 to 20 minutes
To serve: 6

Metric/Imperial/American
2 peppers
4 firm salad tomatoes, sliced
½ Spanish onion, peeled and finely chopped, or 6 spring onions (scallions), finely chopped
small bunch of fresh coriander leaves or parsley, chopped
Dressing:
4 tablespoons (¼ cup) olive oil
1 to 2 tablespoons wine vinegar
salt
freshly ground black pepper

Spear the peppers with a fork and turn them over or under a flame until they are soft and the skin has blistered all over. Peel off the thin skin and remove any charred bits under cold running water. Cut the peppers into ribbons, removing stalks and seeds.

Put them in a serving bowl with the rest of the ingredients and toss in the dressing.

41

Fish dishes

Baked Fish with Ratatouille

Gigot de Mer

Gigot means leg in French and this dish is so called because the fish is cooked exactly like a leg of lamb. Use a whole bass or bream, or a thick piece of cod, haddock or monkfish. The recipe is from Provence.

Preparation time: 10 minutes
Cooking time: 30 to 40 minutes
Oven temperature: 190°C, 375°F, Gas Mark 5
To serve: 6

Metric/Imperial/American
2 to 2½ kg/4½ to 5½ lb whole fish or thick slice, cleaned and scaled
2 cloves garlic, peeled and cut into slivers
1 tablespoon olive oil
2 onions, peeled and thinly sliced
2 bay leaves
salt
freshly ground black pepper
1 sprig of fresh thyme
2 sprigs of fresh parsley
1 lemon, thinly sliced
150 ml/¼ pint (⅔ cup) dry white wine or dry vermouth
ratatouille (see page 127)

Cut diagonal slits all over the surface of the fish, and insert a sliver of garlic in each.

Line a baking dish with foil and oil the foil with about 1 teaspoon of the olive oil. Use half the sliced onion to make a bed for the fish, top with a bay leaf and lay the fish on top. Put salt, pepper, thyme and parsley inside the fish and cover with the remaining onion and bay leaf and half the lemon slices. Dribble on the remaining olive oil. Pour over the wine or vermouth and bake for 30 to 40 minutes, basting from time to time, until the fish is just cooked. Test by inserting a knife gently near the backbone – the fish should come away fairly easily and be only the palest pink.

Spread the ratatouille in a shallow ovenproof dish.

Remove the fish carefully from the baking dish onto a plate. Discard the bay leaves and lemon slices, then pour the remaining contents of the baking dish over the ratatouille.

Fillet the fish carefully and lay it, skin side up, on top of the ratatouille. Return to the oven briefly to heat through, and serve decorated with the remaining lemon slices.

Stuffed Bass

Loup Farci à la Niçoise

Though sea bass is the fish most frequently cooked in this way in Nice, bream or grey mullet may also be cooked in the same fashion.

Preparation time: 20 minutes
Cooking time: 40 minutes
Oven temperature: 190°C, 375°F, Gas Mark 5
To serve: 6

Metric/Imperial/American
2 to 2½ kg/4½ to 5½ lb fish, or 2 smaller ones, cleaned and scaled
salt
freshly ground black pepper
½ tablespoon French mustard
bunch of fresh fennel
2 bay leaves
2 tablespoons olive oil
1 onion, peeled and finely chopped
1 clove garlic, peeled and finely chopped
100 g/4 oz (½ cup) salt pork or bacon, finely chopped
0.5 kg/1 lb mushrooms, finely chopped
2 tablespoons capers, finely chopped
100 g/4 oz (¾ cup) black olives, stoned (pitted) and finely chopped
bunch of fresh parsley or chives, finely chopped
0.5 kg/1 lb tomatoes, skinned and chopped
150 ml/¼ pint (⅔ cup) dry white wine
lemon wedges to garnish

Rub the prepared fish inside and out with salt and pepper. Place a sprig of fennel inside and spread a little mustard inside the cavity. Make some slits all over the surface of the fish, and insert a small sprig of fennel in each. Lay bay leaves and another sprig of fennel on top of the fish, and wrap in foil oiled with 1 teaspoon of the oil. Bake for 30 to 40 minutes, until the fish is just cooked.

Meanwhile, mix together the onion, garlic, salt pork or bacon, mushrooms, capers, olives and parsley or chives. Heat the remaining oil in a large frying pan (skillet) and cook this mixture over a brisk heat for 5 minutes, stirring frequently. Add the tomatoes and wine and cook gently, uncovered, for a further 20 to 30 minutes, or until the mixture is very smooth and concentrated. Season to taste.

When the fish is ready, fillet it very carefully, and discard the backbone. Place the bottom half on a heated serving platter, spread on the filling and place the other fillet on top, so that the fish appears stuffed. Pour on any juices

from the foil and serve very hot, garnished with lemon wedges.

Fish with Fennel

Poisson Grillé au Fenouil

Bass, bream, mullet and denté are all excellent cooked in this way, but, of course, the fish should be very fresh and not too large. Traditionally, it should be cooked over a charcoal fire, but an indoor grill (broiler) will also do very well.

Preparation time: 10 minutes
Cooking time: 15 to 25 minutes
To serve: 6

Metric/Imperial/American
3 kg/6½ lb fish (see above), allowing 1 small or ½ larger fish per person, cleaned and scaled
bunch of fresh fennel
salt
freshly ground black pepper
lemon juice
2 tablespoons olive oil
Montpelier butter (see page 132) to garnish

Cut deep diagonal slashes in the sides of the fish, and insert a sprig of fennel in each. Place a sprig of fennel in the cavity of each fish also, together with a good sprinkling of salt and pepper. Rub the outside of each fish with salt and pepper and place them on the grid of the barbecue or wire rack of the grill (broiler) pan. If using a grill (broiler) pan, line it with foil to catch the juices.

Dribble some lemon juice and olive oil over each fish, put another sprig of fennel on top of each one and place under the very hot grill (broiler) or over the hot charcoal embers.

When one side of the fish is done, and its skin is lightly charred, turn over carefully. Sprinkle the other side with lemon juice and oil, place another branch of fennel on top and cook until this side is done also. Pour the cooking juices over the fish when serving, with Montpelier butter.

Above left: Baked Fish with Ratatouille
Above right: Stuffed Bass
Below: Fish with Fennel

Bouillabaisse

Marseillaise Fish Soup

A great deal of mystique surrounds this most famous of all fish soups. There are those who say it is not worth eating outside the harbour of Marseille, and certainly it is hard to produce a truly authentic *bouillabaisse* away from the Mediterranean, because the fish should be very fresh, and strictly speaking should include a *rascasse* or gurnard. However, a bouillabaisse can be exceedingly enjoyable to eat, and to make, even without a rascasse, given a sufficient variety of fish.

Choose three or four of the following: bass, bream, cod, eel, flounder, gurnard, haddock, hake, halibut, John Dory, monkfish, sole, perch, plaice, porgy, mullet, snapper and turbot. A little shellfish adds an extra touch of luxury, but is not essential.

Though referred to as a soup, this is really a very filling main dish, and it would be hard to think of eating anything other than some fruit afterwards. Serve with a dry white wine.

Preparation time: 50 minutes
Cooking time: 50 minutes
To serve: 8 (This dish is not worth making in smaller quantities)

Metric/Imperial/American
2 kg/4½ lb fish (see above), cleaned, scaled and thickly sliced
1 onion, peeled and quartered
1 carrot, peeled and quartered
1 sprig of fresh fennel
2 bay leaves
fresh parsley stalks
2.5 litres/4½ pints (2½ quarts) water
4 tablespoons (¼ cup) olive oil
2 onions, peeled and finely chopped
2 leeks, white parts only, finely chopped
4 cloves garlic, peeled and finely chopped
2 tomatoes, skinned and roughly chopped
1 tablespoon tomato purée (paste)
salt
freshly ground black pepper
large pinch of saffron powder
1 sprig of fresh thyme
2 strips of orange rind
16 slices of French bread (2 per person)
1 clove garlic, peeled and halved
1 tablespoon Pernod
1 tablespoon finely chopped fresh parsley

Put the fish heads and trimmings in a large saucepan with the quartered onion, carrot, fennel, bay leaves and parsley stalks. Cover with the cold water, bring to the boil, skim and simmer for 30 minutes. Heat 2 tablespoons of the olive oil in another large saucepan, add the finely chopped onions, leeks and garlic and fry until softened. Stir in the tomatoes and tomato purée, then add the slices of the firmer of the fish and turn well. Strain on the hot fish stock and add seasoning, the saffron, thyme and orange rind. Bring just to the boil and simmer gently for 10 minutes. Add the more delicate fish and simmer for a further 10 minutes or until the fish is cooked.

Meanwhile, dry the slices of bread in the oven or under the grill (broiler). Rub each with the cut surface of the halved clove of garlic and dribble a little of the remaining oil on each.

Just before serving bring the soup to a rapid boil and add the remaining olive oil, which should become amalgamated with the stock. Add the Pernod and sprinkle with the parsley.

Serve in deep soup plates, floating two slices of bread on top of each serving.

Hand round a bowl of rouille (see page 132) or aioli (see next recipe) so that everyone who wishes can add a dollop to their plates.

Mediterranean Fish Stew

La Bourride

Use almost any white fish for this creamy, garlicky 'soup': bass, brill, cod, haddock, halibut, John Dory, mullet, porgy, sea bream, turbot or whiting. Serve with plain boiled potatoes, followed by a salad, and accompanied by a dry white wine.

Preparation time: 40 to 50 minutes
(more if making *aioli* by hand)
Cooking time: 40 minutes
To serve: 6 to 8

Metric/Imperial/American
1.5 kg/3 lb white fish (see above), cleaned and scaled
Stock:
1 onion, peeled and quartered
1 carrot, peeled and chopped
2 leeks, pale green part only
1 strip of lemon rind
1 bay leaf
sprigs of fresh fennel and parsley
2 tablespoons wine vinegar
3.5 litres/6 pints (3½ quarts) water
salt
freshly ground black pepper

Aioli:
2 or 3 cloves garlic, peeled
salt
2 egg yolks
300 ml/½ pint (1¼ cups) olive oil
good (large) squeeze of lemon juice
freshly ground black pepper
Soup:
2 tablespoons olive oil
2 leeks, white part only, thinly sliced
12 to 16 slices of French bread (2 per person)
2 egg yolks
2 tablespoons finely chopped fresh parsley

Fillet the fish or cut into thick slices. Put the fish heads and trimmings into a large saucepan with the onion, carrot, green part of the leeks, lemon rind, bay leaf, fennel, parsley and vinegar. Cover with the cold water, bring to the boil, skim and simmer for 20 minutes. Strain into a clean saucepan and boil rapidly for 5 minutes to reduce. Season.

Meanwhile, make the aioli. Crush the garlic cloves with a little salt and stir into the egg yolks. Add the olive oil drop by drop at first, beating in well so that the oil is amalgamated. When the sauce begins to thicken you can add the oil a little more rapidly, but it should never be added in more than a thin stream. An electric beater or Magimix is invaluable for this operation. Season to taste with lemon juice, salt and pepper.

To make the soup, heat the oil in a large saucepan, add the white parts of the leeks and sweat gently until soft. Lay the fish fillets or slices on top, placing the firmest fish, such as cod, turbot or halibut, at the bottom, the most delicate, such as whiting or bream, on top. Strain on the fish stock (there should be just enough to cover the fish) and poach for 10 to 15 minutes. Meanwhile, toast or bake the French bread and put the prepared slices at the bottom of a large heated soup tureen.

When the fish is ready, lift the pieces out with a slotted spoon and lay on top of the bread in the tureen. Cover and keep hot.

Put two-thirds of the aioli into a large heatproof bowl set over a pan of simmering water, or into the top of a double boiler. Stir in the 2 egg yolks, then slowly whisk in the hot fish stock a ladleful at a time. Stir until thick and creamy, but do not allow to boil. Taste for seasoning. Pour over the fish in the tureen. Sprinkle with the parsley and serve.

Pass the remaining aioli separately so that those who wish can add an extra spoonful to their soup.

Above and centre: Bouillabaisse
Below: Mediterranean Fish Stew

Zarzuela de Pescados

Exotic Fish Stew

Literally translated, this is something like a 'seafood operetta', or a 'musical comedy of fish'. A classic Catalan dish, the *zarzuela* uses any suitable seafood available cooked together in a rich reddish-brown sauce.

Preparation time: 20 minutes
Cooking time: 20 to 25 minutes
To serve: 4 to 6

Metric/Imperial
about 1 kg/2 lb assorted fish, which should include 1 small cooked lobster, if possible, Dublin Bay prawns, mussels or clams, hake or halibut, a few very small squid (optional), or any other fish or shellfish available, cleaned and cut up where necessary
4 tablespoons olive oil
2 onions, peeled and finely chopped
2 red or green peppers, cored, seeded and chopped
2 cloves garlic, peeled and finely chopped
4 ripe tomatoes, skinned and chopped
1 tablespoon chopped lean cooked ham
12 blanched almonds, hazelnuts or pine nuts, ground

Zarzuela de Pescados

¼ teaspoon saffron powder, or pinch of saffron threads
½ teaspoon paprika
1 teaspoon salt
freshly ground black pepper
200 ml/⅓ pint dry white wine
juice of 1 lemon
600 ml/1 pint water
1 tablespoon finely chopped or minced fresh parsley
120 ml/4 fl oz brandy (optional)

American
about 2 lb assorted fish, which should include 1 small cooked lobster, if possible, jumbo shrimp, clams or mussels, hake or halibut, a few very small squid (optional), or any other fish or shellfish available, cleaned and cut up where necessary
¼ cup olive oil
2 onions, peeled and finely chopped
2 red or green peppers, cored, seeded and chopped
2 cloves garlic, peeled and finely chopped
4 ripe tomatoes, skinned and chopped
1 heaping tablespoon chopped lean cooked ham
12 blanched almonds, hazelnuts or pine nuts, ground
¼ teaspoon saffron powder or pinch of saffron threads
½ teaspoon paprika

1 teaspoon salt
freshly ground black pepper
1 cup dry white wine
juice of 1 lemon
2½ cups water
1 tablespoon finely chopped or ground fresh parsley
½ cup brandy (optional)

Cut the tail section off the lobster, if using. Remove the stomach sac and any bits of dark intestine and cut the tail into sections. Twist off the large claws and cut the remaining piece of lobster in half lengthways.

Heat the oil in large heavy flameproof casserole. Add the onions, red or green peppers and garlic and cook gently for 4 to 5 minutes or until softened. Add the tomatoes, ham, nuts, saffron, paprika and seasoning. Stir gently and cook for another 5 minutes. Then add the wine, lemon juice and water and stir thoroughly. Bring to the boil. Put in any raw fish or shellfish and cover the pot. Simmer for about 8 minutes, then add the lobster and prawns (shrimp) and discard any shellfish that have not opened. Stir in the parsley and brandy, if used. Cover again and cook for a further 5 to 7 minutes or until all the fish is cooked. Adjust the seasoning, then serve very hot, in the casserole, with a good white wine.

Stewed Octopus

Stewed Octopus

Pulpo Quisado

Octopus is a popular dish in nearly all Mediterranean countries, although this particular recipe is Spanish. The best octopus to use are the small ones, as they are not so likely to be tough. If there is any doubt about toughness, the octopus may be pre-cooked in a pressure cooker for 15 to 20 minutes, or thoroughly beaten before cooking. Adding the salt after cooking also helps.

Preparation time: 15 minutes
Cooking time: about 1½ hours
To serve: 4

Metric/Imperial
1 kg/2 lb small octopus
2 tablespoons olive oil
2 cloves garlic, peeled and chopped
8 large spring onions or shallots, sliced
1 red or green pepper, cored, seeded and sliced
pinch of cayenne pepper
2 tablespoons lemon juice
about 150 ml/¼ pint white wine
2 tablespoons chopped fresh parsley
salt

American
2 lb small octopus
2 tablespoons olive oil
2 cloves garlic, peeled and chopped
8 large scallions or shallots, sliced
1 red or green pepper, cored, seeded and sliced
pinch of cayenne pepper
2 tablespoons lemon juice
about ⅔ cup white wine
2 tablespoons chopped fresh parsley
salt

Clean the octopus, turning them inside out under cold running water. Remove the eyes and beaks. Cut them into small pieces, including the bodies and tentacles.

Heat the olive oil in a saucepan over gentle heat and put in the octopus and garlic. Let them stew for about 20 minutes; they will probably give off quite a lot of their own liquid. Add the vegetables and cook for a further 10 minutes, stirring occasionally.

Add the cayenne, lemon juice and enough white wine just to cover everything. Bring to the boil, then partially cover the pan and simmer very gently for about 1 hour. Test the octopus for tenderness, and if need be cook a little longer. (One hour would be long enough if you have used a pressure cooker to pre-cook the octopus.)

When the octopus is tender, stir in the parsley and salt to taste. Serve hot, in individual earthenware dishes, with plenty of crusty bread and a dry white wine.

Casserole of Fresh Sardines

Cacerola de Sardinas Frescas

Fresh sardines are a feature of Spanish life and come in a variety of sizes. For this recipe you need sprat-sized sardines. Sprats could be used instead, if necessary.

Preparation time: 30 minutes
Cooking time: 40 minutes
Oven temperature: 180°C/350°F, Gas Mark 4.
To serve: 4

Metric/Imperial
2 potatoes, peeled and sliced
about 24 fresh sardines, cleaned and heads and tails removed
4 cloves garlic, peeled and chopped
2 tablespoons chopped fresh parsley
salt (preferably sea salt)
freshly ground black pepper
2 large onions, peeled and sliced in rings
6 large tomatoes, skinned and sliced
2 green peppers, cored, seeded and sliced
4 tablespoons olive oil
outside leaves of a cos lettuce (optional)

American
2 potatoes, peeled and sliced
about 24 fresh sardines, cleaned and heads and tails removed
4 cloves garlic, peeled and chopped
2 tablespoons chopped fresh parsley
salt (preferably coarse salt)
freshly ground black pepper
2 large onions, peeled and sliced in rings
6 large tomatoes, skinned and sliced
2 green peppers, cored, seeded and sliced
¼ cup olive oil
outside leaves of a romaine lettuce (optional)

Oil a shallow ovenproof dish. Put a layer of sliced potato on the bottom, then some of the sardines. Sprinkle with a little garlic, parsley, salt and pepper. Add a layer of onion rings and one of tomato slices, then more sardines, followed by some green pepper. Continue making layers until all the fish and vegetables are used up, alternating the layers as you wish and sprinkling garlic, parsley, salt and pepper over each layer of fish. When the dish is full sprinkle it liberally with olive oil and pour a little more oil down the sides. Cover the dish with a layer of lettuce leaves, as they do in Mallorca, or use a sheet of foil instead. (The lettuce leaves will give a pleasant flavour.)

Put into the oven and cook for about 40 minutes, or until done.

Take the dish to the table to serve, with plenty of fresh crusty bread and a dry red wine.

Baked Mediterranean Bream

Dentón Asada

There are numerous kinds of bream in the Mediterranean. The best one to use for this recipe is the Dentex or Dente, which is exceptionally good. Sea bream could also be used with success, or red snapper or porgy. Variations of this recipe are popular all over Spain.

Preparation time: 20 minutes
Cooking time: about 40 minutes
Oven temperature: 180°C/350°F, Gas Mark 4
To serve: 4

Metric/Imperial
0.5 kg/1 lb onions, peeled and sliced
1 kg/2 lb bream, or 2 smaller bream, cleaned and scaled, head left on
1 lemon, cut in thin wedges
4 cloves garlic, peeled and finely chopped
2 tablespoons finely chopped fresh parsley
3 tablespoons dry breadcrumbs
1 tablespoon paprika
salt
freshly ground black pepper
2 tablespoons olive oil
150 ml/¼ pint dry sherry
1 black olive (optional)
strips of red pepper (optional)

American
1 lb onions, peeled and sliced
2 lb red snapper or porgy, or 2 smaller fish, cleaned and scaled, head left on
1 lemon, cut in thin wedges
4 cloves garlic, peeled and finely chopped
2 tablespoons finely chopped fresh parsley
3 tablespoons dry breadcrumbs
1 tablespoon paprika
salt
freshly ground black pepper
2 tablespoons olive oil
⅔ cup dry sherry
1 black olive (optional)
strips of red pepper (optional)

Oil a large oval ovenproof dish, preferably earthenware, into which the fish will fit neatly. Cover the bottom with the sliced onions. Make parallel incisions in the fish, about 5 cm/2 inches long and running from top to bottom, and insert a wedge of lemon in each, skin side up. Put the fish on to the layer of onion in the dish. Mix together the garlic, parsley, breadcrumbs and paprika and sprinkle over the fish, followed by salt and pepper to taste and the olive oil. Pour the sherry down the sides of the dish. Put the olive in the fish's eye socket, if you like. You can also add a few strips of red pepper for decoration.

Put the dish into the oven and cook for about 40 minutes, or until the fish feels cooked through to the bone when pierced with a skewer, and is a golden brown. Serve in the dish.

Red Mullet

Salmonetes a la Parilla

Red mullet is one of the delicacies of the Mediterranean. When you clean these fish leave on the heads, and also the liver if you can.

Preparation time: 10 minutes, excluding marinating time
Cooking time: 8 to 10 minutes
To serve: 4

Metric/Imperial
4 large or 8 small red or grey mullet, cleaned as above
salt
8 tablespoons olive oil
juice of 1 lemon
2 tablespoons finely chopped fresh parsley
Romescu (see page 132)

American
4 large or 8 small red or gray mullet, cleaned as above
salt
½ cup olive oil
juice of 1 lemon
2 tablespoons finely chopped fresh parsley
Romescu (see page 132)

Prepare the fish a few hours before you need them: sprinkle them with salt, oil and lemon juice and leave to marinate. (During this time make the sauce.)

When ready to cook, preheat the grill (broiler) and drain the fish, leaving on a film of oil. Grill (broil) the fish until crisp and serve with the parsley scattered over. Serve the sauce separately.

Above: Casserole of Fresh Sardines
Centre: Baked Mediterranean Bream
Below: Red Mullet

Paella

Rice with Chicken and Seafood

The ingredients of a paella can, within limits, be adapted to suit your taste. However, it always has a basis of saffron-flavoured rice, and in Spain a special medium-grain rice grown around Valencia is used. You might be able to buy this at a specialist Spanish food store (ask for Valencia rice); otherwise use Italian risotto rice or Carolina rice.

Preparation time: 20 minutes
Cooking time: 30 minutes
To serve: 4 to 6

Metric/Imperial
1 small live lobster or 8 Dublin Bay prawns
150 ml/¼ pint olive oil
2 cloves garlic, peeled and chopped

Paella

1 onion, peeled and thinly sliced
2 tomatoes, skinned and chopped
1 red or green pepper, cored, seeded and cut into thin strips
1.5 kg/3 lb oven-ready chicken, jointed
a few small squid, if available, cleaned and cut into strips
2 teaspoons paprika
salt
450 g/1 lb medium-grain rice
800 ml to 1 litre/1⅓ to 1¾ pints chicken stock
½ teaspoon saffron powder or saffron threads infused in a little boiling water
100 g/4 oz shelled fresh or frozen peas
8 mussels or clams, scrubbed
2 lemons, cut into wedges

American
1 small live lobster or 8 jumbo shrimp
⅔ cup olive oil
2 cloves garlic, peeled and chopped
1 onion, peeled and thinly sliced
2 tomatoes, skinned and chopped
1 red or green pepper, cored, seeded and cut into thin strips
3 lb oven-ready chicken, cut up
a few small squid, if available, cleaned and cut into strips
2 teaspoons paprika
salt
2¼ cups rice
3¼ to 4 cups chicken stock
½ teaspoon saffron powder or saffron threads infused in a little boiling water
1 cup shelled fresh or frozen peas
8 clams or mussels, scrubbed
2 lemons, cut into wedges

If you cannot face cutting up a live lobster, plunge it into boiling water and boil for about 4 minutes to kill it. Cut off the tail section and twist off the large claws. Remove the stomach sac and the dark line that runs the length of the body. Cut the tail section into slices and split the rest of the lobster in two, lengthways.

Heat the olive oil in a *paellera* (a two-handled iron pan made especially for the purpose) or in any large shallow pan or flameproof casserole. Put in the garlic and swirl it around to flavour the oil. Remove or leave in, according to your taste for garlic. Add the onion, tomatoes, red or green pepper, the pieces of chicken and squid. Fry gently for about 10 minutes, turning the chicken over to brown evenly. Sprinkle with the paprika and salt, then spread the rice evenly over the contents of the pan. Turn it in the hot oil until it starts to colour slightly.

Bring the stock to the boil in a saucepan and add the saffron. Remove the *paellera* from the heat and carefully pour in the boiling stock. Stir thoroughly and put back on a low heat. Add the pieces of lobster, pushing them down into the rice and sprinkle the peas over. Cook very gently for about 20 minutes, without stirring, then add the prawns (shrimp), if used, and mussels or clams (which should remain on the surface). Cover the pan and continue to cook gently for 5 minutes. The mussels or clams should open by this time; remove any that do not. Remove from the heat and allow to stand for about 5 minutes before serving in the *paellera*, with wedges of lemon pushed on to the rim.

Vermicelli with Clams and Mussels

Vermicelli con Vongole e Cozze

This is one of the most characteristic and colourful dishes of the Bay of Naples. According to what shellfish happen to be available, it is made with either clams or mussels, or a mixture of both. Spaghetti can be used instead of vermicelli, but Neapolitans prefer the finer pasta. The shellfish must, of course, be very fresh, and the dish eaten as soon as it is cooked.

Preparation time: 30 minutes (plus 2 hours soaking)
Cooking time: 30 minutes
To serve: 4

Metric/Imperial
1.2 litres/2 pints small fresh clams or cockles
1.5 litres/2½ pints fresh mussels
salt
5 tablespoons olive oil
1 medium onion, peeled and finely chopped
2 large cloves garlic, peeled and crushed
0.5 kg/1 lb ripe tomatoes, skinned, seeded and chopped
350 g/12 oz vermicelli or spaghetti
freshly ground black pepper
2 tablespoons chopped fresh parsley

American
2½ pints small fresh clams
1½ quarts fresh mussels
salt
5 tablespoons olive oil
1 medium onion, peeled and finely chopped
2 large cloves garlic, peeled and crushed
1 lb ripe tomatoes, skinned, seeded and chopped
¾ lb vermicelli or spaghetti
freshly ground black pepper
2 tablespoons chopped fresh parsley

Thoroughly wash all the shellfish and tug away the beards from the mussels. Discard any fish that gape open and refuse to shut tight when given a sharp tap. Put into a deep pail, cover with cold water, add 2 tablespoons of salt and leave for about 2 hours to release any sand.

When ready to cook, heat 3 tablespoons of the oil in a saucepan, add the onion and fry gently until soft. Add the garlic and fry for 1 minute, then stir in the tomatoes. Cook gently, covered, for about 20 minutes, or until pulped.

Meanwhile, lower the vermicelli into a large pan of boiling salted water and cook until just tender but still firm, about 8 minutes.

Scoop the shellfish from the pail, leaving the sand behind, and put into a wide saucepan. Set the pan over brisk heat and cook for 5 to 6 minutes, shaking frequently. As the shells open take them from the pan. Remove the fish from their shells, discarding the shells, and add to the tomato sauce. Leave about one-quarter of the fish in their shells for garnishing the dish.

Drain the vermicelli, return to the pan and toss with the remaining olive oil until the strands glisten, then pile on a large hot serving dish. Taste and season the sauce as necessary. Pour over the pasta and scatter liberally with chopped parsley. Garnish with the fish in shells.

Vermicelli with Clams and Mussels

A Provençal seafood stall

Fish Salad

Salatat Samak

For this Middle Eastern recipe, too, you are always told to use any fish you like, but firm fish that flakes well is best. Use more than one type. You may also add large prawns (jumbo shrimp) or freshly cooked mussels. It makes a marvellous alfresco meal served with vegetables of the season, either boiled or raw. It also makes a light first course to be followed by a meat dish.

Preparation time: 10 minutes
Cooking time: 10 to 40 minutes, depending on whether you boil or bake
To serve: 6

Metric/Imperial
1 kg/2 lb fish fillets or steaks (use salmon, salmon trout, John Dory, bream, bass, grey mullet, cod, haddock or halibut)
0.5 kg/1 lb cooked large prawns, mussels
finely chopped fresh parsley to garnish
Dressing:
4 to 5 tablespoons olive oil
juice of 1 lemon, or more
salt
freshly ground black pepper
Alternative dressing (tahina sauce):
150 ml/¼ pint tahina (sesame meal)
150 ml/¼ pint plain yogurt
salt
freshly ground black pepper
2 cloves garlic, peeled and crushed
juice of 2 lemons

American
2 lb fish fillets or steaks (use salmon, porgy, bass, gray mullet, cod, haddock or halibut)
1 lb cooked jumbo shrimp, mussels
finely chopped fresh parsley to garnish
Dressing:
4 to 5 tablespoons olive oil
juice of 1 lemon, or more
salt
freshly ground black pepper
Alternative dressing (tahina sauce):
⅔ cup tahina (sesame meal)
⅔ cup plain yogurt
salt
freshly ground black pepper
2 cloves garlic, peeled and crushed
juice of 2 lemons

Poach, steam or bake the fish in foil. It is better to undercook it than overcook it. The time required depends on the size of the steaks or of the fish if cooked whole. Meanwhile, mix together the dressing ingredients.

Drain the fish, remove the skin and bones, and pour the dressing over. Sprinkle generously with finely chopped parsley.

The alternative dressing is an Arab favourite. Mix together the ingredients and pour over the fish.

Fish with Rice

Sayadieh

Fish served with rice cooked in a fish broth rich and brown with fried onions is popular throughout the Arab world. Bass is often used but other fish will also do. In this recipe the fish is poached, but you may prefer to fry it lightly in oil or butter and serve it in the same way.

Preparation time: about 20 minutes
Cooking time: 1 hour
To serve: 6

Metric/Imperial/American
150 ml/¼ pint (⅔ cup) oil (preferably olive oil)
2 tablespoons halved blanched almonds
2 tablespoons pine nuts
2 large onions, peeled and chopped
fish heads and trimmings
salt
freshly ground black pepper
1 teaspoon ground cumin
1 kg/2 lb fish
0.5 kg/1 lb (2⅓ cups) long-grain rice
25 g/1 oz (2 tablespoons) butter
juice of 1 lemon

Heat the oil in a large saucepan, add the almonds and fry until they are golden. Add the pine nuts and stir until lightly browned. Remove the nuts and reserve them. Fry the onions in the oil until they are a light brown. Add about 1.5 litres/2½ pints (3 US pints) of water. Put in the fish heads and trimmings and add salt and pepper to taste and the cumin.

Bring to the boil, then simmer for about 30 minutes. Put in the fish pieces and cook for a further 10 minutes or until just tender. Lift out the fish and keep aside. Strain the broth, pressing the onions through the strainer.

Put the rice in the pan with 1 litre 1¾ pints (1 quart) of the fish broth and the butter. Bring to the boil, then simmer, covered, on very low heat for 15 to 20 minutes or until the rice is tender. Add more broth or water, if necessary.

Serve on a large platter, arranging the fish pieces around or on top of the rice. Sprinkle with the almonds and pine nuts.

A good way of presenting the dish if you want everything to be very hot is to put the almonds and nuts at the bottom of a large greased mould. Lay the fish on top and cover with the rice. Press it down well and put in the oven to heat through. Unmould onto the platter just before serving.

Reduce the remaining broth by boiling, add the lemon juice and serve as a sauce.

Fish Sticks

Blehat Samak

Most Middle East fish recipes will work with any fish, at least that is what everyone tells you. In this case you certainly can use any fish or a mixture. As good hot as it is cold, serve this as an appetizer, or main dish with rice and salad. Excellent for a buffet meal.

Preparation time: 15 minutes
Cooking time: 30 minutes
To serve: 6

Metric/Imperial
175 g/6 oz sliced white bread, crusts removed
0.75 kg/1½ lb fish, skinned, boned and finely chopped or minced
1 small onion, peeled and grated or minced

Left: Fish Salad
Centre: Fish with Rice
Right: Fish Sticks

2 cloves garlic, peeled and crushed
3 tablespoons finely chopped fresh parsley
½ teaspoon ground cumin
½ teaspoon ground coriander
salt
freshly ground black pepper
1 egg
flour
oil for frying
chopped fresh parsley to garnish
Sauce:
2 tablespoons oil
1 medium onion, peeled and finely chopped
1 x 64 g/2¼ oz can tomato purée
300 ml/½ pint water
1 bay leaf

American
6 slices of white bread, crusts removed
1½ lb fish, skinned, boned and finely chopped or ground
1 small onion, peeled and grated or minced
2 cloves garlic, peeled and crushed
3 tablespoons finely chopped fresh parsley
½ teaspoon ground cumin
½ teaspoon ground coriander
salt
freshly ground black pepper
1 egg
flour
oil for frying
chopped fresh parsley to garnish
Sauce:
2 tablespoons oil
1 medium onion, peeled and finely chopped
1 x 2¼ oz can tomato paste
1¼ cups water
1 bay leaf

Soak the bread in a little water, squeeze dry and crumble. Put the bread in a large bowl with the fish, onion, garlic, parsley, cumin, coriander, salt and pepper and the egg. Mix and knead together thoroughly by hand. Take walnut-sized lumps of the mixture and roll them into small finger shapes. Coat them in flour and fry in hot oil, turning them over until they are golden brown all over. Drain on paper towels.

To make the sauce, heat the oil in a large saucepan, add the onion and fry until golden. Stir in the tomato paste and water. Season to taste with salt and pepper and add the bay leaf. Stir well. Bring to the boil, then simmer for about 5 minutes. Drop in the fish sticks carefully. Add more water, if necessary, to cover, and cook for a further 15-20 minutes. Remove the bay leaf.

Serve hot or cold, garnished with chopped parsley.

Salt Cod with Garlic Sauce

Bakaliaro Tighanito Scorthaliá

The Greeks retain their fondness for this very traditional form of preserved fish. Before cooking, dried salt cod must be soaked in cold water for 12 to 24 hours, depending on saltiness, with the water changed several times. In Greece fish fried in batter, whether salt cod or fresh fish, is especially notable for the lightness and crispness of the coating. The batter, for which the recipe is given below, is also used for frying delectable vegetable fritters.

Preparation time: 50 minutes, plus previous soaking of fish
Cooking time: 20 minutes
To serve: 4

Metric/Imperial
675 g/1½ lb salt cod, soaked as above
flour for coating
oil for frying
Batter:
100 g/4 oz plain flour
1 teaspoon baking powder
¼ teaspoon salt
1 egg, lightly beaten
150 ml/¼ pint plus 2 tablespoons warm water
Garlic sauce:
100 g/4 oz crustless white bread
a little cold water
1 to 3 cloves garlic, peeled
½ teaspoon salt
6 tablespoons hot water
3 tablespoons white wine vinegar
6 tablespoons olive oil

American
1½ lb salt cod, soaked as above
flour for coating
oil for frying
Batter:
1 cup all-purpose flour
1 teaspoon baking powder
¼ teaspoon salt
1 egg, lightly beaten
¾ cup warm water
Garlic sauce:
4 slices crustless white bread
a little cold water
1 to 3 cloves garlic, peeled
½ teaspoon salt
6 tablespoons hot water
3 tablespoons white wine vinegar
6 tablespoons olive oil

At least 30 minutes before required make the batter. Sift the flour, baking powder and salt into a bowl and beat in the egg and the water, mixing to a smooth batter. Cover and leave at room temperature for 30 minutes or longer.

For the garlic sauce put the bread into a bowl, moisten with cold water and leave to absorb it. Put the garlic cloves on a chopping board. Sprinkle with the salt and crush to a paste with a knife, then transfer to a mixing bowl. Squeeze the bread as dry as possible, add to the garlic and beat well with a wooden spoon. Gradually add half of the hot water and the vinegar, beating all the time. Then little by little beat in the olive oil and the remaining hot water. If necessary add a little more water to give the sauce a pouring consistency. Leave to stand.

Pour enough oil into a frying pan (skillet) to give a depth of 1 cm/½ inch and heat gently to 190°C/375°F, or until a bead of batter sizzles when dropped into the fat.

Meanwhile cut the fish into serving portions and pat dry with kitchen paper. One at a time coat the pieces of fish with flour, shaking off the excess. Lower the fish into the batter, coat thoroughly, then lift out with two skewers and put into the hot fat. Fry, three or four pieces at a time, for 7 to 8 minutes, turning, until the batter is crisp and golden on both sides and the fish cooked through. Drain on crumpled kitchen paper and keep hot. The Garlic Sauce is poured over the hot fish or handed separately.

Arcadian Baked Fish

Psari Plaki

There are as many variations of this colourful, flexible way of cooking fish as there are cooks in Greece. For instance, the sauce can be poured over a gutted whole fish instead of fish portions, and the cooked dish can be served hot or cold, usually with bread and a salad. In many Greek kitchens the dish is simmered on top of the stove, in which case a more liquid sauce is used, and reduced later if need be. Almost any kind of fish can be cooked in this way.

Preparation time: 15 minutes
Cooking time: 20 to 30 minutes
Oven temperature: 190°C/375°F, Gas Mark 5
To serve: 4 or 5

Metric/Imperial
5 tablespoons olive oil
225 g/8 oz onions, peeled and thinly sliced
1 clove garlic, peeled and crushed
4 large ripe tomatoes, skinned and chopped
4 tablespoons white wine
salt
freshly ground black pepper
1 kg/2 lb fish, cut in portions
2 tablespoons lemon juice
2 firm tomatoes, sliced
2 tablespoons chopped parsley or *mint*

American
5 tablespoons olive oil
½ lb onions, peeled and thinly sliced
1 clove garlic, peeled and crushed
4 large ripe tomatoes, skinned and chopped
¼ cup white wine
salt
freshly ground black pepper
2 lb fish, cut in portions
2 tablespoons lemon juice
2 firm tomatoes, sliced
2 tablespoons chopped parsley or *mint*

Heat 3 tablespoons of the oil in a sauté pan and fry the onions gently until soft, about 10 minutes. Add the garlic, chopped tomatoes, wine and a little salt and pepper. Bring to simmering point and cook gently, uncovered, for 15 to 20 minutes, stirring now and then, until reduced to a sauce consistency.

Heat the oven, and oil a baking dish large enough to hold the fish in a single layer. Arrange the fish in the dish, season with salt and pepper and sprinkle with the lemon juice.

Spoon the sauce over the fish. Arrange the tomato slices on top of each portion and sprinkle with the remaining oil.

Bake, uncovered, in the centre of the oven for 20 to 30 minutes depending on the thickness of the fish, until cooked through. Sprinkle with parsley or mint.

Above: Salt Cod with Garlic Sauce
Below: Arcadian Baked Fish

Mackerel in Paper Cases

Sgombro in Cartoccio

This is a favourite Italian way of cooking small whole fish such as mackerel, trout and red mullet. Choose portion-size fish and serve them still in their paper cases complete with their cooking juices. Make the paper cases of double greaseproof (wax or parchment) paper or foil.

Preparation time: 30 minutes
Cooking time: 25 to 30 minutes
Oven temperature: 190°C/375°F, Gas Mark 5
To serve: 4

Metric/Imperial/American
*4 fresh mackerel, about 350 g/12 oz
(¾ lb) each, cleaned but heads and tails
left on*
salt
freshly ground black pepper
olive oil
*1 medium onion, peeled and finely
chopped*
2 sticks celery, finely chopped
1 clove garlic, peeled and finely crushed
1 tablespoon chopped fresh parsley
1 teaspoon dried basil or dill
2 tablespoons lemon juice

Season the cavity in the fish with salt and pepper and brush all over with oil. Cut out a heart-shaped piece of paper for each fish, about 5 cm/2 inches longer than the fish, and brush all over with oil. Lay a fish on one side of each paper heart.

Heat 2 tablespoons of oil in a small pan, add the onion and celery and fry gently for 10 minutes. Stir in the garlic, parsley, basil or dill, lemon juice and a seasoning of salt and pepper. Spoon a little of the vegetable mixture over each fish. Bring the edges of the paper together and twist firmly to seal in the fish.

Lay the parcels on an oiled baking sheet and bake for 25 minutes if using greaseproof (wax or parchment) paper but 30 minutes if foil. Serve in the paper cases.

Hake with Spinach

Merluza con Acelgas

Acelga is the name given to a rather coarse, spinach-like vegetable very popular in Spain, which is sometimes called Swiss chard in English. Spinach may be used instead.

Preparation time: 20 minutes
Cooking time: 30 minutes
Oven temperature: 180°C/350°F, Gas Mark 4
To serve: 4

Metric/Imperial
3 tablespoons olive oil
1 onion, peeled and very finely chopped
2 cloves garlic, peeled and chopped
4 thick slices of hake or cod
salt
2 tablespoons flour
*1 kg/2 lb Swiss chard or spinach, coarse
stalks removed and finely chopped*
freshly ground black pepper
*50 g/2 oz pine nuts or split blanched
almonds*

Above: Hake with Spinach. Below: Mackerel in Paper Cases

120 ml/4 fl oz dry sherry
2 tablespoons chopped fresh parsley

American
3 tablespoons olive oil
1 onion, peeled and very finely chopped
2 cloves garlic, peeled and chopped
4 thick slices of hake or cod
salt
2 tablespoons flour
2 lb Swiss chard or spinach, coarse
    stalks removed and finely chopped
freshly ground black pepper
½ cup pine nuts or split blanched
    almonds
½ cup sherry
2 tablespoons chopped fresh parsley

Heat 2 tablespoons of the oil in a shallow flameproof casserole. Add the onion and garlic and cook gently for a few minutes, stirring often. Flatten the slices of fish, sprinkle with salt and coat lightly with flour. Add to the casserole, clearing a space in the onion, and brown on both sides.

Meanwhile, cook the chard or spinach in very little boiling water until reduced to a purée. Mash the chard or spinach down and drain off any liquid. Season and mix in the nuts.

Remove the pieces of fish carefully from the casserole and keep hot. Stir the chard or spinach mixture into the oil and onion and flatten it down to cover the bottom of the casserole. Replace the fish on top, sprinkle with the remaining olive oil, the sherry and parsley and transfer to the oven. Bake for about 15 minutes. Serve in the casserole.

Lobster, Fish and Vegetable Salad

Maionese di Pesce alla Genovese

This sumptuous seafood salad, a simplification of a classic Genoese recipe, makes a perfect party piece. Crawfish is an excellent substitute for lobster, similar in all respects except that it lacks the large claws. Cook the vegetables in separate pans, timing each carefully to avoid overcooking any of them. And give yourself time to enjoy arranging and garnishing the salad to your own taste.

Preparation time: 1 hour (plus cooling)
Cooking time: 30 minutes
To serve: 6 to 8

Metric/Imperial
1 kg/2 lb firm white fish fillets,
    eg turbot, halibut or sea bass

salt
freshly ground black pepper
olive oil
0.75 kg/1½ lb lobster or crawfish, freshly
    cooked
225 g/8 oz potatoes, peeled, cooked and
    diced
225 g/8 oz carrots, peeled, diced and
    cooked
225 g/8 oz green beans, cooked and cut
    in short pieces
225 g/8 oz shelled fresh peas, cooked
about 600 ml/1 pint homemade
    mayonnaise
4 hard-boiled eggs, quartered
24 large unshelled cooked prawns
100 g/4 oz large stoned olives

American
2 lb firm white fish fillets, eg turbot,
    halibut or bass
salt
freshly ground black pepper
olive oil
1½ lb lobster or crawfish, freshly cooked
½ lb potatoes, peeled, cooked and diced
½ lb carrots, peeled, diced and cooked
½ lb green beans, cooked and cut in short
    pieces
1½ cups shelled fresh peas, cooked
about 1 pint homemade mayonnaise
4 hard-cooked eggs, quartered

Lobster, Fish and Vegetable Salad

24 unshelled jumbo shrimp
¾ cup large pitted olives

Steam or poach the fish fillets until just cooked, then drain, remove any skin or bone and cut into bite-size pieces. Put into a bowl, season with salt and pepper and sprinkle with oil. Leave to cool.

Meanwhile, remove the head, claws and legs from the lobster and reserve. Slit the shell beneath the tail, discard the intestine; remove the meat in one piece and cut neatly into slanting slices. Remove the meat from the claws, chop roughly and add to the fish fillets.

Combine the cooked potatoes, carrots, beans and half of the peas. Mix with enough mayonnaise to moisten them thoroughly. Season to taste.

Pile the fish mixture down the centre of a long oval serving dish. Arrange the lobster head at one end, some legs or feelers at the other end, and lay the slices of lobster tail meat, overlapping each other, along the top of the fish mixture. Border the fish with the vegetable mayonnaise and garnish with the remaining peas. Finally encircle the vegetables with alternating pieces of hard-boiled egg and the unshelled prawns (shrimp). Garnish with the olives.

Meat dishes

Casserole of Beef with Wine and Herbs

Boeuf en Daube Provençale

Each housewife will make this age-old country dish according to her own well-tried recipe. Originally, such *daubes* would have been carried to the village baker, to slip into the oven after the bread had been baked. The important point is that the beef is cooked with wine and herbs very slowly in a well-sealed casserole, until it becomes so tender it could be eaten with a spoon. An irresistible aroma will steal through the house during the long slow cooking. Serve with a *macaronade* (see page 114). Any beef left over can be used to make *Boeuf Mironton* (see page 71).

Preparation time: 30 minutes
Cooking time: 4 to 5 hours
Oven temperature: 140°C, 275°F, Gas Mark 1
To serve: 6 to 8

Metric/Imperial
1 tablespoon olive oil
225 g/8oz salt pork or streaky bacon, diced
2 onions, peeled and sliced
2 carrots, peeled and sliced
2 cloves garlic, peeled and finely chopped
1 kg/2¼ lb chuck or braising steak, trimmed of fat and cut into large cubes
600 ml/1 pint red wine
2 sprigs each of fresh thyme, rosemary and parsley
1 bay leaf
2 strips of orange rind
3 tomatoes, skinned and roughly chopped
salt
freshly ground black pepper
50 g/2 oz black olives, stoned (optional)

American
1 tablespoon olive oil
½ lb salt pork or bacon, diced
2 onions, peeled and sliced
2 carrots, peeled and sliced
2 cloves garlic, peeled and finely chopped
2¼ lb beef chuck steak, trimmed of fat and cut into large cubes
2½ cups red wine
2 sprigs each of fresh thyme, rosemary and parsley
1 bay leaf
2 strips of orange rind
3 tomatoes, skinned and roughly chopped

salt
freshly ground black pepper
⅓ cup pitted black olives (optional)

Heat the oil in a flameproof casserole, add salt pork or bacon and fry until transparent. Add the onions, carrots and garlic and continue frying until softened. Raise the heat, add the meat and brown on all sides.

Bring the wine to the boil in a separate saucepan and boil fiercely for 5 minutes. Pour it over the meat and add the herbs, orange rind, tomatoes and seasoning. Cover closely with a double thickness of foil and then the lid of the casserole and transfer to the very low oven. Cook for 4 to 5 hours. Add the olives to the dish 5 minutes before serving, if using.

Marinated Beef with Wine and Olives

Boeuf en Daube Niçoise

A more pungent type of *boeuf en daube*, this is characterized by the addition of the sharp little black olives of the region. Serve cold with a salad, or hot with potatoes baked with herbs (see page 130) or a *macaronade* (see page 114).

Preparation time: 20 minutes (plus 12 hours marinating)
Cooking time: 3 hours
Oven temperature: 150°C, 300°F, Gas Mark 2
To serve: 8 to 10

Metric/Imperial/American
Marinade:
4 tablespoons (¼ cup) olive oil
1 onion, peeled and sliced
1 carrot, peeled and sliced
1 stick (stalk) celery, chopped
300 ml/½ pint (1¼ cups) red wine
2 cloves garlic, peeled and sliced
6 peppercorns
2 sprigs each of fresh thyme, rosemary and parsley
2 bay leaves
2 cloves
2 strips of finely pared orange rind (dried, if possible)
Daube:
1.5 kg/3 lb piece of beef topside (round) or other rolled joint (boneless cut)
4 medium carrots, peeled and quartered lengthwise
2 cloves garlic, peeled
3 tomatoes, skinned, seeded and roughly chopped
2 sprigs of fresh thyme

225 g/8 oz salt pork or bacon, in one piece (not necessary if beef is wrapped in fat)
225 g/8 oz (1½ cups) black olives, stoned (pitted)
salt
black peppercorns, roughly crushed
Garnish (optional):
1 clove garlic, peeled and finely chopped
4 anchovy fillets, finely chopped
½ tablespoon capers, finely chopped
½ onion, peeled and finely chopped
small bunch of fresh parsley, finely chopped

To make the marinade, heat the oil in a small pan. Add the onion, carrot and celery and fry until lightly browned. Add the wine and let it bubble for 1 minute. Lower the heat and stir in the garlic, peppercorns, herbs, bay leaves, cloves and strips of orange rind. Simmer gently for 15 minutes. Leave to cool, then pour over the piece of beef in a large earthenware bowl. Leave to marinate for at least 12 hours, or longer if possible, turning the meat over several times.

The next day, place the beef in a frame-proof casserole just large enough to hold it. Arrange the carrots around the sides, add the garlic, tomatoes and thyme and place the piece of salt pork or bacon on top. Pour on the strained marinade. Bring just to the boil, then cover with a double thickness of foil and the lid and transfer to the slow oven. Cook for 2½ hours. Add the olives and seasoning, re-cover and cook for a further 30 minutes.

If the dish is to be served hot, cut the meat into thick slices and arrange on a deep serving platter surrounded by the carrots and olives. Pour over the sauce and garnish, if you like, with the garlic, anchovy, capers, onion and parsley mixed together.

If the dish is to be served cold, leave overnight in the refrigerator, then lift off the lid of fat which will have set on top.

Slice the meat thickly and arrange on a deep serving platter. Warm the remaining contents of the casserole gently, lift out the carrots and olives and arrange them around the meat. Strain the sauce over the dish, and leave to set in the refrigerator.

Above: Casserole of Beef with Wine and Herbs
Below: Marinated Beef with Wine and Olives

Beef and Potato Casserole

Kreas me Patates

Nothing could be simpler to prepare than this family dish combining beef and potatoes in one pot. It is a satisfying dish and a winter favourite all over Greece. The tomato gives the potatoes a rich colour, but try to choose the type of potatoes that keep their shape when cooked. With it serve a leafy green vegetable.

Preparation time: 30 minutes
Cooking time: 2¼ to 2½ hours
To serve: 6

Metric/Imperial
1 kg/2 lb braising beef
3 tablespoons oil
1 large onion, peeled and chopped
2 bay leaves
1 clove garlic, peeled and crushed
salt
freshly ground black pepper
3 tablespoons tomato purée
450 ml/¾ pint water
1 kg/2 lb potatoes, peeled

American
2 lb chuck steak
3 tablespoons oil
1 large onion, peeled and chopped
2 bay leaves
1 clove garlic, peeled and crushed
salt
freshly ground black pepper
3 tablespoons tomato paste
1 pint water
2 lb potatoes, peeled

A herd of cattle in a Turkish village

Cut the meat into 2.5 cm/1 inch cubes and pat them dry with kitchen paper. Heat the oil in a deep flameproof casserole and when hot fry one-third of the meat fairly briskly until browned on all sides. Remove to a plate with a slotted spoon. Repeat with the remaining two-thirds of the meat.

Add the onion to the casserole and fry gently for several minutes, then return the meat to the pot with the bay leaves, garlic and salt and pepper to taste. Mix the tomato purée (paste) with the water, pour over the meat and stir. Bring the casserole to simmering point, cover tightly and simmer very gently for 1½ to 2 hours until the meat is almost tender, stirring occasionally and adding a little more water if necessary.

Cut the potatoes into quarters if small, into thick wedges if large. Stir the potatoes gently into the casserole, mixing them with the meat and gravy. Cover and simmer for a further 15 to 20 minutes, until the potatoes are tender and the sauce thick; avoid stirring again so as not to break up the potatoes. By the time the meat and potatoes are cooked only a small amount of sauce should be left. Serve from the casserole.

Winter Casserole

Stifatho

There are various ways of preparing this favourite Greek family recipe, but whether the meat used is veal, beef or something else the special features of the dish are a large number of small onions and a small amount of rich, well-reduced tomato sauce.

Preparation time: 35 minutes
Cooking time: 2 to 3 hours
To serve: 6

Metric/Imperial
1 kg/2 lb lean braising beef or veal
4 tablespoons olive oil
1 kg/2 lb shallots or small onions, peeled
2 large cloves garlic, peeled and crushed
3 tablespoons tomato purée
450 ml/¾ pint water
150 ml/¼ pint red wine
2 tablespoons wine vinegar
2 bay leaves
salt
freshly ground black pepper
2 tablespoons chopped fresh parsley

American
2 lb lean beef or veal stew meat
¼ cup olive oil
2 lb shallots or small onions, peeled
2 large cloves garlic, peeled and crushed
3 tablespoons tomato paste
1 pint water
⅔ cup red wine
2 tablespoons wine vinegar
2 bay leaves
salt
freshly ground black pepper
2 tablespoons chopped fresh parsley

Cut the meat into 2.5 cm/1 inch cubes and pat dry with kitchen paper. Heat the oil in a large flameproof casserole and fry one-third of the meat, turning the pieces to brown on all sides. Remove with a slotted spoon and reserve. Fry the remaining meat, one-third at a time, in the same way. Fry the onions in the same oil for about 10 minutes, stirring them now and again, until lightly browned, then remove with a slotted spoon and reserve separately.

Put the garlic, tomato purée (paste), water, wine, vinegar, bay leaves and salt and pepper to taste into the casserole, stir well and bring to the boil. Return the meat to the pot, and stir. When the liquid regains boiling point lower the heat, cover tightly and simmer very gently for about 1½ hours.

Add the onions to the casserole, pushing them under the liquid. Re-cover and continue cooking gently for another 30 to 60 minutes depending on how long the onions take to become tender. By the time both meat and onions are cooked the sauce should be thick and rich; if not uncover the pan and cook a little longer and faster until the sauce is reduced, but watch that it does not burn. Remove the bay leaves and serve the casserole sprinkled with parsley.

Above: Beef and Potato Casserole
Below: Winter Casserole

Casserole of Veal

Spezzatino di Vitello

This is a tasty family dish popular in Italy usually made with mature veal, but equally good when made with lamb. Serve with plain boiled potatoes. If no white wine is available replace it with equal quantities of dry white vermouth and water.

Preparation time: 20 minutes
Cooking time: about 2 hours
To serve: 6

Metric/Imperial
1 kg/2 lb boneless shoulder or leg of
   veal, cut into 2.5 cm/1 inch cubes
flour for coating
40 g/1½ oz butter
3 thick rashers unsmoked streaky bacon,
   cut into 1 cm/½ inch cubes
1 onion, peeled and chopped
150 ml/¼ pint dry white wine
2 to 3 chilli peppers, cut into thin strips
1 stick celery, sliced
1 tablespoon tomato purée
300 ml/½ pint stock
salt
225 g/8 oz shelled fresh peas

American
2 lb boneless shoulder or leg of veal, cut
   into 1 inch cubes
flour for coating
3 tablespoons butter
3 thick slices bacon, cut into ½ inch cubes
1 onion, peeled and chopped
⅔ cup dry white wine
2 to 3 chili peppers, cut into thin strips
1 stalk celery, sliced
1 tablespoon tomato paste
1¼ cups stock
salt
1½ cups shelled fresh peas

Coat the veal cubes with flour. Put the butter and bacon cubes into a flame-proof casserole and cook gently for 5 minutes or until the bacon fat begins to run. Add the onion and fry for a few minutes, then add the veal and fry, stirring frequently, until golden. Stir in the wine and allow to bubble until well reduced.

Add the chillis, celery, tomato purée (paste), stock and a little salt. Bring to the boil, stirring, then cover and simmer very gently for about 1½ hours. Check the seasoning, add the peas and continue cooking for another 20 to 30 minutes or until the peas are tender. Serve from the casserole.

Fried Lamb Chops with Piquant Dressing

Costolette di Agnello Appetitose

This is a simple Italian way of adding flavour and interest to a dish of lamb chops.

Preparation time: 15 minutes (plus 2
   hours marinating)
Cooking time: 15 minutes
To serve: 4

Metric/Imperial/American
8 lamb chops
salt
freshly ground black pepper
2 cloves garlic, peeled and crushed
4 tablespoons (¼ cup) olive oil
2 tablespoons finely chopped fresh
   parsley
1 teaspoon finely chopped fresh oregano
2 tablespoons lemon juice
2 tablespoons capers, chopped
To serve:
diced sautéed potatoes
1 lemon, cut into 8 wedges

Lay the chops side by side in a shallow dish. Season them generously with salt and pepper, sprinkle over the garlic and oil, cover and leave in a cool place to marinate for at least 2 hours.

When ready to cook, pour the marinade into a large frying pan (skillet), add the chopped herbs and heat. When hot fry the chops briskly until golden on each side, then lower the heat and fry gently until cooked, about 5 to 6 minutes on each side. Squeeze the lemon juice over the chops and add the capers and a light seasoning of salt and pepper. Cook gently for another minute or so.

Arrange the chops around a pile of sautéed potatoes on a hot serving dish and spoon the pan juices over them. Garnish with the segments of lemon and serve immediately.

Left: Casserole of Veal
Centre: Fried Lamb Chops with Piquant Dressing

Right: Sweetbreads with Marsala and Sage

Sweetbreads with Marsala and Sage

Animelle al Marsala con Salvia

The bland flavour of sweetbreads is enhanced by this combination of Marsala with sage and bacon. Served with braised spinach they make a pleasant main course.

Preparation time: 20 minutes (plus 1 hour for soaking sweetbreads)
Cooking time: 20 minutes
To serve: 4

Metric/Imperial
450 g/1 lb lambs' sweetbreads
salt
1 tablespoon wine vinegar
50 g/2 oz butter
1 tablespoon oil
2 good sprigs of fresh sage,
   or 1 teaspoon dried sage
75 g/3 oz thin rashers lean bacon, cut
   into matchstick strips
freshly ground black pepper
6 tablespoons Marsala
To serve:
4 slices of bread, fried in butter
slim wedges of lemon

American
1 lb lamb sweetbreads
salt
1 tablespoon wine vinegar
¼ cup butter
1 tablespoon oil
2 large sprigs of fresh sage, or 1 teaspoon
   dried sage
3 oz Canadian bacon, cut into
   matchstick strips
freshly ground black pepper
6 tablespoons Marsala
To serve:
4 slices of bread, fried in butter
slim wedges of lemon

Cover the sweetbreads with cold water and leave to soak for at least 1 hour. Drain, put in a saucepan and cover with fresh cold water. Add 2 teaspoons salt and the wine vinegar and bring slowly to the boil. Drain and cover again with fresh cold water. When cool enough to handle cut away any tubes or thick pieces of membrane. Divide the sweetbreads into small pieces and pat dry.

Melt the butter with the oil in a wide saucepan, add the sage and the sweetbreads and toss over fairly brisk heat until beginning to look glazed and golden. Add the bacon and some pepper and cook, stirring gently, for another 2 minutes. Add half the Marsala and continue stirring and cooking until the winc has almost evaporated, then add the rest of the wine and stir and cook until it has reduced to a syrupy glaze. Remove the sage, check the seasoning and serve the sweetbreads on slices of fried bread, garnished with slim wedges of lemon.

Tongue with Sauce

Lenqua en Salsa

This is a dish which is best cooked in advance, so cook the tongue early, or better still the day before.

Preparation time: 40 minutes (plus 1 to 2 hours soaking)
Cooking time: about 4 hours
To serve: 4 to 6

Metric/Imperial
1 kg/2 lb salted ox tongue
1 carrot, peeled
1 stick celery
1 onion, peeled
2 cloves garlic, peeled
1 bay leaf
Sauce:
50 g/2 oz butter or dripping
75 g/3 oz flour
150 ml/¼ pint milk
150 ml/¼ pint dry sherry
1 tablespoon chopped fresh parsley
salt if necessary
freshly ground black pepper

American
2 lb salted beef tongue
1 carrot, peeled
1 celery stalk
1 onion, peeled
2 cloves garlic, peeled
1 bay leaf
Sauce:
¼ cup butter or drippings
¾ cup flour
⅔ cup milk
⅔ cup dry sherry
1 tablespoon chopped fresh parsley
salt if necessary
freshly ground black pepper

Soak the tongue for 1 to 2 hours, then bring to the boil in a saucepan of fresh water. Throw the water away and re-fill the saucepan with more fresh water; this should get rid of surplus salt. Add the carrot, celery, onion, garlic and bay leaf and simmer for 2½ to 3 hours or until the tongue is tender. Lift it out and peel off the skin. Trim off any fatty bits and small bones in the base and curl the tongue around itself. Put it into a tight-fitting straight-sided casserole or cake pan and press the top down with a weighted plate. Allow to cool completely and leave in the container overnight if possible.

Strain the stock and reserve 300 ml/½ pint (1¼ cups) for the sauce.

About 20 minutes before you want to serve the tongue make the sauce. Melt the butter or dripping in a saucepan, stir in the flour and when it thickens gradually stir in the reserved stock and milk. Cook, stirring until it forms a smooth sauce. (Taste the stock first to make sure it is not too salty; if so dilute with more milk.) Stir in the sherry and parsley and adjust the seasoning. Simmer very gently while you remove the tongue from its bowl and slice it neatly. Arrange the slices in a shallow flame-proof dish. Pour over the hot sauce and warm on a very low heat for about 5 minutes or until it just starts to bubble. Serve at once in the same dish. Plainly boiled potatoes and broad (Lima) beans go well with this.

Braised Beef with Pomegranate

Ternera en Salsa de Granada

This recipe is from Mallorca, where meat cooked with pomegranate is popular. *Ternera* is very young beef, but not quite veal. Choose the tenderest beef you can find.

Preparation time: 15 minutes
Cooking time: about 1 hour
Oven temperature: 180°C/350°F, Gas Mark 4
To serve: 4

Metric/Imperial
50 g/2 oz beef dripping or lard
4 thick slices of lean beef
16 small onions or shallots, peeled
salt
300 ml/½ pint red wine
seeds and pulp of 2 pomegranates

68

American

¼ cup beef drippings or lard
4 thick slices of lean beef
16 pearl onions or shallots, peeled
salt
1¼ cups red wine
seeds and pulp of 2 pomegranates

Heat the fat in shallow flameproof casserole and seal the meat briefly on both sides. Add the onions and turn them in the hot fat. Remove from the heat, sprinkle with salt and pour in the red wine. Cover the casserole and transfer to the oven. Cook for about 45 minutes.

Add the pomegranate seeds and pulp to the casserole and cook for another 15 minutes.

Take the casserole straight to the table and serve with baked potatoes and green salad as a side dish.

Left: Tongue with Sauce
Centre: Braised Beef with Pomegranate
Right: Kidneys in Sherry Sauce

Kidneys in Sherry Sauce

Riñones al Jerez

This is a classic dish from Andalucia in southern Spain.

Preparation time: 20 minutes
Cooking time: 20 minutes
To serve: 4

Metric/Imperial

3 tablespoons olive oil
1 large onion, peeled and finely chopped
2 cloves garlic, peeled and finely chopped
1 tablespoon flour
300 ml/½ pint beef or chicken stock (or use a stock cube)
1 tablespoon tomato purée
1 bay leaf
salt
freshly ground black pepper
50 g/2 oz lard or butter
1 kg/2 lb calves' kidneys, all skin, fat and white tissue removed, thinly sliced
150 ml/¼ pint dry sherry
1 tablespoon chopped fresh parsley

American

3 tablespoons olive oil
1 large onion, peeled and finely chopped
2 cloves garlic, peeled and finely chopped
1 tablespoon flour
1¼ cups beef or chicken stock (or use a bouillon cube)
1 tablespoon tomato paste
1 bay leaf
salt
freshly ground black pepper
¼ cup lard or butter
2 lb veal kidneys, all skin, fat and white tissue removed, thinly sliced
⅔ cup dry sherry
1 tablespoon chopped fresh parsley

Heat the oil in a saucepan and fry the onion and garlic until the onions are transparent, about 7 minutes. Stir in the flour, cook for 1 to 2 minutes, stirring constantly, then stir in the stock, tomato paste and bay leaf. Bring to the boil and stir until a thick sauce is formed. Season to taste. Lower the heat and continue to simmer for 3 minutes. Remove from heat and keep hot.

Melt the lard or butter in a large frying pan (skillet) and put in the kidneys. Cook briefly, turning them over all the time to brown evenly on all sides. Remove and keep hot. Pour the sherry into the pan and let it bubble for about 1 minute, stirring in all the bits left sticking to the pan. Return the kidneys to the pan with the sauce and the parsley and cook gently, stirring, for another 2 minutes or so. Adjust the seasoning and remove the bay leaf. Serve with rice.

Lamb and Vegetable Casserole

Daube d'Avignon

A hearty and warming peasant dish, you might be offered this anywhere in Provence, although it is associated particularly with the town famous for the dancing lords and ladies on its lovely old Ròman bridge.

Serve with a robust red or white wine, and follow with a refreshing salad.

Preparation time: 40 minutes (plus overnight marinating)
Cooking time: 3 to 4 hours
To serve: 6 to 8

Metric/Imperial/American
1 leg or *shoulder of lamb, boned and cut into 5 cm/2 in cubes*
2 *large onions, peeled and quartered*
1 *large carrot, peeled and quartered*
3 *cloves garlic, peeled and finely chopped*
1 *teaspoon salt*
½ *teaspoon freshly ground black pepper*
2 *sprigs each of fresh thyme, rosemary and marjoram* or 2 *teaspoons each dried*
2 *bay leaves*
3 *strips of finely pared orange rind*
450 ml/¾ (1 US) *pint red wine*
2 *tablespoons brandy*

Lamb and Vegetable Casserole

A quayside scene on the island of Corfu

5 tablespoons olive oil
100 g/4 oz (½ cup) bacon or salt pork, diced
225 g/8 oz onions, peeled and thinly
   sliced
0.5 kg/1 lb carrots, peeled and cut into
   rings
0.5 kg/1 lb (2 cups) dried haricot (navy)
   beans, soaked overnight
1 sprig of fresh rosemary
1 tablespoon finely chopped fresh
   parsley

Place the meat in a large bowl with the quartered onions and carrot, 1 clove of garlic, the salt, pepper, herbs, orange rind, wine, brandy and 2 tablespoons of the olive oil. Leave to marinate for 4 to 5 hours, or overnight, turning the meat occasionally.

Heat the remaining olive oil in a flameproof casserole, add the bacon or salt pork and fry until it has rendered most of its fat. Add the sliced onions,

the carrot rings and the remaining garlic. Raise the heat and allow the vegetables to brown. Add the meat and pour on the marinade. Bring to the boil and simmer for 5 minutes, then cover and leave to simmer very gently for 3 to 4 hours, by which time the meat should be very tender, and the sauce much reduced. Taste for seasoning.

Meanwhile, cook the drained haricot (navy) beans in fresh boiling water with the sprig of rosemary. Remove the rosemary when the beans are cooked. Drain well and stir in 2 or 3 tablespoons of sauce from the *daube*, together with the parsley, before serving. You can make the *daube* a day ahead, keep it in the refrigerator, and skim the fat off the sauce before reheating gently.

Beef Baked with Capers

Beef Baked with Capers

Boeuf Mironton

This is the Niçois version of shepherd's pie – a tasty way of using up cooked beef, from a *daube*, for instance, or a *pot-au-feu*. Serve with potatoes, plain boiled noodles or a *macaronade* (see page 114).

Preparation time: 15 minutes
Cooking time: 30 to 40 minutes
Oven temperature: 190°C, 375°F, Gas
   Mark 5
To serve: 6

Metric/Imperial
3 tablespoons olive oil
2 onions, peeled and finely chopped
1 clove garlic, peeled and finely chopped
4 tomatoes, skinned and roughly
   chopped
½ tablespoon wine vinegar
150 ml/¼ pint beef stock or sauce from
   the daube
pinch of grated nutmeg
salt
freshly ground black pepper
about 0.5 kg/1 lb cooked beef, sliced or
   chopped
2 tablespoons capers
100 g/4 oz fresh breadcrumbs

American
3 tablespoons olive oil
2 onions, peeled and finely chopped
1 clove garlic, peeled and finely chopped
4 tomatoes, skinned and roughly
   chopped
½ tablespoon wine vinegar
⅔ cup beef stock or sauce from the daube
pinch of grated nutmeg
salt
freshly ground black pepper
about 1 lb (2 cups) cooked beef, sliced or
   chopped
2 tablespoons capers
½ cup fresh breadcrumbs

Heat 2 tablespoons of the oil in a large frying pan (skillet), add the onions and garlic and fry gently until golden brown. Raise the heat, add the tomatoes and cook for a few minutes to evaporate their moisture. Stir in the vinegar and then the stock or sauce, nutmeg and seasoning. Simmer for 5 minutes.

Butter or oil a baking dish and pour in half the sauce. Put the meat on top, scatter on the capers and cover with the remaining sauce. Sprinkle on the breadcrumbs, the remaining oil and bake for 30 to 40 minutes, until golden brown.

Pot-au-feu
Provençal

Boiled Beef and Lamb with Vegetables

Provence is not only a region of sun-baked olive trees, fruit blossom and Van Gogh landscapes; the mistral sweeps ruthlessly across the area in winter and spring, and stomachs need lining against the bitter cold. The *pot-au-feu* is the French housewife's all-purpose stock-pot dish, which provides at least two courses from one pot. The proportion of the different kinds of meat to each other is not important, but what is important is that each piece of meat should be of a substantial size, so that it does not disintegrate in the long slow cooking.

A really large cooking pot is essential for this dish.

Preparation time: 40 minutes
Cooking time: 3½ hours
To serve: 10 to 12

Metric/Imperial

1 kg/2 lb lamb (½ shoulder or leg, or best end of neck)
1 kg/2 lb piece of beef (topside, top rib, brisket or silverside)
1 beef marrow bone
1 knuckle of veal (optional)
1 chicken carcass or small boiling fowl
4 litres/7 pints water
2 large onions, washed not peeled
4 cloves
2 cloves garlic, peeled
2 leeks
2 carrots, peeled
4 tomatoes, halved and lightly grilled
1 stick celery
12 juniper berries
1 bouquet garni
1 tablespoon salt
150 ml/¼ pint white wine
freshly ground black pepper
To serve:
0.5 kg/1 lb carrots, peeled and cut into rings or quartered lengthways
0.5 kg/1 lb potatoes, peeled
0.5 kg/1 lb turnips, peeled
1 French loaf
1 tablespoon finely chopped fresh parsley

American

2 lb lamb (½ shoulder or leg, or rack)
2 lb piece of beef (top round or brisket)
1 beef marrow bone
1 veal shank (optional)
1 chicken carcass or small stewing chicken
4 quarts water
2 large onions, washed not peeled

4 cloves
2 cloves garlic, peeled
2 leeks
2 carrots, peeled
4 tomatoes, halved and lightly broiled
1 stalk celery
12 juniper berries
1 bouquet garni
1 tablespoon salt
⅔ cup white wine
freshly ground black pepper
To serve:
1 lb carrots, peeled and cut into rings or quartered lengthwise
1 lb potatoes, peeled
1 lb turnips, peeled
1 French loaf
1 tablespoon finely chopped fresh parsley

Trim excess fat off the lamb, and make sure both pieces of meat are securely tied. Tie the marrow bone in a piece of muslin or cheesecloth, so as not to lose the marrow.

Put the meat, knuckle of veal and chicken into a large pot. Cover with the cold water and bring very slowly to the boil. Skim off all the grey scum that will rise to the top for the next 30 minutes. When the water is clear, add the onions stuck with the cloves, the garlic, leeks, carrots, tomatoes, celery, juniper berries, bouquet garni and salt. Cover and simmer very gently, so that the water just barely moves, for 2 hours. Add the marrow bone and cook for another hour.

Meanwhile, cook the carrots, potatoes and turnips separately in boiling water. Alternatively, they can be added to the pot to cook in the broth for the last 30 minutes but will not have as fresh a taste. When the dish is ready to be served, lift out the pieces of meat, slice thickly and arrange on a serving platter. Surround with the carrots, potatoes and turnips and keep hot. Strain the broth through a damp cloth into a clean saucepan to get a really clear broth. Skim off excess fat, bring to the boil and boil rapidly for 5 minutes. Add the wine and pepper and taste for seasoning. Toast one slice of French bread per person, or dry the slices in the oven. Spread on the marrow from the bone, and serve these with the strained broth for the first course.

Moisten the meat and vegetables with a ladleful of the broth, sprinkle with the parsley and serve for the second course.

Fried Lamb with
Garlic

Cordero Frito con Ajo

Lamb and garlic go well together and this is a favourite Spanish way of using up cold leftover lamb.

Preparation time: 15 minutes
Cooking time: about 30 minutes
To serve: 4

Metric/Imperial

1 kg/2 lb cooked boneless lamb, cut into walnut-size pieces
flour for coating
4 tablespoons olive oil
3 onions, peeled and finely chopped
3 cloves garlic, peeled and crushed
4 tomatoes, skinned and chopped
150 ml/¼ pint dry white wine
salt
freshly ground black pepper
a few black or green olives

American

2 lb cooked boneless lamb, cut into walnut-sized pieces
flour for coating
¼ cup olive oil
3 onions, peeled and finely chopped
3 cloves garlic, peeled and crushed
4 tomatoes, skinned and chopped
⅔ cup dry white wine
salt
freshly ground black pepper
a few black or green olives

Dust the lamb with flour. Heat the oil in a frying pan (skillet) or saucepan and brown the pieces of lamb, turning them carefully. Remove and set aside.

Put the onions, garlic and tomatoes into the pan and cook gently until almost a purée. Return the meat to the pan and stir in the wine. Season with salt and pepper and cook for a few minutes to heat through. Serve on a bed of rice, garnished with the olives.

Above: Pot-au-feu Provençal
Below: Fried Lamb with Garlic

Mousaka

Minced Meat and Vegetable Pie

Mousaka is the shepherd's pie of Greece. Every cook varies the recipe and seasoning to suit her own family or the state of the larder. Aubergine (eggplant) is the favourite vegetable ingredient, but courgette (zucchini) or potato are popular alternatives. Served with a green salad, mousaka makes an excellent luncheon or buffet supper dish and needs no last-minute preparation.

Preparation time: 30 minutes
Cooking time: 45 minutes
Oven temperature: 180°C/350°F, Gas Mark 4
To serve: 6

Mousaka

Metric/Imperial
3 large aubergines, about 1 kg/2 lb
salt
olive oil
1 large onion, peeled and thinly sliced
675 g/1½ lb minced lean lamb or beef
1 x 400 g/14 oz can peeled tomatoes, drained and chopped
1 clove garlic, peeled and crushed
2 tablespoons chopped fresh parsley
freshly ground black pepper
75 g/3 oz cheese, finely grated
Sauce:
25 g/1 oz butter
25 g/1 oz flour
450 ml/¾ pint hot milk
salt
pepper
¼ teaspoon grated nutmeg
2 small eggs

American
3 large eggplants, about 2 lb
salt
olive oil
1 large onion, peeled and thinly sliced
1½ lb ground lean lamb or beef
1 x 14 oz can peeled tomatoes, drained and chopped
1 clove garlic, peeled and crushed
2 tablespoons chopped fresh parsley
freshly ground black pepper
¾ cup finely grated cheese
Sauce:
2 tablespoons butter
¼ cup flour
1 pint hot milk
salt
pepper
¼ teaspoon grated nutmeg
2 eggs

Cut off the green stems from the aubergines (eggplants), wipe them and cut lengthwise into 1 cm/½ inch thick slices. Put the slices in a colander, sprinkling salt liberally between each layer, and leave for 30 minutes to allow the bitter juices to drain away.

Heat 2 tablespoons oil in a saucepan and fry the onion gently for 6 minutes, until soft and golden. Add the meat and fry, stirring, until lightly browned. Add the tomatoes, garlic, parsley and salt and pepper to taste and cook gently for 15 minutes. The mixture should become fairly thick so, if necessary, increase the heat towards the end of the cooking, but stir frequently to prevent it sticking.

Rinse the aubergine (eggplant) slices in cold water and pat dry with kitchen paper. Heat 3 mm/⅛ inch depth of oil in a large heavy frying pan (skillet) and fry the aubergine (eggplant) slices, in batches, until lightly browned on each side. They absorb rather a lot of oil, so add more oil to the pan as necessary. Drain the fried slices on kitchen paper.

Cover the bottom of a 25 x 20 cm/ 10 x 8 inch baking dish, that is 5 cm/ 2 inches deep, with aubergine (eggplant) slices. Then arrange alternate layers of the meat mixture, a sprinkling of cheese and aubergine (eggplant) slices on top, finishing with aubergine (eggplant). Reserve a little of the cheese.

To make the sauce melt the butter in a saucepan, add the flour and stir and cook for 1 to 2 minutes. Gradually stir in the hot milk and whisk until the sauce boils and thickens. Season to taste with salt, pepper and nutmeg. Simmer gently for 5 minutes and remove from the heat.

Beat the eggs lightly in a bowl with 2 tablespoons of the sauce, then return to the pan of sauce, stirring well. Spoon the sauce evenly over the surface of the mousaka and sprinkle with the remaining cheese. Bake in the centre of the oven for 45 minutes until golden brown and bubbling.

Lamb on Skewers

Arni Souvlákia

The sharp aromatic scent of skewered lamb cooking over charcoal is part of the magic of a Greek island holiday. Lean shoulder lamb can be substituted for leg, but it is important to allow time for the meat to marinate for several hours before cooking. Use long, flat-bladed kebab skewers, if possible, which hold the meat firmly while cooking.

Preparation time: 15 minutes, plus 2 to
 4 hours to marinate
Cooking time: 8 to 12 minutes
To serve: 4

Metric/Imperial
675 g/1½ lb boneless leg of lamb
salt
freshly ground black pepper
1 teaspoon dried marjoram
2 small onions, peeled
4 tablespoons olive oil
1 tablespoon lemon juice
4 bay leaves, halved

American
1½ lb boneless leg of lamb
salt
freshly ground black pepper
1 teaspoon dried marjoram
2 small onions, peeled
¼ cup olive oil
1 tablespoon lemon juice
4 bay leaves, halved

Trim away skin or excess fat from the lamb. Cut the meat into 2 cm/¾ inch cubes. Put into a mixing bowl, season with salt and pepper and sprinkle with the marjoram.

Cut the onions into quarters. Keep the thick outer pieces for the kebabs, and chop and reserve the inner core for a tomato salad to accompany the cooked lamb.

Add the outer onion pieces, olive oil and lemon juice to the meat, stir gently, cover and leave to marinate in a cool place for 2 to 4 hours.

When ready to cook divide the meat between four long skewers, impaling a piece of onion or half a bay leaf between every two pieces of meat. Push the meat into the centre of the skewers, leaving the ends free.

Arrange the skewers about 7.5 cm/ 3 inches below a preheated grill (broiler), or over a glowing charcoal fire, and cook for about 8 to 12 minutes, until nicely browned outside but still pink and juicy inside. Turn the skewers once and keep well basted with the marinade. Serve on the skewers with a wedge of lemon, thick slices of crusty bread and a tomato salad.

For snack meals the meat can be pushed off the skewers and served in a *pitta* bread.

Lamb on skewers

Casserole of Beans with Pork and Lamb

Cassoulet de Toulouse

Three towns in the Languedoc – Castel-naudry, Toulouse and Carcassone – claim this classic dish as their own. Each has its own particular variation, but the basic ingredients of any cassoulet are haricot (navy) beans, a well-flavoured pork sausage, and a piece of preserved goose (*confit d'oie*). The latter can be bought canned, but if it is not available a perfectly good *cassoulet* can be made without it. This version, from Toulouse, which includes lamb as well as pork, is particularly satisfying.

Essential is a really large cassoulet pot, or casserole.

Preparation time: 1 hour
Cooking time: about 3 hours
Oven temperature: 150°C, 300°F, Gas Mark 2
To serve: 10 to 12

Metric/Imperial
1 kg/2 lb dried white haricot beans
225 g/8 oz salt pork or bacon, in one piece
0.5 kg/1 lb loin or shoulder of pork, boned
2 tablespoons oil or fat from preserved goose
2 onions, peeled and thinly sliced
3 cloves garlic, peeled and finely chopped
1 small shoulder of lamb (or ½ large one), boned
1 piece preserved goose (optional)
0.5 kg/1 lb coarse pork and garlic sausage (whole)
4 tablespoons concentrated tomato purée
1.75 litres/3 pints water
salt
freshly ground black pepper
1 bouquet garni
100 g/4 oz fresh breadcrumbs (or more, see below)

American
2 lb (4 cups) dried navy beans
½ lb salt pork or bacon, in one piece
1 lb loin or shoulder of pork, boned
2 tablespoons oil or fat from preserved goose
2 onions, peeled and thinly sliced
3 cloves garlic, peeled and finely chopped
1 small shoulder of lamb (or ½ large one), boned
1 piece preserved goose (optional)

1 lb coarse pork and garlic sausage (whole)
¼ cup tomato paste
1¾ quarts water
salt
freshly ground black pepper
1 bouquet garni
2 cups fresh breadcrumbs (or more, see below)

Rinse the beans in cold water, then put into a large saucepan. Cover with cold water, bring slowly to the boil and simmer for 5 minutes. Remove from the heat, cover and leave to soak in the water while you prepare the remaining ingredients.

Remove the rind from the salt pork or bacon, and from the pork, and cut it into small squares.

Heat the oil or goose fat in a large frying pan (skillet) and fry the onions and garlic until softened. Add the pieces of rind and fry gently for 5 minutes. Raise the heat and brown on all sides, in turn, the piece of pork, the shoulder of lamb, the piece of goose and the sausage. Remove each from the pan when it is browned and set aside. Add the tomato purée (paste) to the pan with a little of the water, stir well to amalgamate any sediment and bring quickly to the boil.

Drain the beans, rinse them and put them in a clean saucepan with the remaining cold water. Bring to the boil, then pour the beans and water into the cassoulet pot. Add the contents of the frying pan (skillet) and seasoning, and stir well. Bury the salt pork or bacon, the pork, the shoulder of lamb, the preserved goose and the sausage among the beans, add the bouquet garni, and bring everything to simmering point on top of the stove.

Sprinkle on a thick layer of breadcrumbs and place the cassoulet pot in the oven. Cook for 2 to 3 hours. From time to time press down the crust which will have formed on top and sprinkle on a further layer of breadcrumbs. Tradition has it that the crust must be pressed down and renewed seven times, but after three times you should have a lovely golden crust. Larger pieces of meat should be cut up before serving.

Lamb with Anchovy and Garlic

Gigot d'Agneau à l'Aillade

A typical Provençal dish, this makes liberal use of two of the region's most popular ingredients. The marinating of

the lamb gives it a full-bodied, almost gamey flavour, while the gentle stewing of the garlic cloves takes the sting out of their aroma and reduces them to a rich – but harmless – sauce.

Preparation time: 20 minutes (plus 3 to 4 hours marinating)
Cooking time: 1½ to 2 hours
Oven temperature: 220°C, 425°F, Gas Mark 7, reduced to 190°C, 375°F, Gas Mark 5
To serve: 6 to 8

Metric/Imperial/American
2 tablespoons olive oil
1 teaspoon dried rosemary, crumbled
1 teaspoon dried thyme
1 teaspoon sea (coarse) salt
1 teaspoon freshly ground black pepper
1 leg of lamb
12 to 18 cloves garlic, peeled
12 anchovy fillets, halved lengthways and chopped
150 ml/¼ pint (⅔ cup) white wine
1 tablespoon finely chopped fresh parsley or mint

Combine the olive oil with the herbs, salt and pepper, and rub this mixture liberally into the leg of lamb.

Cut about 6 of the garlic cloves into thin slivers. Using a sharp-pointed kitchen knife, make shallow incisions all over the leg of lamb and insert a sliver of garlic and a piece of anchovy into each incision. Leave the lamb to marinate for 3 to 4 hours.

Place the lamb on a rack in a roasting pan and put in the centre of the hot oven. Roast for 20 minutes, then reduce the oven temperature and continue roasting until cooked medium rare, allowing about 20 minutes to each 450 g/1 lb at the lower temperature. The flesh when pierced should produce a clear pale liquid, and the meat, when carved, should be pale pink.

Meanwhile, put the remaining cloves of garlic into a small saucepan with a little water and stew gently for 10 to 15 minutes, until they are soft. Drain and mash with a fork or in a mortar.

When the meat is cooked, remove it from the pan and leave to breathe for 5 minutes before carving into thick slices. Keep warm on a heated platter.

Pour the wine into the roasting pan, place it over a gentle heat on top of the stove and stir well to combine with the juices in the pan. Bring quickly to the boil, then stir in the mashed garlic. Add the parsley or mint and pour over the meat before serving.

Left: Casserole of Beans with Pork and Lamb
Right: Lamb with Anchovy and Garlic

Meat Balls with Egg and Lemon Sauce

Youvarlákia me Saltsa Avgholemono

In Greece, the best and most delicate meat balls are made from good quality finely minced (ground) veal, or failing that lean pork; but lamb or beef can also be used. The broth in which the meat balls are poached forms the basis of the egg and lemon sauce in which they are served. The dish goes well with fluffy boiled rice, and salad is usually served separately.

Preparation time: 30 minutes
Cooking time: 40 minutes
To serve: 4

Metric/Imperial
25 g/1 oz butter
2 tablespoons grated onion
450 g/1 lb finely minced shoulder veal or pork
75 g/3 oz fresh fine white breadcrumbs
1 egg, beaten
6 tablespoons white wine or water
salt
freshly ground black pepper
600 ml/1 pint good chicken or veal stock
Sauce:
3 eggs
1 tablespoon water
3 tablespoons lemon juice
Garnish:
350 g/12 oz cooked rice (about 175 g/6 oz raw rice)
chopped fresh parsley

American
2 tablespoons butter
2 tablespoons grated onion
1 lb finely ground shoulder veal or pork
1½ cups fresh fine white breadcrumbs
1 egg, beaten
6 tablespoons white wine or water
salt
freshly ground black pepper
2½ cups chicken or veal stock
Sauce:
3 eggs
1 tablespoon water
3 tablespoons lemon juice
Garnish:
2 cups cooked rice (about ¾ cup raw rice)
chopped fresh parsley

Melt the butter in a heavy based saucepan and fry the onion over gentle heat for about 5 minutes until soft and golden. Off the heat add the meat, breadcrumbs, egg, wine or water with a generous seasoning of salt and pepper, and beat together until smoothly mixed.

Above: Pork with Celery. Below: Meat Balls with Egg and Lemon Sauce

Take one rounded tablespoon of the mixture at a time and roll between well floured hands to form balls. Set the balls aside in a cool place until ready to cook.

Pour the stock into a wide saucepan and bring to the boil over moderate heat. Put in the meat balls and allow the stock to regain boiling point. Lower the heat, cover and simmer gently for 30 to 35 minutes, shaking the pan occasionally or moving the balls around with a spoon so that they cook evenly. Remove from the heat.

To complete the sauce beat the eggs, water and lemon juice together, then stir in several spoonfuls of the hot stock. Pour this mixture over the meat balls in the pan and heat very gently, stirring, until the sauce thickens, but on no account allow it to boil. Check the seasoning, then spoon into the centre of a hot dish bordered with cooked rice. Sprinkle with parsley and serve.

Pork with Celery

Hirino me Selinoriza

Another simple meat dish, this is stewed gently on top of the stove like so many Greek dishes. The sauce is made piquant by a final addition of egg and lemon juice. Celeriac can be used instead of celery; simply cut the peeled root into 1 cm/½ inch cubes and parboil them for 5 minutes before draining and adding to the meat.

Preparation time: 20 minutes
Cooking time: 1¾ to 2 hours
To serve: 6

Metric/Imperial
1 kg/2 lb boneless lean shoulder pork
3 tablespoons olive oil
1 large onion, peeled and chopped
4 tablespoons white wine
2 tablespoons flour
150 ml/¼ pint plus 1 tablespoon cold water
150 ml/¼ pint chicken stock

Pork with Eggplants

Lomo de Cerdo con Berenjenas

Use the long cylindrical pork fillets (tenderloin) for this Spanish dish.

Preparation time: 20 minutes (plus 1 hour draining the aubergines (eggplants))
Cooking time: about 1 hour
To serve: 4

Metric/Imperial/American
*4 aubergines (eggplants), sliced into
   rounds
salt
1 tablespoon flour
freshly ground black pepper
0.5 kg/1 lb pork fillet (tenderloin), sliced
   into rounds
olive oil
2 onions, peeled and sliced
2 tomatoes, skinned and chopped
150 ml/¼ pint (⅔ cup) dry white wine or
   cider
1 small sprig of fresh rosemary
about 12 blanched almonds, split,
   toasted and crushed*

Put the sliced aubergines (eggplants) into a colander, sprinkle with salt and leave to drain for about 1 hour. Rinse and pat dry with paper towels.

Mix the flour with salt and pepper and use to coat the slices of pork. Heat 2 tablespoons of oil in a saucepan or flameproof casserole, add the onions and tomatoes and fry gently until softened. Remove from the pan. Add the aubergine (egg plant) slices with more oil as needed and brown them on both sides. Remove and keep hot. Put in the slices of pork on a slightly higher heat and brown them on both sides. Add the wine or cider and let it bubble for a second or two, then stir in about the same amount of water. Lower the heat and return the tomatoes, onions and aubergines (eggplants) to the pan, making sure they are just covered by liquid. Season to taste and put in the rosemary in one piece. (It will be removed later.) Simmer very gently, partially covered, for 45 minutes or until the pork is tender. Just before serving, remove the sprig of rosemary and add the crushed toasted almonds. Serve with rice or potatoes.

Pork with Eggplants

*1 clove garlic, peeled and crushed
salt
freshly ground black pepper
1 head tender celery, divided into sticks
3 egg yolks
3 tablespoons lemon juice
2 tablespoons chopped fresh parsley*

American
*2 lb boneless lean shoulder pork
3 tablespoons olive oil
1 large onion, peeled and chopped
¼ cup white wine
2 tablespoons flour
⅔ cup plus 1 tablespoon cold water
⅔ cup chicken stock
1 clove garlic, peeled and crushed
salt
freshly ground black pepper
1 bunch tender celery, divided into stalks
3 egg yolks
3 tablespoons lemon juice
2 tablespoons chopped fresh parsley*

Cut the meat into 2.5 cm/1 inch cubes. Heat the oil in a flameproof casserole and fry the meat in batches over moderate heat, stirring frequently. Remove with a slotted spoon to a plate as soon as the pieces of pork are coloured.

Add the onion to the casserole, stir and fry for a few minutes, then add the wine. Mix the flour smoothly with the 150 ml/¼ pint (⅔ cup) cold water, add the chicken stock and stir all into the casserole. Add the garlic and salt and pepper to taste and bring to the boil. Return the pork to the pot, cover tightly and simmer gently for 1 hour.

Remove any discoloured or stringy pieces from the celery and cut the stalks into 2.5 cm/1 inch cubes. Add to the casserole and push under the liquid. Cover and continue simmering for 40 minutes, or until both pork and celery are tender.

Mix the egg yolks, lemon juice, the remaining 1 tablespoon of water and the parsley together in a bowl. Stir in several tablespoons of hot liquid from the casserole. Stir gently into the pork and celery and continue cooking and stirring over low heat for a few minutes until the sauce thickens. Do not allow to boil. Check the seasoning and serve with cooked rice or pasta.

Left: Pork with Sage and Capers
Centre: Roast Pork with Fennel
Right: Provençal Roast Pork

Pork with Sage and Capers

Porc à la Sauge et aux Capres

The combination of the pungent herbs and sharp capers of the Languedoc region make pork cooked this way particularly light and digestible.

This dish is excellent served with braised fennel (see page 130) or celery and accompanied by a dry white wine or a rosé.

Preparation time: 20 minutes
Cooking time: 1½ hours
To serve: 6

Metric/Imperial/American
1.5 kg/3 lb loin or *shoulder of pork,
  boned, trimmed of fat and cubed*
salt
freshly ground black pepper
3 tablespoons olive oil
2 onions, peeled and chopped
150 ml/¼ pint (⅔ cup) white wine
1 tablespoon chopped fresh sage

2 sprigs of fresh thyme
2 bay leaves
150 ml/¼ pint (⅔ cup) dry vermouth
2 tablespoons capers
*1 tablespoon finely chopped fresh
  parsley*

Sprinkle the meat with salt and pepper. Heat the oil in a flameproof casserole and quickly brown the meat on all sides. Remove the meat and set aside.

Add the onions to the casserole, lower the heat and fry until softened. Add the wine and let it bubble for a moment, scraping the bottom of the casserole to loosen any sediment. Return the meat to the casserole with the sage, thyme and bay leaves. Cover and cook gently for 1 to 1½ hours, or until the meat is tender.

When the meat is cooked, lift it out of the casserole and keep it hot. Add the vermouth to the juices, and bring quickly to the boil, stirring well. Return the meat, add the capers and allow to heat through. Remove the thyme sprigs and bay leaves. Adjust the seasoning, sprinkle with the parsley and serve, in the casserole.

Roast Pork with Fennel

Rôti de Porc au Fenouil

Prepare the meat as described for Provençal Roast Pork (see page 80). Serve with braised fennel (see page 130) or celery.

Preparation time: 15 minutes (plus at
  least 12 hours marinating)
Cooking time: 2 hours
Oven temperature: 220°C, 425°F, Gas
  Mark 7, reduced to 190°C, 375°F, Gas
  Mark 5
To serve: 6

Metric/Imperial/American
1.5 kg/3 lb loin or *leg of pork*
*1 large (Florence) fennel bulb, trimmed
  and cut into small strips*
salt
freshly ground black pepper
1 tablespoon finely chopped fresh sage
150 ml/¼ pint (⅔ cup) white wine
1 tablespoon olive oil
1 tablespoon Pernod
*1 tablespoon finely chopped fresh fennel
  leaves* or *parsley*

Cut some shallow incisions all over the surface of the meat, and slip a strip of fennel into each one. Rub the meat with plenty of salt and pepper, place in a large earthenware bowl, sprinkle with half the sage, add the stalks and outer leaves of the fennel and pour over the wine. Leave to marinate overnight, turning once or twice.

When the meat is ready to be cooked, remove it from the marinade and place in a roasting pan. Reserve the marinade. Sprinkle the meat with a little more salt and pepper, the remaining sage and the olive oil and place in the hot oven. Roast for 20 minutes, then reduce the temperature and cook for a further 1½ hours, or a little longer, depending on the type of cut.

When the meat is cooked, remove to a carving board or dish and keep hot. Add the strained marinade to the juices in the roasting pan and bring to the boil, scraping well to amalgamate any sediment. Add the Pernod and adjust the seasoning.

Carve the pork into thick slices and arrange on a heated serving platter. Pour over the sauce and sprinkle with the chopped fennel or parsley before serving.

Provençal Roast Pork

Rôti de Porc Provençal

Pork loin is the most popular cut for roasting in France, but a leg may also be cooked in the same way. The rind and all but a thin layer of fat are usually removed from a pork cut before roasting, making it much less fatty. The rind is used to enrich soups and stews, and the strips of fat for lining pâtés or terrines.

Preparation time: 15 minutes (plus 1 hour marinating)
Cooking time: 2 hours
Oven temperature: 220°C, 425°F, Gas Mark 7, reduced to 190°C, 375°F, Gas Mark 5
To serve: 6

Metric/Imperial/American
2 cloves garlic, peeled and cut into slivers
1.5 kg/3 lb loin or leg (fresh ham) of pork
salt
freshly ground black pepper
3 sprigs of fresh thyme or rosemary
150 ml/¼ pint (⅔ cup) white wine
100 g/4 oz (2 cups) fresh white breadcrumbs
2 tablespoons finely chopped fresh parsley
1 clove garlic, peeled and finely chopped
½ teaspoon finely grated lemon rind

Insert the slivers of garlic near the bones of the meat and into the thin layer of fat. Rub the meat with plenty of salt and pepper.

Place the meat in the roasting pan, lay the sprigs of thyme or rosemary on top, pour over the wine and leave to marinate for at least 1 hour. Place the meat in the hot oven, roast for 20 minutes, then lower the heat. Add a little water to the pan if it is getting too dry. Mix together the breadcrumbs, parsley, chopped garlic, lemon rind and seasoning.

When the meat has been cooking for 1 hour, spread the breadcrumb mixture over the top, pressing it down firmly. Cook for another 1 hour, basting with the pan juices from time to time, until a crisp golden crust has formed on top.

Family Style Meat Loaf

Polpettone alla Casalinga

What makes this meat loaf deliciously different from others is the grated cheese added to the minced (ground) meat and the ham, hard-boiled egg and cheese hidden in the centre. The recipe comes from Campania where provolone and mozzarella are the cheeses used, but other cheeses that melt readily can be substituted. Serve the *polpettone* hot, surrounded with cooked vegetables such as green beans, carrot sticks and cauliflower sprigs, or eat it cold with salad.

Preparation time: 30 minutes
Cooking time: 45 to 50 minutes
Oven temperature: 190°/375°F, Gas Mark 5
To serve: 4 to 6

Metric/Imperial
225 g/8 oz minced beef or *veal*
225 g/8 oz minced pork
50 g/2 oz firm bread, soaked in a little milk
2 eggs, lightly beaten
1 tablespoon chopped fresh parsley
1 clove garlic, peeled and crushed
2 tablespoons grated Parmesan cheese
salt
freshly ground black pepper
2 tablespoons olive oil
50 g/2 oz cooked ham or *salami, rinded and sliced*
2 hard-boiled eggs, sliced
75 g/3 oz provolone or *mozzarella cheese in one piece, sliced*

American
½ lb ground beef or *veal*
½ lb ground pork
2 slices of firm bread, soaked in a little milk
2 eggs, lightly beaten
1 tablespoon chopped fresh parsley
1 clove garlic, peeled and crushed
2 tablespoons grated Parmesan cheese
salt
freshly ground black pepper
2 tablespoons olive oil
2 oz cooked ham or *salami, rinded and sliced*
2 hard-cooked eggs, sliced
3 oz provolone or *mozzarella cheese in one piece, sliced*

Put the minced (ground) meats into a mixing bowl. Squeeze the bread dry and add to the meats with the eggs, parsley, garlic, grated cheese and salt and pepper to taste. Mix together very thoroughly.

Pour 1 tablespoon of the oil into a loaf pan of 1 litre/1¾ pints (1 US quart) capacity and grease it thoroughly. Press half of the meat mixture into the bottom of the pan, then arrange the ham, hard-boiled egg and cheese slices over it. Cover with the remaining meat mixture and smooth the surface. Sprinkle with the remaining oil. Bake for 45 to 50 minutes or until cooked through. Turn out and serve hot or cold.

Family Style Meat Loaf

Stuffed Veal Rolls with Peas

Involtini di Vitello con Piselli

Italians are very fond of combining veal, ham and cheese in quickly cooked and delicious dishes like this one. The Gruyère cheese softens nicely in the time it takes to cook the veal, but does not melt or ooze out as many soft cheeses would do.

Preparation time: 20 minutes
Cooking time: 15 minutes
To serve: 4

Metric/Imperial
8 thin veal escalopes, about 50 g/2 oz each
4 thin slices of lean cooked ham, halved
100 g/4 oz thick slice Gruyère cheese, cut into 8 fingers
50 g/2 oz butter
2 tablespoons oil
0.5 kg/1 lb shelled fresh peas
salt
freshly ground black pepper
1 teaspoon sugar

American
8 thin veal scallops, about 2 oz each
4 thin slices of lean cooked ham, halved
¼ lb thick slice Gruyère cheese, cut into 8 fingers
¼ cup butter
2 tablespoons oil
1 lb shelled fresh peas (about 3 cups)
salt
freshly ground black pepper
1 teaspoon sugar

Place the slices of veal between dampened greaseproof (wax) paper and beat with a wooden rolling pin, cleaver or mallet to flatten them as much as possible. Lay one slice of ham and a cheese finger on top of each slice of veal. Roll up each slice of veal neatly and secure with a wooden cocktail stick or with white cotton thread.

Melt the butter with the oil in a wide flameproof oven-to-table casserole, add the veal rolls and fry gently for 12 to 15 minutes, turning to brown on all sides.

Meanwhile, cook the peas in boiling salted water for 10 to 15 minutes (or 5 minutes, if using frozen peas), draining them as soon as they are tender.

When cooked lift out the veal rolls and remove the cocktail sticks or thread. Tip the peas into the pan the veal was cooked in, quickly stir around so that they absorb the buttery cooking juices, and season with salt, pepper and sugar. Replace the veal rolls and serve.

Stuffed Meat Roll

Polpettone alla Siciliana

Stuffed meat rolls with tasty fillings are very popular in Southern Italy. A thick slice of topside (top round) of beef is the best cut for beating out thinly. Creamed potatoes go well with this recipe, and for special occasions it can be piped decoratively around the edge of the serving dish.

Preparation time: 40 minutes
Cooking time: 1¾ to 2 hours
To serve: 7

Metric/Imperial

0.5 kg/1¼ lb topside of beef, cut as one
   1 cm/½ inch slice
salt
freshly ground black pepper
50 g/2 oz bread, soaked in a little milk
2 eggs, lightly beaten
225 g/8 oz minced shoulder pork
225 g/8 oz minced lean beef
40 g/1½ oz Pecorino or Parmesan cheese,
   grated
50 g/2 oz cooked ham, coarsely chopped
2 hard-boiled eggs, coarsely chopped
50 g/2 oz provolone or Gruyère cheese,
   coarsely chopped

3 tablespoons olive oil
1 onion, peeled and sliced
150 ml/¼ pint robust red wine
1 tablespoon tomato purée dissolved in
   4 tablespoons hot water

American

1¼ to 1½ lb top round of beef, cut as one
   ½ inch slice
salt
freshly ground black pepper
2 slices of bread, soaked in a little milk
2 eggs, lightly beaten
½ lb ground shoulder pork
½ lb ground lean beef
⅓ cup grated Pecorino or Parmesan
   cheese
¼ cup coarsely chopped cooked ham
2 hard-cooked eggs, coarsely chopped
½ cup coarsely chopped provolone or
   Gruyère cheese
3 tablespoons olive oil
1 onion, peeled and sliced
⅔ cup robust red wine
1 tablespoon tomato paste dissolved in
   ¼ cup hot water

Lay the slice of meat flat and beat with a wooden rolling pin, cleaver or mallet until the meat is about 5 mm/¼ inch thick and roughly 25 cm/10 inches square. Season it with salt and pepper.

Squeeze the bread dry, put into a bowl and beat with a fork. Add the beaten eggs, minced (ground) pork and beef, grated cheese and seasonings of salt and pepper. Mix thoroughly, then spread over the surface of the meat to within 2.5 cm/1 inch of the edges.

Mix together the chopped ham, eggs and chopped cheese and arrange the mixture across the centre of the meat. Starting at one end roll up the meat to form a thick sausage shape and secure by tying with string in the centre and near both ends.

Heat the oil in an oval flameproof casserole, add the onion and fry gently for a few minutes. Put in the meat roll and brown lightly on all sides. Add the wine, tomato purée (paste) and a seasoning of salt and pepper. Cover tightly and simmer very gently until tender, turning once, and adding a little hot water if too much of the liquid evaporates.

Lift the meat on to a carving board and remove the strings. Carve into thick slices and arrange, overlapping, on a hot serving dish. Keep hot. Skim the fat off the pan juices and boil the juices rapidly until reduced to a thick sauce. Check the seasoning and spoon over the meat slices.

Left: Stuffed Meat Roll. Right: Stuffed Veal Rolls with Peas

Potato and Salami Pie

Torta di Patate e Salami

A substantial family dish from Campania, serve this with a mixed green salad. Cooked ham can be used instead of the salami, and any soft cheese that melts readily would be suitable.

Preparation time: 40 minutes
Cooking time: 25 to 30 minutes
Oven temperature: 200°C/400°F, Gas Mark 6
To serve: 4 to 6

Metric/Imperial
0.75 kg/1½ lb potatoes, scrubbed
salt
50 g/2 oz butter
50 g/2 oz Parmesan or Pecorino cheese, grated
1 egg
freshly ground black pepper
grated nutmeg
175 g/6 oz mozzarella or Bel Paese cheese, diced
175 g/6 oz salami, rinded, or cooked ham, diced
3 hard-boiled eggs, sliced
2 tablespoons dry white breadcrumbs

Potato and Salami Pie

American
1½ lb potatoes, scrubbed
salt
¼ cup butter
½ cup grated Parmesan or Pecorino cheese
1 egg
freshly ground black pepper
grated nutmeg
6 oz mozzarella or Bel Paese cheese, diced
6 oz salami, rinded, or cooked ham, diced
3 hard-cooked eggs, sliced
2 tablespoons dry white breadcrumbs

Cook the potatoes in boiling salted water until tender, about 20 minutes. Drain, cool a little then peel. Put into a bowl and mash smoothly, then beat in 25 g/1 oz (2 tablespoons) of the butter, the grated cheese, egg, salt, pepper and nutmeg. Generously butter a 23 cm/9 inch pie plate (pan) and spread half of the potato mixture evenly over the bottom.

Spread the cheese and meat dice over the potato base with the egg slices, leaving a 1 cm/½ inch margin around the edge. Cover completely with the remaining potato mixture and smooth the top with a knife. Sprinkle with the breadcrumbs and dot with the rest of the butter. Bake for 25 to 30 minutes or until well browned. Cut into wedges and serve hot in the pie dish.

Ribbon Noodles Capri Style

Fettuccine alla Capricciosa

This is a rather special pasta dish especially when made with *proscuitto*, the famous Italian raw ham. But cooked ham makes a delicious sauce, too, with the peas and mushrooms adding colour and texture. For a family dish many Italians would omit the meat and the wine and be happy with a simple but colourful tomato, pea and mushroom sauce. The amount of pasta is entirely a question of appetite – the greater amount for the very hungry and for Italians!

Preparation time: 20 minutes
Cooking time: 35 minutes
To serve: 4

Metric/Imperial
2 tablespoons olive oil
100 g/4 oz lean boneless veal or pork, finely chopped
salt
freshly ground black pepper
150 ml/¼ pint white wine, or half dry white vermouth and half water
300 ml/½ pint tomato sauce (see page 135)
350 to 450 g/12 oz to 1 lb fettuccine
65 g/2½ oz butter
50 g/2 oz sliced raw or cooked ham, cut in matchsticks
100 g/4 oz button mushrooms, sliced
175 g/6 oz shelled fresh peas, cooked
grated Parmesan cheese

American
2 tablespoons olive oil
½ cup finely chopped lean boneless veal or pork
salt
freshly ground black pepper
⅔ cup white wine, or half dry white vermouth and half water
1¼ cups tomato sauce (see page 135)
¾ to 1 lb fettuccine
5 tablespoons butter
2 oz sliced raw or cooked ham, cut in matchsticks
1 cup sliced button mushrooms
1 cup shelled fresh peas, cooked
grated Parmesan cheese

Heat the oil in a saucepan and fry the meat for about 5 minutes, stirring frequently, until golden. Season with salt and pepper. Add the wine and allow to bubble briskly until most of it has evaporated. Stir in the tomato sauce, bring to the boil, cover and simmer very gently for 30 minutes.

Meanwhile lower the fettuccine into a large saucepan of boiling salted water. When the water returns to the boil simmer for 5 to 10 minutes, or until the pasta is tender but still has a 'bite'. Drain thoroughly. Melt 25 g/1 oz (2 tablespoons) of the butter in the pan, return the pasta and toss lightly with two forks. Transfer to one large hot serving dish or 4 individual bowls. Keep hot.

Melt the remaining butter in a frying pan (skillet), add the ham and mushrooms and fry, stirring frequently, for 2 to 3 minutes. Add the peas and cook, stirring, for another couple of minutes until the peas are hot. Tip all into the meat and tomato sauce, check the seasoning and pour over the pasta. Hand the grated cheese separately.

Stuffed Rice Balls

Arancine di Riso

Rice dishes belong to northern Italy and are not usually popular in the south, but this Sicilian recipe is an exception. The stuffing can be a thick and tasty cooked minced (ground) meat mixture or the simpler one given below. Serve *arancine* hot, with a good homemade tomato sauce.

Preparation time: 40 minutes (plus 1 hour chilling)
Cooking time: 40 minutes
To serve: 4

Metric/Imperial
225 g/8 oz short grain Italian rice
75 g/3 oz Pecorino Sardo or *Parmesan cheese*, grated
2 eggs, lightly beaten
1 tablespoon thick tomato sauce (see page 135)
a few leaves of parsley to garnish
450 ml/¾ pint thick tomato sauce to serve
Filling:
50 g/2 oz salami, rinded and finely chopped
75 g/3 oz mozzarella or *Bel Paese cheese*, finely chopped
salt
freshly ground black pepper
2 tablespoons thick tomato sauce
Coating and Frying:
2 small eggs, beaten
fine dry breadcrumbs
oil for deep frying

American
1¼ cups short grain Italian rice
¾ cup grated Pecorino Sardo or *Parmesan cheese*
2 eggs, lightly beaten
1 tablespoon thick tomato sauce (see page 135)
a few leaves of parsley to garnish
1 pint thick tomato sauce to serve

Filling:
¼ cup finely chopped salami
3 oz mozzarella or *Bel Paese cheese*, finely chopped
salt
freshly ground black pepper
2 tablespoons thick tomato sauce
Coating and Frying:
2 small eggs, beaten
fine dry breadcrumbs
oil for deep frying

Cook the rice in boiling salted water until tender, about 17 to 20 minutes. Drain thoroughly, then add the grated cheese, eggs and tomato sauce and mix thoroughly. Leave to become cold. Meanwhile, mix together the filling ingredients.

To form the *arancine*, put 2 tablespoons of rice in the palm of your cupped left hand. Make a well in the rice, put a teaspoon of filling into the hollow and mould the rice around the meat into a ball (roughly the size of a golf ball). When all the *arancine* are prepared, coat the balls with beaten egg and breadcrumbs and chill for about 1 hour.

Deep fry the balls in oil heated to 190°C/375°F, a few at a time, for about 3 to 5 minutes or until golden. Drain and keep hot until all are cooked. Decorate each ball with a tiny leaf of parsley. Serve with the tomato sauce thinned with a little water and heated to boiling point.

Left: Stuffed Rice Balls. Right: Ribbon Noodles Capri Style

Tunisian Meat Pie

Tagine Malsouka

This pie is traditionally made with a very thin dough resembling phyllo (page 148). Several sheets are used, brushed with melted butter in between, for the top and bottom crust. Ordinary short-crust (pie) or puff pastry may be used for a simpler alternative. This meal-in-itself needs only a vegetable or a salad to accompany it.

Preparation time: 20 minutes
Cooking time: 3 hours
Oven temperature: 180°C/350°F, Gas Mark 4, increased to 220°/425°F, Gas Mark 7
To serve: 8

Metric/Imperial
2 tablespoons oil
0.5 kg/1 lb lean boneless lamb, cubed
100 g/4 oz dried haricot beans, soaked overnight
freshly ground black pepper
1 teaspoon ground cinnamon
salt
5 eggs
1 x 400 g/14 oz packet frozen shortcrust or puff pastry, thawed
beaten egg to glaze

American
2 tablespoons oil
1 lb lean boneless lamb, cubed
½ cup dried navy beans, soaked overnight
freshly ground black pepper
1 teaspoon ground cinnamon
salt
5 eggs
1 x 14 oz package frozen pie or puff pastry, thawed
beaten egg to glaze

Heat the oil in a large heavy saucepan, add the meat and brown on all sides. Add the drained beans, cover with fresh water and season with pepper and cinnamon. Bring to the boil, then simmer gently for about 2 hours, or until the beans are soft, adding salt when the beans are almost tender. The liquid should be reduced but must not have dried out. Add more water if necessary.

Remove from the heat. Break the eggs into the pan, stir well and taste to see if more salt and pepper is required. Return to the heat and stir until the eggs have become creamy.

Cut the pastry dough in two so as to have one slightly larger piece. Roll out the larger piece on a floured board into the proper shape to line a greased baking sheet or shallow ovenproof dish. Let it come well over the edge. Fill with the meat and egg mixture. Roll out the other piece of dough and use to cover the filling. Stick the edges together by pinching and twisting into a festoon shape. Brush the top with lightly beaten egg and bake for 40 minutes. Raise the temperature and bake for a further 10 minutes or until well browned and the eggs have set firmly.

Lamb and Rice Patties

Kadin Budu

The soft texture and succulence of these patties is evoked by their Turkish name which means 'ladies' thighs'. Serve with potatoes or rice. Although lamb is the usual meat, try them also with beef or veal.

Preparation time: 30 minutes
Coking time: 20 minutes
To serve: 6

Metric/Imperial
0.5 kg/1 lb minced lamb
100 g/4 oz rice, cooked
1 onion, peeled and grated
2 tablespoons finely chopped fresh parsley
salt
freshly ground black pepper

Left: Tunisian Meat Pie
Centre: Lamb and Rice Patties

2 eggs
flour
oil for frying

American
1 lb ground lamb
½ cup rice, cooked
1 onion, peeled and grated
2 tablespoons finely chopped fresh
    parsley
salt
freshly ground black pepper
2 eggs
flour
oil for frying

Mix together the meat, rice, onion, parsley, salt and pepper, kneading well with your hands. Add one egg and work it into the mixure to make a smooth paste. Take walnut-sized lumps, shape into balls and flatten slightly. Dip into the remaining beaten egg, then into flour. Deep fry in hot oil in batches until they are coloured and done, turning over once. Drain on paper towels and serve hot.

Right: Ground Meat Kebabs

Ground Meat Kebabs

Kofta Kebab

Most cafés and restaurants of the Middle East offer a choice of meats, cubed or minced (ground), grilled on charcoal. Often, they are threaded together on skewers. The advantage of using mince (ground meat) is that it can be better flavoured and is usually beautifully tender. Lamb is the preferred meat but beef is a good alternative. The secret of the special soft texture is to work the meat to a paste. Each country has its own flavourings among which cinnamon, allspice, cumin and coriander are usual favourites. Make your own choice. Serve with salad or rice, or drop into a pouch of *pitta* bread.

Preparation time: 20 minutes
Cooking time: 7 to 10 minutes
To serve: 6

Metric/Imperial
1 kg/2 lb finely minced lamb or beef
1 large onion, peeled and grated or
    minced
25 g/1 oz fresh parsley, finely chopped
2 teaspoons ground cinnamon, or 1
    teaspoon ground cinnamon and 1
    teaspoon ground allspice, or 1
    teaspoon ground cumin and 1
    teaspoon ground coriander

salt
freshly ground black pepper
a sprinkling of cayenne pepper
    (optional)

American
2 lb finely ground lamb or beef
1 large onion, peeled and grated or
    minced
¾ cup finely chopped fresh parsley
2 teaspoons ground cinnamon, or 1
    teaspoon ground cinnamon and 1
    teaspoon ground allspice, or 1
    teaspoon ground cumin and 1
    teaspoon ground coriander
salt
freshly ground black pepper
a sprinkling of cayenne pepper
    (optional)

Put the meat in a large bowl with the rest of the ingredients and work it well with your hands to a smooth pasty texture.

You will need good skewers for this kebab (the flat-edged twisted sword type are the best) or the meat will fall apart or slip on the skewer and not get cooked all over.

Take smallish lumps of the meat mixture and press firmly around the skewer in sausage shapes so that it holds well together. Grill over the glowing embers of a charcoal fire on a well-oiled grid. Turn the skewers until the meat is browned all over but still soft and juicy inside. A good amount of fat should keep it moist.

Couscous with a Lamb Stew

It is not only those who have travelled to Morocco, Algeria or Tunisia who know the fine semolina steamed over a rich and juicy stew. For this speciality of the North African countries, part of their old Berber food, has now invaded France as well as Spain and Portugal together with the new immigrant workers and the old French settlers from the south of the Mediterranean. France with its insular tastes has been conquered by couscous.

So much goes in the stew that nothing need be served with it. Only fruit to follow.

The handling of the fine grain might seen difficult but it becomes easy with practice, and there is a pre-cooked variety on the market which is as quick and easy as anything to prepare. Follow the instructions on the box.

Preparation time: 30 minutes
Cooking time: 2 hours
To serve: 8

Metric/Imperial
1 kg/2 lb stewing lamb (the neck will do)
2 large chicken portions
2 large onions, peeled and chopped
50 g/2 oz chick peas, soaked overnight
2 turnips, peeled and quartered
½ small cabbage, cored and shredded
freshly ground black pepper
½ teaspoon ground ginger
½ teaspoon saffron powder (optional)
salt
0.5 kg/1 lb couscous
2 tablespoons oil
50 g/2 oz raisins
4 courgettes, sliced, or 1 small marrow, cubed
100 g/4 oz fresh shelled or frozen broad beans
2 tomatoes, skinned and chopped
4 tablespoons finely chopped fresh parsley
small bunch of fresh coriander leaves (if available), chopped
25 g/1 oz butter to serve
Sauce:
cayenne pepper or chilli powder
1 teaspoon paprika

American
2 lb lamb stew meat
2 large chicken portions
2 large onions, peeled and chopped
⅓ cup chick peas, soaked overnight
2 turnips, peeled and quartered
½ small head cabbage, cored and shredded
freshly ground black pepper
½ teaspoon ground ginger
½ teaspoon saffron powder (optional)
salt
1 lb couscous
2 tablespoons oil
⅓ cup raisins
4 zucchini, sliced
¾ cup fresh shelled or frozen lima beans
2 tomatoes, skinned and chopped
¼ cup finely chopped fresh parsley
small bunch of fresh coriander leaves (if available), chopped
2 tablespoons butter to serve
Sauce:
cayenne or chili powder
1 teaspoon paprika

Put the meat, chicken, onions, drained chick peas, turnips and cabbage in a large pan. Cover with water, add pepper, ginger and saffron and bring to the boil. Remove any scum and simmer for about 1 hour, or until the chick peas and meat are tender. Add salt when the chick peas have softened.

Now prepare the couscous. If you do not have a *cous-cousier*, the traditional sieve which sits on top of the stew-pan, improvise with another fine sieve. Moisten the grain with a little cold water, working it in with your fingers to prevent lumps from forming. Turn it into the sieve and place it over the pan with the simmering stew. Cook for 30 minutes, raking the grain occasionally to help it to swell evenly with the steam. Turn the couscous into a bowl. Sprinkle with cold water and stir with a wooden spoon to break up any lumps and separate and air the grain. Add only a little water just enough to swell the grain and not so as to make it stodgy. Add a little salt and the oil.

Now add the rest of the ingredients, which need less cooking, to the stew and stir well. Return the couscous to the sieve and steam over the simmering stew for a further 30 minutes.

Take about 150 ml/¼ pint (⅔ cup) of liquid from the stew and stir in cayenne or chilli powder and paprika, enough to make it as fiery as you like.

To serve, pile the couscous on a large warmed dish. Add the butter and work it into the grain as it melts. Arrange the meat and vegetables over it and pass the hot, peppery sauce separately in a sauce-boat or little bowl.

If you prefer, serve the couscous and the stew separately.

Couscous with a Lamb Stew

Lamb Pilaf

Lamb Pilaf

Piláv Kuzulu

Each country in the Middle East has its own variety of meat and rice dishes. This delicious Turkish version, a good winter dish, is a meal in itself and needs only plain yogurt, slightly warmed, as an accompaniment.

Preparation time: about 20 minutes
Cooking time: about 1 hour
To serve: 6

Metric/Imperial
40 g /1½ oz butter, or 3 tablespoons oil
1 large onion, peeled and finely chopped
0.5 kg/1 lb lean boneless lamb, cut into small pieces
50 g/2 oz pine nuts
25 g/1 oz sultanas
salt
freshly ground black pepper
1 teaspoon ground cinnamon
3 tablespoons finely chopped fresh parsley
3 tablespoons tomato purée
0.5 kg/1 lb long-grain rice
1 litre/1¾ pints water

American
3 tablespoons butter or oil
1 large onion, peeled and finely chopped
1 lb boneless lean lamb, cut into small pieces
½ cup pine nuts
3 tablespoons seedless white raisins
salt
freshly ground black pepper
1 teaspoon ground cinnamon
3 tablespoons finely chopped fresh parsley
3 tablespoons tomato paste
2⅓ cups long-grain rice
1 quart water

Melt the butter or heat the oil in a large heavy saucepan, add the onion and fry until it is soft. Add the lamb and fry gently, turning over the pieces until they are browned all over. Add the pine nuts and let them brown. Stir in the sultanas (raisins), salt, pepper, cinnamon, parsley and tomato purée (paste). Cover with water and stir well. Bring to the boil, then simmer gently for at least 30 minutes, or until the meat is really tender, adding water if necessary so that it does not dry out.

Add the rice and cover with the water. Add salt and stir well. Simmer gently, covered and undisturbed, for 20 minutes or until the rice is cooked and all the water has been absorbed.

Cracked Wheat
Baked with Meat

Kibbeh bel Sania

This is one version of a whole family of dishes which symbolize the food of Syria and Lebanon. In all of them cracked wheat and meat, usually lamb, are worked to a smooth paste. Although this is traditionally done by pounding in a mortar, a food processor gives excellent results, while a blender or a dough hook is a good alternative. Layers of paste sandwich a layer of fried meat filling.

Preparation time: varies with the process used – up to 1 hour
Cooking time: 30 to 40 minutes
Oven temperature: 200°C/400°F, Gas Mark 6
To serve: 8

Metric/Imperial
350 g/12 oz burghul (cracked wheat)
0.75 kg/1½ lb finely minced lean lamb
2 medium onions, peeled and grated or minced
1 teaspoon ground allspice
salt
freshly ground black pepper
50 g/2 oz butter, melted

Filling:
2 tablespoons oil
1 medium onion, peeled
0.5 kg/1 lb minced lamb or beef
½ teaspoon ground allspice, or 1 teaspoon ground cinnamon
3 tablespoons pine nuts or chopped walnuts
2 tablespoons raisins

American
2½ cups cracked wheat
1½ lb finely ground lean lamb
2 medium onions, peeled and grated or ground
1 teaspoon ground allspice
salt
freshly ground black pepper
¼ cup butter, melted
Filling:
2 tablespoons oil
1 medium onion, peeled
1 lb ground lamb or beef
½ teaspoon ground allspice, or 1 teaspoon ground cinnamon
3 tablespoons pine nuts or chopped walnuts
2 tablespoons raisins

Wash the cracked wheat in cold water and drain it. Turn the meat and onions into a paste by pounding them in a mortar. Or use a food processor, or a blender with a very little cold water, or the dough hook of a mixer. Add the allspice, salt, pepper and cracked wheat and continue to work into a smooth, well-blended paste.

To make the filling, heat the oil in a frying pan (skillet), add the onion and fry until it is soft. Add the meat and fry, stirring, until it browns. Stir in the spice, pine nuts or walnuts and the raisins.

Grease a shallow round or square baking pan or ovenproof dish. Spread half the meat and wheat paste on the bottom, cover with the filling and top with the rest of the meat and wheat paste. Cut diamond shapes in the top and run the knife around the sides of the dish. Pour the melted butter over the top and bake for 30 to 40 minutes or until well browned.

Serve hot or cold with cucumber and yogurt salad (page 25) or with any other and *Humus bi Tahina.*

90

Left: Cracked Wheat Baked with Meat
Right: Rice with Meat and Nuts

Rice with Meat and Nuts

Roz bil Tatbila

This attractive way of presenting rice, popular in Egypt, makes a good party piece. If you want it to be the main dish increase the quantity of minced (ground) meat to about 1 kg/2 lb. Though a ring mould is traditionally used, other types may be used.

Preparation time: 20 minutes
Cooking time: 30 minutes
To serve: 6

Metric/Imperial
40 g/1½ oz butter
0.5 kg/1 lb long-grain rice
1 litre/1¾ pints water
salt
4 tablespoons oil
1 large onion, peeled and chopped
350 g/12 oz lean minced beef
freshly ground black pepper
¼ teaspoon ground allspice
1 teaspoon ground cinnamon
50 g/2 oz blanched almonds, slivered
25 g/1 oz pine nuts, or 50 g/2 oz
   walnuts, chopped

American
3 tablespoons butter
2⅓ cups long-grain rice
1 quart water
salt
¼ cup oil
1 large onion, peeled and chopped
¾ lb lean ground beef
freshly ground black pepper
¼ teaspoon ground allspice
1 teaspoon ground cinnamon
½ cup slivered blanched almonds
¼ cup pine nuts, or ½ cup chopped
   walnuts

Melt the butter in a saucepan. Stir in the rice until it is thoroughly coated with butter and translucent. Add the water and 1 to 2 teaspoons of salt and stir. Bring to the boil, then reduce the heat and barely simmer, covered, for about 20 minutes, or until the rice is tender but not too soft.

In a large frying pan (skillet) heat 2 tablespoons of oil, add the onion and fry until it is golden. Add the minced (ground) meat with salt and pepper to taste, the allspice and cinnamon. Fry, stirring, until browned and crumbly, about 10 minutes, adding a little water if too dry.

In another frying pan (skillet) heat the remaining oil and fry the nuts until lightly browned. Stir into the meat mixture. Spread half of this over the bottom of an oiled ring mould. Press the hot cooked rice over it to fill the mould, then turn out into a serving dish. Pour the rest of the meat mixture into the hollow in the centre.

The whole could be put together in the mould ahead of time and warmed up in the oven before serving.

91

Poultry and game

Garlic Chicken

Poulet à Quarante Cousses d'Ail

A legendary Provençal dish, which any lover of garlic should try at least once. The garlic mellows beautifully in the cooking, and amazingly you will not reek of it for days, but a most delicate perfume will steal through the house during the cooking. Serve with dry white wine and the French bread only, and follow with a plain salad.

Preparation time: 10 minutes
Cooking time: 1¼ to 1½ hours
Oven temperature: 190°C, 375°F, Gas Mark 5
To serve: 6

Metric/Imperial
1.75 kg/4 lb oven-ready roasting chicken, trussed
salt
freshly ground black pepper
2 sprigs of fresh rosemary
2 sprigs of fresh thyme
2 bay leaves
2 tablespoons olive oil
150 ml/¼ pint white wine
about 40 cloves garlic, unpeeled
toasted slices of French bread

American
4 lb oven-ready roasting chicken, trussed
salt
freshly ground black pepper
2 sprigs of fresh rosemary
2 sprigs of fresh thyme
2 bay leaves
2 tablespoons olive oil
⅔ cup white wine
about 40 cloves garlic, unpeeled
toasted slices of French bread

Rub the chicken inside and out with plenty of salt and pepper and stuff one sprig each of rosemary and thyme and one bay leaf in the cavity. Heat the oil in a flameproof casserole and brown the chicken all over. Remove the chicken and take the casserole off the heat. Pour in the wine and stir well to loosen any sediment, then add the garlic to the casserole. Put the chicken on top and lay the remaining herbs on top of the chicken. Cover and seal the casserole well and place in the oven. Cook for 1¼ to 1½ hours.

Serve with toasted French bread, and let everyone help himself to as many cloves of garlic as he wishes. These will be meltingly tender, and will slide easily out of their skins. They can be eaten as they are, or spread on the toast.

Chicken with Peppers, Tomatoes and Olives

Poulet à la Niçoise

This is a simple and refreshing way of cooking chicken.

Preparation time: 20 minutes
Cooking time: 45 minutes
To serve: 6

Metric/Imperial
1.75 kg/4 lb oven-ready roasting chicken, jointed
1 clove garlic, peeled and halved
salt
freshly ground black pepper
2 tablespoons olive oil
225 g/8 oz onions, peeled and thinly sliced
500 g/1 lb peppers (mixed colours if possible), cored, seeded and cut into strips
500 g/1 lb tomatoes, skinned and roughly chopped
100 g/4 oz black olives, stoned

American
4 lb oven-ready roasting chicken, cut up
1 clove garlic, peeled and halved

Garlic Chicken

salt
freshly ground black pepper
2 tablespoons olive oil
½ lb onions, peeled and thinly sliced
1 lb peppers (mixed colors if possible),
  cored, seeded and cut into strips
1 lb tomatoes, skinned and roughly
  chopped
¾ cup pitted black olives

Rub the pieces of chicken with the cut surface of the clove of garlic and season well. Heat the oil in a flameproof casserole and brown the chicken on all sides. Remove from the casserole and keep warm.

Lower the heat and add the onions to the casserole. Cook until golden and soft. Add the peppers and tomatoes, raise the heat and allow to bubble for 5 minutes to expel excess moisture. Lower the heat, place the chicken pieces on top of the bed of vegetables, season and cover. Cook over a moderate heat for 30 to 35 minutes, or until the chicken is tender.

Add the olives to the casserole 5 minutes before serving and allow to heat through.

Left: Chicken in Anchovy and Olive Sauce
Right: Chicken with Peppers, Tomatoes
and Olives

Chicken in Anchovy and Olive Sauce

Poulet en Saupiquet

A quickly made chicken dish, this embodies the most pungent flavours of Provence.

Preparation time: 20 minutes
Cooking time: 45 minutes
To serve: 6

Metric/Imperial
1.75 kg/4 lb oven-ready roasting
  chicken, jointed
lemon juice
1 clove garlic, peeled and halved
1 teaspoon finely chopped fresh thyme
  or rosemary
salt
freshly ground black pepper
1 tablespoon flour
2 tablespoons olive oil
150 ml/¼ pint white wine
6 anchovy fillets, finely chopped
2 cloves garlic, peeled and crushed
225 g/8 oz tomatoes, skinned and
  roughly chopped
100 g/4 oz black olives, stoned and
  roughly chopped

American
4 lb oven-ready roasting chicken, cut up
lemon juice

1 clove garlic, peeled and halved
1 teaspoon finely chopped fresh thyme
  or rosemary
salt
freshly ground black pepper
1 tablespoon flour
2 tablespoons olive oil
⅔ cup white wine
6 anchovy fillets, finely chopped
2 cloves garlic, peeled and crushed
½ lb tomatoes, skinned and roughly
  chopped
¾ cup pitted black olives, roughly
  chopped

Rub the pieces of chicken with lemon juice and with the cut surface of the halved garlic clove. Mix the herbs and seasoning into the flour and dust the chicken pieces with this mixture. Heat the oil in a deep frying pan (skillet) and brown the chicken pieces on all sides. When each piece is golden brown, remove to a flameproof casserole. Pour over the juice from the frying pan (skillet), cover and cook over a gentle heat for 30 minutes.

Meanwhile, pour the wine into the frying pan (skillet) and bring to the boil, stirring to amalgamate any sediment. Lower the heat and add the anchovy, crushed garlic, tomatoes and olives. Simmer until the sauce thickens. Season to taste.

Pour the sauce over the chicken just before serving.

Chicken in Tomato with Noodles

Kotopoulo Rapama me Hilopites

This easily prepared chicken dish has a rich colour and flavour and is cooked on top of the stove. If red wine is not available use white wine or chicken stock instead. In summer fresh ripe tomatoes, skinned and chopped, can be used instead of canned ones, with a little tomato purée (paste) added to strengthen the flavour. Kefalotiri is a hard, salty Greek cheese, mostly used dry and grated, like Parmesan.

Preparation time: 25 minutes
Cooking time: 1¼ hours
To serve: 4

Metric/Imperial
1.5 kg/3 lb oven-ready chicken, cut into
   8 pieces
salt
freshly ground black pepper
25 g/1 oz butter
2 tablespoons olive oil
1 medium onion, peeled and finely
   chopped
6 tablespoons red wine
1 x 400 g/14 oz can peeled tomatoes
½ teaspoon dried marjoram (optional)
350 g/12 oz noodles
freshly grated kefalotiri or Parmesan
   cheese

American
3 lb oven-ready chicken, cut into 8 pieces
salt
freshly ground black pepper
2 tablespoons butter
2 tablespoons olive oil
1 medium onion, peeled and finely
   chopped

View from a Greek island

6 tablespoons red wine
1 x 14 oz can peeled tomatoes
½ teaspoon dried marjoram (optional)
¾ lb noodles
freshly grated kefalotiri or Parmesan
   cheese

Rinse the chicken pieces, pat dry with kitchen paper and season liberally with salt and pepper. Heat the butter and oil in a flameproof casserole and when hot fry the chicken pieces fairly briskly, turning until golden on all sides. Lift out the pieces as they brown and reserve them on a plate.

Add the onion to the casserole and fry over gentle heat for 5 to 6 minutes, stirring frequently. Add the wine and tomatoes with their juice and bring to the boil. Taste and add the herbs, if used, and salt and pepper to taste. Return the chicken pieces to the casserole and turn them in the sauce. Cover the pot tightly and simmer gently for about 1 hour, when the chicken should be very tender and the tomatoes reduced to a sauce.

About 15 minutes before the end of the cooking time, cook the noodles in a large pan of boiling salted water until just tender. Drain and arrange on a hot serving platter.

Place the cooked chicken on the bed of noodles and pour the sauce over them. Hand the cheese separately.

Chicken with Yogurt

Ornitha Tis Sha Ras me Yaóurti

To be at its very best, this dish should be cooked outdoors over a glowing charcoal fire. When this is not possible these marinated chicken pieces still taste delicious cooked under the grill (broiler). Start preparations early enough

for the marinade to flavour the chicken thoroughly. In Greece they like to serve the chicken straight from the grill (broiler) with the refreshingly crisp sauce poured over them. Alternately put a bowl of sauce in the centre of a dish and arrange the chicken around. Serve a salad separately.

Preparation time: 30 minutes, plus time
   to marinate
Cooking time: 25 to 30 minutes
To serve: 4

Metric/Imperial
4 chicken quarters
½ recipe of Cucumber in Yogurt
(see page 25)
Marinade:
4 tablespoons olive oil
4 tablespoons lemon juice
1 strip thinly pared lemon rind
6 black peppercorns, slightly crushed
2 sprigs thyme
1 clove garlic, peeled and crushed
1 teaspoon salt

American
4 chicken quarters
½ recipe of Cucumber in Yogurt
(see page 25)
Marinade:
¼ cup olive oil
¼ cup lemon juice
1 strip thinly pared lemon rind
6 black peppercorns, slightly crushed
2 sprigs thyme
1 clove garlic, peeled and crushed
1 teaspoon salt

Wipe the chicken pieces with a damp cloth. Mix all the marinade ingredients together in a deep bowl. Add the chicken pieces, turn them in the marinade, then cover and chill for about 4 hours, turning once or twice.

Prepare the Cucumber in Yogurt, cover and leave to chill in the refrigerator.

When ready to cook, preheat the grill (broiler). Drain the chicken pieces, reserving the marinade. Remove the grill (broiler) rack and arrange the chicken, cut sides uppermost, in a single layer in the grill (broiler) pan. Position the pan 13 to 15 cm/5 to 6 inches below the source of heat and grill (broil) *gently* for 12 to 15 minutes. Turn the pieces, brush with marinade and continue cooking *gently* for another 12 to 15 minutes, until the skin is crisp and golden and the juices are colourless when the deepest part of the thigh is pierced with a fine skewer. Baste the chicken with marinade frequently throughout the cooking.

Above: Chicken in Tomato with Noodles
Below: Chicken with Yogurt

Chicken Grilled over Charcoal

Ferakh Meshwi

A lovely way to plan a barbecue is around chicken. The special flavour imparted by glowing embers is one much appreciated in the Middle East where eating outdoors is a way of life. A good second best is to use an indoor grill (broiler), either gas or electric. Choose young and tender chicken. Serve it with salads and rice or potatoes.

Preparation time: 10 minutes (plus 2 hours marinating)
Cooking time: about 25 minutes
To serve: 4

Metric/Imperial/American
2 kg/4 lb oven-ready chicken
Marinade:
4 tablespoons (¼ cup) olive oil
3 cloves garlic, peeled and crushed (optional)
juice of 1 lemon, or more
freshly ground black pepper or a few crushed peppercorns
about 2 teaspoons salt

Chicken Grilled over Charcoal

Garnish:
watercress or *parsley*
lemon wedges

Cut the chicken into four portions. Remove the skin and bones.

Prepare a marinade in a bowl with the oil, garlic if used, lemon juice, pepper or crushed peppercorns but not the salt. Turn the chicken pieces in this and leave for at least 2 hours in a cold place, turning once. If you are picnicking, you can prepare the chicken at home, put it in a plastic bag and store it in an insulated food bag.

When the fire has died down to embers, sprinkle the chicken with salt and lay it on a well-oiled grid over the fire. Cook for about 25 minutes, turning once, until it is just coloured and tender at the pricking of a fork but still juicy inside. As chicken dries out more quickly than meat, especially fatty meat, it must be basted frequently with the marinade or simply with oil.

Serve garnished with watercress or parsley and lemon wedges.

This recipe can also be made with the chicken left on the bone, but extra cooking time should be allowed.

Circassian Chicken

Çerkes Tavaǧu

Many variations exist of this famous Turkish dish which makes use of an ancient local way of thickening sauces with ground walnuts. It is a lovely summer dish usually eaten cooled rather than cold. An excellent buffet dish, it can also be served as an appetizer with young lettuce leaves or as a main dish with rice.

Preparation time: 30 minutes
Cooking time: 1 hour
To serve: 6

Metric/Imperial/American
2.5 kg/5 lb oven-ready chicken
1 large onion, peeled and quartered
2 sticks celery with leaves
1 bay leaf
2 cloves garlic, peeled and crushed
Sauce:
225 g/8 oz (2 cups) shelled walnuts
2 medium slices of wholemeal (wholewheat) bread, crusts removed
Garnish:
2 teaspoons paprika

2 tablespoons light oil (preferably
   walnut)
a few sprigs of fresh parsley

Put the chicken, onion, celery, bay leaf
and garlic in a large saucepan and cover
with water. Bring to the boil and simmer
for 45 minutes to 1 hour or until the
chicken is tender. Lift out the chicken.
Strain the broth and boil to reduce it to
about 300 ml/½ pint (1¼ cups).

To make the sauce, pound, mince or
grind the walnuts. Soak the bread in the
reduced chicken broth in the saucepan,
then mash it. Stir in the walnuts and
cook over gentle heat, stirring, until the
sauce thickens. Alternatively the bread,
broken into pieces, walnuts and a little
broth can be worked to a smooth purée
in an electric blender, then cooked for a
few minutes in the remaining broth.

Skin and bone the chicken. Cut the
meat into thin strips. Serve in a large
platter with the sauce poured over it.
Stir the paprika into the oil and dribble
over the dish, then sprinkle with parsley.

Left: Circassian Chicken
Right: Chicken with Chick Peas

Chicken with Chick Peas

Ferakh bi Humus

A sustaining winter dish especially
popular in Morocco makes delightful
use of a vegetable much loved in that
part of the world. Turmeric gives it a
light yellow colour. It is filling and needs
only salads as an accompaniment.

Preparation time: 15 minutes
Cooking time: up to 1½ hours
To serve: 6

Metric/Imperial
3 tablespoons oil
1 large onion, peeled and finely chopped
1 teaspoon turmeric
2.5 kg/5 lb oven-ready chicken
225 g/8 oz chick peas, soaked for at least
   4 hours or overnight
juice of 1 lemon, or more
2 to 3 cloves garlic, peeled and crushed
freshly ground black pepper
salt
Garnish:
100 g/4 oz blanched almonds
oil

American
3 tablespoons oil
1 large onion, peeled and finely chopped
1 teaspoon turmeric
5 lb oven-ready chicken
1 cup chick peas, soaked for at least
   4 hours or overnight
juice of 1 lemon, or more
2 to 3 cloves garlic, peeled and crushed
freshly ground black pepper
salt
Garnish:
1 cup blanched almonds
oil

Heat the oil in a large saucepan, add the
onion and fry until golden. Stir in the
turmeric. Put the chicken in the saucepan and let it cook slowly in the oil,
turning it over until it is a nice yellow
colour all over. Add the drained chick
peas and enough fresh water to cover
them. Stir in the lemon juice, garlic and
pepper. Bring to the boil and simmer
gently for 1 to 1½ hours or until the
chick peas are soft and the chicken very
tender, adding salt when the chick peas
are cooked.

Just before serving, fry the almonds in
oil until they are lightly browned all
over. Cut the chicken into serving pieces
and arrange on the chick pea mixture in
a warmed serving dish. Garnish with the
almonds.

Chicken Cooked with Dried Fruit

Djaj bal Barcouck

Many dishes of meat and chicken cooked with fresh and dried fruits have come to Morocco from Persia by way of the conquering armies of Islam. This one is a fine example of an ancient tradition continued. Serve it with rice, couscous (page 88) or bread to dip into the sauce.

Preparation time: 5 minutes
Cooking time: 1 to 1½ hours
To Serve: 6

Metric/Imperial
2.5 kg/5 lb oven-ready chicken
2 onions, peeled and chopped
½ teaspoon ground ginger
1 teaspoon ground cinnamon
225 g/8 oz prunes
225 g/8 oz dried apricots
50 g/2 oz blanched almonds, halved
salt
freshly ground black pepper

American
5 lb oven-ready chicken
2 onions, peeled and chopped
½ teaspoon ground ginger
1 teaspoon ground cinnamon
1½ cups prunes
1½ cups dried apricots
½ cup halved blanched almonds
salt
freshly ground black pepper

Put all the ingredients together into a large saucepan. Cover with water, bring to the boil and remove any scum. Simmer for 1 to 1½ hours, or until the chicken is so tender that it almost falls off the bone and the sauce much reduced. Taste and add salt and pepper if necessary.

Chicken Pie

Bstila

Made in large trays for festive occasions with pigeons and pastry as fine as paper, this is one of the grand dishes of Morocco. Chicken is best used outside the Middle East, and bought phyllo pastry (see page 148) can be substituted for the very fine round sheets made at home. This makes a chicken go a long way and is a fine party piece.

Preparation time: 20 minutes
Cooking time: up to 3 hours
Oven temperature: 180°/350°F, Gas Mark 4, increased to 200°C/400°F, Gas Mark 6
To serve: about 8

Metric/Imperial
3 kg/6 lb oven-ready chicken
25 g/1 oz butter
1 large onion, peeled and finely chopped
salt
freshly ground black pepper
½ teaspoon ground ginger
¾ teaspoon ground cinnamon
½ teaspoon ground allspice
3 tablespoons finely chopped fresh parsley
6 large eggs
1 tablespoon sugar
100 g/4 oz blanched almonds, chopped and fried in butter
a little sugar and ground cinnamon to garnish
Pastry:
100 g/4 oz butter, melted
16 sheets of phyllo pastry
beaten egg yolk

American
6 lb oven-ready chicken
2 tablespoons butter
1 large onion, peeled and finely chopped
salt
freshly ground black pepper
½ teaspoon ground ginger
¾ teaspoon ground cinnamon
½ teaspoon ground allspice
3 tablespoons finely chopped fresh parsley
6 large eggs
1 tablespoon sugar
1 cup chopped blanched almonds, fried in butter
a little ground cinnamon and sugar to garnish
Pastry:
½ cup butter, melted
16 sheets of phyllo pastry
beaten egg yolk

Put the chicken in a large saucepan. Cover with water and add the butter, onion, salt, pepper, spices (reserving ¼ teaspoon of the cinnamon) and parsley. Simmer gently for 1½ to 2 hours or until the flesh falls off the bones. Remove the

chicken. Skin and bone it and cut the meat into smallish pieces.

Strain the stock and boil to reduce it. Remove about 150 ml/¼ pint (⅔ cup) and beat it with the eggs. Add salt and pepper, pour into a pan and stir over low heat until the mixture is creamy.

Brush a large 33 cm/13 inch round or square baking pan or ovenproof dish, 4 to 5 cm/1½ to 2 inches deep, with a little of the melted butter. Fit a sheet of phyllo in the dish so that the ends fold well up and overlap the edges. If necessary use more than one sheet. Lay six sheets of pastry on top of each other, brushing melted butter evenly between each layer. Sprinkle the top layer with the sugar, remaining cinnamon and the fried almonds. Spread more than half of the egg mixture over this and sprinkle with a little of the remaining stock. Cover with another four sheets of phyllo, brushing each with melted butter. Spread the pieces of boned chicken on

top and cover with the rest of the egg mixture. Sprinkle with a little more chicken stock. Cover with the remaining phyllo sheets, brushing each with melted butter.

Tuck the top phyllo sheets between the overlapping bottom sheets and the sides of the dish. Brush with beaten egg and bake for 40 minutes. Raise the temperature and bake for a further 15 minutes or until the pastry is crisp and golden.

Serve sprinkled with sugar and cinnamon.

Above left: Chicken Cooked with Dried Fruit
Below left: Chicken Pie
Right: Chicken Served in Bread

Chicken Served in Bread

Msakhan

This simple way of preparing chicken from the Middle East makes a lovely meal in the hand with which you can serve yogurt and a salad. Round, flat hollow Arab and Indian bread (such as *pitta*) must be used.

Preparation time: about 10 minutes
Cooking time: about 25 minutes
Oven temperature: 180°C/350°F, Gas Mark 4
To serve: 4

Metric/Imperial/American
25 to 40 g/1 to 1½ oz (2 to 3 tablespoons) butter
3 tablespoons olive oil
2 onions, peeled and chopped
4 chicken portions, preferably breast, boned
salt
freshly ground black pepper
½ teaspoon ground cinnamon
juice of ½ lemon
1 cardamom pod, cracked (crushed)
2 pitta breads, cut in half

Melt the butter with the oil in a frying pan (skillet), add the onions and fry until soft. Add the chicken pieces, salt, pepper, cinnamon, lemon juice and the cardamom pod. Cook gently, turning over the chicken occasionally until tender but still juicy (about 15 minutes). Remove the cardamom.

Put a piece of chicken in each pouch of bread with some onions and sauce. Lay the stuffed bread halves on a baking sheet and heat in the oven for about 10 minutes.

Chicken in Almond Sauce

Pollo en Salsa de Almendra

For this you need a well-flavoured chicken. Choose a boiling fowl (stewing chicken) if you can, or at least a free-range fresh chicken. Almonds are widely used in Spain.

Preparation time: 20 minutes
Cooking time: 1½ to 2½ hours, depending on the age of the chicken
To serve: 4

Metric/Imperial
2 tablespoons flour
salt
freshly ground black pepper
1.5 kg/3½ lb oven-ready chicken, cut into serving pieces
75 g/3 oz lard
1 onion, peeled and finely chopped
2 cloves garlic, peeled and roughly chopped
150 ml/¼ pint dry sherry
about 15 blanched toasted almonds
1 tablespoon finely chopped fresh parsley
100 g/4 oz shelled fresh peas (optional)

American
2 tablespoons flour
salt
freshly ground black pepper

Chicken in Almond Sauce

3½ lb oven-ready chicken, cut into serving pieces
6 tablespoons lard
1 onion, peeled and finely chopped
2 cloves garlic, peeled and roughly chopped
⅔ cup dry sherry
about 15 blanched toasted almonds
1 tablespoon finely chopped fresh parsley
1 cup shelled fresh peas (optional)

Mix the flour with salt and pepper and use about half of it to coat the chicken pieces. Melt the lard in a saucepan, add the onion and garlic and fry gently until softened. Add the pieces of chicken a few at a time and fry until they are golden brown all over. Remove and keep warm. Stir the remaining seasoned flour into the hot fat and cook for 1 minute, then stir in the sherry. Bring to the boil, stirring. Add a little boiling water to stop it burning, if necessary. Put back the chicken and just enough hot water to cover. Simmer, partially covered, for about 1½ hours or until the chicken is tender.

Crush the almonds with a pestle and mortar or in a blender and mix with a little of the liquid from the chicken. About 10 minutes before serving, add the almonds to the pan with the parsley and peas (if used), stirring well. The sauce should be fairly thick, so you could remove the lid from the pan and let it reduce a little if necessary. Serve with saffron-flavoured rice.

Roast Stuffed Turkey

Ghallos Yemistos

In Greece, as elsewhere, roast stuffed turkey is served at special family gatherings. Traditionally Greek turkeys range freely on the farms, and to ensure tenderness they are cooked in a large covered pan, initially with a little water to create steam. It is a succulent way of cooking any turkey, but frozen birds must always be thawed completely before cooking commences.

Preparation time: 40 minutes
Cooking time: 3½ to 4 hours
Oven temperature: 180°C/350°F, Gas Mark 4
To serve: 12 to 14

Metric/Imperial
4.5 kg/10 lb oven-ready turkey
salt
freshly ground black pepper
½ lemon
olive oil or melted butter for basting and greasing
Stuffing:
225 g/8 oz chestnuts
3 tablespoons olive oil
1 medium onion, peeled and finely chopped
the turkey giblets, except the neck
350 g/12 oz minced pork or sausage meat
150 g/5 oz long-grain rice
scant 300 ml/½ pint water
75 g/3 oz seedless raisins or currants
50 g/2 oz pine nuts or blanched shredded almonds
3 tablespoons chopped fresh parsley
2 teaspoons dried thyme or sage
salt
freshly ground black pepper

American
10 lb oven-ready turkey
salt
freshly ground black pepper
½ lemon
olive oil or melted butter for basting and greasing
Stuffing:
½ lb chestnuts
3 tablespoons olive oil
1 medium onion, peeled and finely chopped
the turkey giblets, except the neck
¾ lb ground pork or sausagemeat
⅔ cup long-grain rice
1¼ cups water
½ cup seedless raisins or currants
½ cup pine nuts or blanched shredded almonds
3 tablespoons chopped fresh parsley

Roast Stuffed Turkey

2 teaspoons dried thyme or *sage*
salt
freshly ground black pepper

Remove the giblets from the turkey and rinse them. Reserve the neck for stock. Chop the liver, heart and gizzard and keep for the stuffing.

Rinse and dry the turkey and season inside and out with salt and pepper. Rub over with the cut lemon, squeezing the juice over the bird. Leave in a cool place while preparing the stuffing.

Cut a small slit in the pointed end of each chestnut, put them in a pan, cover with cold water and bring to the boil. Simmer for 15 minutes. Drain, peel off the outer and inner skins and chop the nuts roughly.

Heat the oil in a saucepan, add the onion and fry gently until soft. Add the chopped giblets and cook, stirring constantly, until they lose their red colour. Add the pork or sausage meat and stir until crumbly. Add the rice and water and cook over moderate heat, stirring frequently, until the water is absorbed and the rice half cooked, about 15 minutes. Remove from the heat. Add the raisins or currants, nuts, parsley, herbs, salt and pepper to taste and the chestnuts. Mix gently and leave to become cold and firm.

Heat the oven. Spoon the stuffing loosely into the neck end of the bird and secure the flap of skin under the bird with a small skewer. Put any surplus stuffing in a separate covered dish, and cook with the turkey in the lower part of the oven.

Place the bird breast up on a rack in a roasting pan and pour 150 ml/¼ pint (⅔ cup) hot water into the pan. Brush the bird all over with olive oil or melted butter. Thoroughly grease a piece of kitchen foil large enough to cover the bird loosely and secure it in place by twisting it under the rim of the pan.

Cook in the centre of the oven for 3 hours. Then remove the foil, baste the bird with the pan drippings and continue cooking for another 30 to 45 minutes until the bird is golden brown. If the juices run clear when the thickest part of the thigh is pierced with a fine skewer, the bird is cooked through.

Transfer the bird to a serving platter, garnish with fresh parsley and serve the juices (from which all fat has been skimmed) separately.

Turkey Breasts with Marsala

Filetti di Tacchino al Marsala

Turkey breast meat can be bought in many supermarkets, and when combined with Marsala, mushrooms and cheese it provides a rather special meal without a great deal of preparation. Chicken breasts or veal escalopes (scallops) can be cooked in exactly the same manner, and it is a dish that can be kept hot in a low oven if guests are delayed.

Preparation time: 20 minutes
Cooking time: 20 minutes
Oven temperature: 160°C/325°F, Gas Mark 3
To serve: 4

Metric/Imperial
450 g/1 lb turkey breast meat, cut into 8 slices
salt
freshly ground black pepper
flour for coating
75 g/3 oz butter
1 tablespoon olive oil
100 g/4 oz button mushrooms, thinly sliced
1 tablespoon lemon juice
2 tablespoons grated Parmesan cheese
6 tablespoons Marsala
2 tablespoons chicken stock

American
1 lb turkey breast meat, cut into 8 slices
salt
freshly ground black pepper
flour for coating
6 tablespoons butter
1 tablespoon olive oil
1 cup thinly sliced button mushrooms
1 tablespoon lemon juice
2 tablespoons grated Parmesan cheese
6 tablespoons Marsala
2 tablespoons chicken stock

Place the turkey slices between greaseproof (wax) paper and beat with a rolling pin, cleaver or mallet to flatten the meat. Dust each piece with salt, pepper and flour. Shake off any surplus flour.

Melt 40 g/1½ oz (3 tablespoons) of the butter with the oil in a large heavy frying pan (skillet) and fry the turkey fillets in two batches (they must lie flat in the pan) over moderate heat for about 5 minutes on each side. Remove from the pan and arrange in a single layer in a shallow ovenproof dish. Cover and put in the oven to continue cooking gently.

Add 25 g/1 oz (2 tablespoons) of the butter to the frying pan (skillet), melt it and fry the mushroom slices gently for about 5 minutes, stirring now and then. Sprinkle with the lemon juice and salt. Using the slotted spoon, lift out the mushrooms and arrange them to cover the turkey fillets. Sprinkle the cheese over the mushrooms and return the dish to the oven, uncovered, so that the cheese can melt.

Pour the Marsala into the frying pan (skillet) and boil rapidly until reduced by half. Add the chicken broth and remaining butter, stir well, scraping up the sediment from the bottom of the pan, and pour over the turkey. Serve hot, with a selection of green beans, sliced courgettes (zucchini), carrot sticks and sprigs of cauliflower.

Braised Chicken Pieces with Peppers

Pollo in Padella con Peperoni

A popular family recipe along the coast of Southern Italy where sweet peppers and tomatoes grow in profusion, serve this with boiled or sauté potatoes.

Preparation time: 20 minutes
Cooking time: about 45 minutes
To serve: 4

Metric/Imperial
4 chicken quarters, about 275 g/10 oz each
salt
freshly ground black pepper
flour for coating
4 tablespoons olive oil
1 large onion, peeled and chopped
2 cloves garlic, peeled and crushed
1 x 400 g/14 oz can peeled tomatoes
2 teaspoons sugar
2 large green peppers
2 tablespoons chopped fresh parsley

American
4 chicken quarters, about 10 oz each
salt
freshly ground black pepper
flour for coating
¼ cup olive oil
1 large onion, peeled and chopped
2 cloves garlic, peeled and crushed
1 x 14 oz can peeled tomatoes
2 teaspoons sugar
2 large green peppers
2 tablespoons chopped fresh parsley

Sprinkle the chicken quarters with salt and pepper and coat with flour. Heat the oil in a wide flameproof casserole, add the onion and fry gently until softened. Add the chicken pieces and fry, turning once or twice, for about 15 minutes, or until golden on both sides.

Left: Braised Chicken Pieces with Peppers. Right: Turkey Breasts with Marsala

Add the garlic, tomatoes and their juice and sugar. Cover and cook gently for 20 minutes.

Meanwhile, grill (broil) the peppers under medium heat for about 10 minutes, turning frequently, until the skin is blackened on all sides. Rinse the peppers in cold water and peel off all the charred skin. Remove the stalks, cut the peppers in half, discard all the white seeds and then cut the flesh in 1 cm/½ in wide strips.

Add the pepper strips to the chicken and continue to simmer, uncovered, for 10 minutes or until the chicken is cooked through and the sauce well reduced. Check the seasoning, sprinkle with parsley and serve from the casserole.

Roast Quails

Codornices al Horno

These tiny, delicately flavoured game birds are still fairly common in Spain. Elsewhere they are obtainable in specialist food stores. Allow two small or one large bird per person.

Preparation time: 20 minutes
Cooking time: 20 minutes
Oven temperature: 200°C/400°F, Gas Mark 6
To serve: 4

Metric/Imperial
4 or 8 quails, cleaned, with giblets
75 g/3 oz butter or bacon fat
1 tablespoon chopped fresh summer savory
1 teaspoon dried thyme
1 teaspoon dried basil
salt
freshly ground black pepper
4 to 8 vine leaves, if available
4 to 8 thin rashers of bacon
juice of 1 lemon
4 slices of white bread, crusts removed
1 tablespoon flour
4 tablespoons red wine
Stock:
300 ml/½ pint water
½ onion, peeled
1 carrot, peeled
1 bay leaf
salt

American
4 or 8 quails, cleaned, with giblets
6 tablespoons butter or bacon fat
1 tablespoon chopped fresh summer savory
1 teaspoon dried thyme
1 teaspoon dried basil

salt
freshly ground black pepper
4 to 8 vine leaves, if available
4 to 8 slices of bacon
juice of 1 lemon
4 slices of white bread, crusts removed
1 tablespoon flour
¼ cup red wine
Stock:
1¼ cups water
½ onion, peeled
1 carrot, peeled
1 bay leaf
salt

Put the giblets and other ingredients for the stock in a saucepan and bring to the boil. Simmer while preparing the quails. Spread a little of the butter or bacon fat on each bird and put a small piece of fat inside. Sprinkle with herbs and a little salt and pepper. Put a vine leaf over the breast of each bird and cover with bacon. Sprinkle with lemon juice.

Roast Quails

Put the birds into a roasting pan with a little more fat, reserving about 25 g/1 oz (2 tablespoons), and roast for 15 to 20 minutes, basting often.

Meanwhile, fry the bread slices in the remaining butter or bacon fat until golden brown on both sides. Drain on paper towels. When the quails are done put one on each slice of bread on a serving platter and keep hot. Strain the giblet stock and reserve 150 ml/¼ pint (⅔ cup).

To make the sauce, pour off most of the fat from the roasting pan, then sprinkle in the flour. Cook on top of the stove, stirring for about 1 minute, then add the reserved giblet stock. Bring to the boil, stirring. Add the wine and continue to stir well, scraping up the particles left in the pan. Cook gently for a few minutes, adjust the seasoning and strain into a hot bowl or jug. Serve the sauce with the quails.

Duck with Olives

Anitra alle Olive

It is the custom in Southern Italy to offset the richness of duck by adding olives. These can be green or black, or a mixture, and preferably plump ones. If using frozen duck make sure it has time to thaw out completely before cooking begins.

Preparation time: 20 minutes
Cooking time: about 2 hours
To serve: 4

Metric/Imperial/American
1.75 to 2.25 kg/4 to 5 lb oven-ready
  duck
salt
freshly ground black pepper
1½ teaspoons dried powdered sage or
  oregano
3 tablespoons oil
1 bay leaf
1 large onion, peeled and thickly sliced
1 large carrot, peeled and sliced
2 stalks celery, sliced
1 tablespoon flour
300 ml/½ pint (1¼ cups) red wine
150 ml/¼ pint (⅔ cup) giblet or chicken
  stock
225 g/8 oz (1½ cups) mixed black and
  green olives, stoned (pitted)

Left: Duck with Olives
Centre: Wild Pigeons Braised with Vegetables
Right: Rabbit Stewed in Roman Style

Prick the skin of the duck well with a fork. Sprinkle inside and out with salt, pepper and the herbs. Heat the oil in a large flameproof oval casserole. Put in the duck and fry briskly until nicely browned all over. Remove from the pot. Add the bay leaf, onion, carrot and celery and fry gently for 5 to 6 minutes. Sprinkle in the flour and stir and cook for 1 to 2 minutes. Stir in the wine, bring to the boil and allow to bubble for several minutes. Add the stock and when simmering replace the duck. Cover the pan tightly and simmer very gently for 2 hours, or until the duck is cooked and tender. Baste with the sauce from time to time and add a little extra stock should it evaporate too much.

 Lift out the duck, cut into serving portions and place in a clean casserole. Keep hot. Pour off as much fat as possible from the sauce and discard the bay leaf. If necessary, reduce the sauce by rapid boiling to about 300 ml/½ pint (1¼ cups). Add the olives, heat gently for 5 minutes, then adjust the seasoning. Pour the sauce over the duck and serve from the casserole.

Wild Pigeons Braised with Vegetables

Colombi Selvatici all' Umbria

The lavish use of herbs is characteristic of Italian country cooking, and this simple Umbrian way with pigeons is no exception. The rough-textured but unthickened vegetable sauce is also characteristic.

Preparation time: 20 minutes
Cooking time: 1¼ to 2 hours
To serve: 4

Metric/Imperial/American
3 tablespoons olive oil
4 plump oven-ready pigeons
1 medium onion, peeled and sliced
1 medium carrot, peeled and sliced
2 sticks celery, sliced
bunch of herbs, consisting of 1 bay leaf,
  1 sprig fresh thyme, 1 sprig fresh
  rosemary and 3 fresh leaves sage, tied
  together

6 tablespoons dry white wine
2 tablespoons white wine vinegar
150 ml/¼ pint (⅔ cup) hot water
salt
freshly ground black pepper
8 small triangles of bread, fried in olive
  oil

Heat the oil in a large flameproof casserole, add the pigeons and brown on all
sides. Lower the heat and add the onion,
carrot, celery and bunch of herbs. Continue frying, stirring frequently, for 5
minutes. Pour in the wine, vinegar and
water and add a seasoning of salt and
pepper. Bring to the boil, cover tightly
and simmer very gently until the pigeons
are tender. This can take from 1 to 2
hours depending on the age of the
pigeons. If more convenient the casserole
can be cooked in the oven preheated to
160°C/325°F, Gas Mark 3.

When the pigeons are tender, remove
them from the casserole, snip off the
bony wing joints and arrange the birds
on a hot serving dish. Keep hot.

Discard the bunch of herbs and pass
the vegetables and liquid through a sieve
or electric blender to produce a rough-
textured sauce. Reheat the sauce, check
the seasoning and pour over the pigeons.
Garnish the dish with the triangles of
fried bread.

Rabbit Stewed in Roman Style

Spezzatino di Coniglio alla Romana

The cooking time for this tasty dish of
rabbit must be adjusted according to the
rabbit's age and can vary from 1 to
nearer 2 hours. Add the pepper strips
about 15 minutes before serving so that
they retain a little crispness. The sauce
should be fairly thick, but if it reduces
too much during cooking add a little
more stock.

Preparation time: 30 minutes (plus 1
  hour to drain aubergine (eggplant)
Cooking time: 1 to 2 hours
To serve: 6

Metric/Imperial

1 medium aubergine, cut into 2.5
  cm/1 inch cubes
salt
2 young rabbits, cut into joints
freshly ground black pepper
3 tablespoons olive oil
50 g/2 oz thickly sliced rashers streaky
  bacon, rinded and cut into strips
1 stick celery, sliced

2 cloves garlic, peeled and crushed
2 teaspoons chopped fresh marjoram, or
  1 teaspoon dried marjoram
6 tablespoons Marsala
1 x 400 g/14 oz can peeled tomatoes
about 300 ml/½ pint hot chicken stock
1 green pepper, cored, seeded and cut
  into thin strips

American

1 medium eggplant, cut into 1 inch cubes
salt
2 young rabbits, cut up
freshly ground black pepper
3 tablespoons olive oil
2 oz thick slices bacon, cut into strips
1 stalk celery, sliced
2 cloves garlic, peeled and crushed
2 teaspoons chopped fresh marjoram, or
  1 teaspoon dried marjoram
6 tablespoons Marsala
1 x 14 oz can peeled tomatoes
about 1¼ cups hot chicken stock
1 green pepper, cored, seeded and cut
  into thin strips

Put the aubergine (eggplant) cubes into
a colander, sprinkle with salt and leave
to drain for about 1 hour.

Meanwhile, season the rabbit pieces
with salt and pepper. Heat the oil in a
large flameproof casserole, add the
bacon and celery and fry gently for a
minute or two. Increase the heat, add the
rabbit pieces and fry, turning frequently,
until nicely browned. Stir in the garlic,
marjoram and Marsala and let it bubble
for several minutes, then add the
tomatoes and their juice. Add enough
hot stock just to cover the rabbit. Cover
the pot tightly and simmer for
30 minutes.

Rinse and dry the aubergine (eggplant) cubes and add to the casserole,
stirring them into the liquid. Re-cover
the casserole and continue simmering
for another 30 minutes. Stir in the green
pepper strips and simmer for another 15
minutes, or until the rabbit is tender.
Check the seasoning and serve from the
casserole.

Light meals, vegetables and sauces

Eggs Flamenca

Huevos a la Flamenca

For this version of a classic Andalucian dish you first make a *sofrito*, a blend of chopped tomatoes, onion, red or green pepper, garlic and parsley, cooked together in olive oil to a thick sauce-like consistency. This *sofrito* is used widely in Spanish cooking, especially along the Mediterranean coasts.

Preparation time: 30 minutes
Cooking time: 20 to 30 minutes
Oven temperature: 180°C/350°F, Gas Mark 4
To serve: 4

Metric/Imperial

4 eggs
100 g/4 oz chorizo or garlic sausage, sliced and slices halved
8 canned or cooked fresh asparagus tips
100 g/4 oz frozen or cooked fresh peas
8 strips canned pimiento
olive oil
Sofrito:
3 tablespoons olive oil
6 tomatoes, skinned and chopped or equivalent amount canned tomatoes
1 large onion, peeled and finely chopped
1 red or green pepper, cored, seeded and chopped
2 cloves garlic, peeled and chopped
about 4 tablespoons water
1 tablespoon chopped fresh parsley
salt
freshly ground black pepper

Young people picnicking on the beach of Otranto, Italy

American

4 eggs
¼ lb chorizo or garlic sausage, sliced and slices halved
8 canned or cooked fresh asparagus tips
1 cup frozen or cooked fresh peas
8 strips canned pimiento
olive oil
Sofrito:
3 tablespoons olive oil
6 tomatoes, skinned and chopped, or equivalent amount canned tomatoes
1 large onion, peeled and finely chopped
1 red or green pepper, cored, seeded and chopped
2 cloves garlic, peeled and chopped
about ¼ cup water
1 tablespoon chopped fresh parsley
salt
freshly ground black pepper

To make the *sofrito*, heat the olive oil in a saucepan, add the tomatoes, onion, red or green pepper and garlic and cook gently for about 5 minutes, stirring often and keeping the pan partially covered. Add the water, parsley and seasoning and cook gently until the vegetables are tender and the sauce is thick.

When the *sofrito* is ready, spread it out in a shallow ovenproof dish. Make four little hollows in the surface. Carefully break the eggs, one by one, into a cup and pour one into each hollow. Decorate the whole of the surface with slices of sausage, asparagus tips, peas and strips of pimiento to make an attractive design. Sprinkle with a little oil and put the now resplendent dish into the oven. Bake for about 15 minutes, or until the eggs are just set. Serve in the dish.

This can also be made in four individual ovenproof dishes.

Spanish Potato Omelette

Tortilla Español de Patatas

An omelette the way the Spanish make it is a robust and solid affair. It is perhaps the most universal of all Spanish dishes, being popular as a snack or a meal, at any time of day and especially as a packed lunch or picnic. It may be varied by the addition of other chopped vegetables or small pieces of chicken, meat or chorizo.

Preparation time: 10 minutes
Cooking time: 20 minutes
To serve: 4

Metric/Imperial/American

150 ml/¼ pint (⅔ cup) olive oil
2 large potatoes, peeled and diced
2 large onions, peeled and finely chopped
3 eggs
½ teaspoon salt

Heat the oil gently in a frying pan (skillet). Add the potatoes and onions and stir well. Cover the pan and cook gently, stirring occasionally, for about 15 minutes or until the vegetables are tender, but not browned.

Meanwhile, beat the eggs and salt together in a large bowl. When the onions and potatoes are cooked, remove them from the oil with a slotted spoon, allow to cool slightly then mix them thoroughly with the beaten eggs. Drain the surplus oil from the pan, leaving just enough to cover the bottom. Scrape off any bits that may have become stuck. Put the pan on a low heat, and when it starts to give off a slight haze, pour in the egg and vegetable mixture. Flatten it down with a spatula and cook on a low heat for a few minutes, shaking the pan gently from time to time to prevent sticking.

The omelette now has to be cooked on the other side. To do this invert a heatproof plate over the pan and tip the omelette onto it, holding plate and pan firmly together. Then slide the omelette back into the pan and cook for a few more minutes. Alternatively, put the pan under a hot grill (broiler) to cook the top. Turn the omelette out when cooked; it should be like a flat round cake. Eat hot or cold, cut into wedges.

Above: Eggs Flamenca
Below: Spanish Potato Omelette

Meat Omelette

Eggah bi Lahma

Thick and firm and more in the character of Spanish omelettes than light French ones, omelettes in the Middle East are usually packed with vegetables and meats. They are as good cold as they are hot and make the perfect picnic or light luncheon meal accompanied by a salad and perhaps yogurt. Though some bake them in the oven, the more traditional way is to cook them in a large frying pan (skillet). This meat version is an Egyptian favourite.

Preparation time: about 20 minutes
Cooking time: 25 minutes
To serve: 6 to 8

Metric/Imperial
4 to 5 tablespoons oil
1 large onion, peeled and chopped
0.5 kg/1 lb lean minced beef
salt
freshly ground black pepper
½ teaspoon ground allspice
1 teaspoon ground cumin
3 tablespoons finely chopped fresh parsley
6 eggs
1 large potato, peeled, cooked and mashed

Meat Omelette

American
4 to 5 tablespoons oil
1 large onion, peeled and chopped
1 lb lean ground beef
salt
freshly ground black pepper
½ teaspoon ground allspice
1 teaspoon ground cumin
3 tablespoons finely chopped fresh parsley
6 eggs
1 large potato, peeled, cooked and mashed

Heat 2 tablespoons of the oil in a frying pan (skillet), add the onion and fry until it is golden. Add the meat and fry, stirring, until it browns. Stir in salt, pepper, the spices and parsley and remove from the heat.

Beat the eggs lightly with a fork in a bowl. Drain the fried meat of all fat and add to the eggs with the mashed potato. Beat well. Taste and add salt and pepper and more spices if necessary.

Heat 2 tablespoons of the oil in the cleaned frying pan (skillet). Pour in the egg mixture. Reduce the heat as low as possible and cover the pan with a lid. Cook for about 20 minutes or until the eggs have set and only the top is still running. Place a plate over the pan, invert the omelette onto it and slip it back carefully into the pan with the remaining oil. Cook and brown the

other side.

Alternatively, put the frying pan (skillet) under a hot grill (broiler) to set and brown the top of the omelette. Turn out on a plate. Serve hot or cold, cut into wedges like a cake.

Ragoût of Peppers and Tomatoes

Pipérade

A simple dish, from the Basque country, which can be served as an appetizer or as a light main dish.

Preparation time: 15 minutes
Cooking time: 30 minutes
To serve: 4 to 6

Metric/Imperial/American
2 tablespoons olive oil or goose or pork dripping
2 large onions, peeled and thinly sliced
1 clove garlic, peeled and finely chopped (optional)
0.5 kg/1 lb peppers, cored, seeded and cut into strips
0.5 kg/1 lb tomatoes, skinned and roughly chopped
6 eggs
salt

Left: Baked Vegetables with Beef. Right: Ragoût of Peppers and Tomatoes

freshly ground black pepper
1 teaspoon finely chopped fresh parsley
*   or basil*
triangles of fried bread to garnish

Heat the oil or dripping in a deep frying pan (skillet) or shallow flameproof casserole, add the onions and garlic and fry gently until golden yellow. Add the peppers and cook for 10 to 15 minutes, or until they are soft. Stir in the tomatoes, raise the heat a little and cook until most of the moisture has evaporated and the tomatoes have cooked down to a thick pulp.

Beat the eggs together with the seasoning and herbs and pour into the pan. Stir gently until they begin to set. Remove the pan from the heat while the mixture is still creamy. Serve garnished with the bread triangles.

Baked Vegetables with Beef

Tumbet

This classic Mallorcan dish can be made either with eggs or minced (ground) beef. The following recipe uses beef.

Preparation time: 40 minutes
Cooking time: 55 minutes
Oven temperature: 180°C/350°F, Gas Mark 4
To serve: 4

Metric/Imperial/American
3 tablespoons olive oil
2 aubergines (eggplants), sliced
4 courgettes (zucchini), sliced
2 potatoes, peeled and thinly sliced
2 green or red peppers, cored, seeded and cut into rings
2 onions, peeled and cut into rings
225 g/8 oz minced (ground) beef
2 tablespoons dry breadcrumbs
a little butter
Sauce:
2 tablespoons olive oil
2 cloves garlic, peeled and crushed

6 tomatoes, skinned and chopped or equivalent amount canned tomatoes
2 tablespoons tomato purée (paste)
salt
freshly ground black pepper
1 teaspoon sugar
1 tablespoon vinegar

To make the sauce, heat the olive oil in a small saucepan and gently fry the garlic until soft. Stir in the tomatoes and tomato paste, season to taste. Add the sugar and vinegar and a little water if necessary. Cook gently for 10 minutes, stirring often. Sieve if you like a smooth texture. Set aside.

Heat the oil in a frying pan (skillet) and fry the vegetables until lightly browned, keeping them separate. Lastly brown the meat, turning it over and over and seasoning with salt and pepper.

Make a layer of aubergine (eggplant) slices in a well-greased baking dish. Add a little meat and then tomato sauce, then cover with a layer of courgettes (zucchini). Continue making layers until all the vegetables, meat and tomato sauce are used up. Sprinkle the top with breadcrumbs and dot with butter. Bake for about 45 minutes. Serve hot in the dish.

113

Provençal Gratin

Tian de Courgettes et Blettes

A *tian* is a Provençal speciality, halfway between a gratin and a thick omelette, and there is hardly any vegetable, or combination of vegetables with meat or fish, which cannot be *tian*-ized. This is a particularly delicious combination, and can be eaten on its own as a light supper dish or served as a vegetable side dish.

Preparation time: 20 minutes (plus 1 hour draining the courgettes/zucchini)
Cooking time: 35 to 40 minutes
Oven temperature: 190°C, 375°F, Gas Mark 5
To serve: 6

Metric /Imperial/American
1 kg/2 lb courgettes (zucchini), coarsely grated
salt
3 tablespoons olive oil
1 onion, peeled and finely chopped
1 clove garlic, peeled and finely chopped (optional)
225 g/8 oz spinach or Swiss chard, or 100 g/4 oz thawed frozen spinach, finely chopped
3 eggs

freshly ground black pepper
1 tablespoon finely chopped fresh parsley
50 g/2 oz (½ cup) grated Parmesan, Gruyère or sharp Cheddar cheese
50 g/2 oz (6 tablespoons) rice, cooked
1 tablespoon fine dry breadcrumbs

Spread out the courgettes (zucchini) on a clean towel, sprinkle with salt and leave to drain in the towel in a colander for 1 hour. Squeeze out all the moisture through the towel.

Heat 2 tablespoons of the oil in a large frying pan (skillet), add the onion and garlic and fry until softened. Add the courgettes (zucchini) and spinach or chard and cook over a moderate heat for 5 minutes. Allow to cool a little.

Beat the egg in a large bowl with salt and pepper. Stir in the parsley and half the grated cheese, then mix in the courgettes (zucchini) and spinach mixture and the rice. Pour into an oiled shallow ovenproof dish, earthenware if possible.

Sprinkle with the breadcrumbs and remaining cheese and dribble on the remaining olive oil. Cover and bake for 35 to 40 minutes, uncovering the dish and moving it to the top of the oven towards the end in order to brown the crust.

Left: Provençal Gratin

Macaroni with Meat Sauce

La Macaronade

This is usually served as an accompaniment to a *daube*, but it can also be served on its own as a simple 'the day after the *daube*' meal.

Preparation time: 20 minutes
Cooking time: 15 to 20 minutes
Oven temperature: 220°C, 425°F, Gas Mark 7
To serve: 4 to 6

Metric/Imperial/American
0.5 kg/1 lb macaroni or noodles
salt
2 tablespoons olive oil or 50 g/2 oz (¼ cup) butter
freshly ground black pepper
100 g/4 oz (1 cup) grated Gruyère, Parmesan or stale Cheddar cheese

Centre: Macaroni with Meat Sauce
Right: Onion, Anchovy and Olive Tart

1 tablespoon finely chopped fresh
  parsley or basil
300 ml/½ pint (1¼ cups) rich meat stock
  from a daube or other meat casserole

Cook the macaroni or noodles in plenty
of boiling salted water until just tender.
Drain and return to the pan with 1
tablespoon of oil or 25 g/1 oz (2 tablespoons) of the butter. Season generously
and stir over a gentle heat to warm
through.

Oil or butter an ovenproof dish and
put in a layer of the pasta. Sprinkle with
a good layer of cheese and a little of the
herbs. Repeat until all the pasta is used,
reserving a little cheese. Pour over the
meat stock and sprinkle with the
remaining cheese and oil, or dot with
the remaining butter.

Place in the oven to heat through, and
serve when the top is golden brown and
crusty.

Onion, Anchovy and Olive Tart

Pissaladière

The pungent Provençal first cousin to
the Italian Pizza, serve *pissaladière* as an
appetizer, or as a light luncheon dish,
accompanied by a salad.

Preparation time: 40 minutes (plus
  1 hour rising for the dough)
Cooking time: 50 minutes
Oven temperature: 200°C, 400°F, Gas
  Mark 6
To serve: 6

Metric/Imperial/American
Crust:
15 g/½ oz (½ cake) fresh (compressed)
  yeast
2 tablespoons lukewarm water
150 g/5 oz (1¼ cups) plain (all-purpose)
  flour
salt
1 egg, beaten
1 tablespoon olive oil
Filling:
4 tablespoons (¼ cup) olive oil
0.5 kg/1¼ lb onions, peeled and thinly
  sliced
salt
freshly ground black pepper

1 x 50 g/1¾ oz can anchovy fillets,
  drained and halved
50 g/2 oz (⅓ cup) black olives, stoned
  (pitted)

Dissolve the yeast in the water and leave
in a warm place until frothy. Sift the
flour and salt into a warmed bowl, and
make a well in the centre. Add the yeast
mixture, egg and olive oil and mix
together with a wooden spoon. Knead
the dough until it is springy and comes
away clean from the sides of the bowl.
Leave in a warm place to rise for about
1 hour, or until it has doubled in bulk.
Meanwhile, heat the olive oil in a heavy
frying pan (skillet), add the onions and
fry gently until they are quite soft and
butter yellow. Do not allow them to
brown. Season to taste.

When the dough has risen, knock
(punch) it down, form into a ball and
place on a well-oiled 30 cm/12 in round
baking tin. Gently press the dough from
the centre outwards until the baking tin
is evenly covered. Spread on the onions,
then make a criss-cross pattern on top
with the halved anchovy fillets and
intersperse with the olives. Leave to rise
again for 15 minutes, then place in the
centre of the oven. Bake for 40 to
50 minutes, turning down the oven to
190°C, 375°F, gas mark 5 for the last
15 minutes if the crust is turning too
dark.

Cut into pieces before serving.

Balearic Pizza

Coca de Baleares

This type of cheese-less, rather simplified pizza is popular throughout Ibiza, Mallorca and Formentera. It is made in a large rectangular piece and cut into squares to suit the customer's requirements. It is usually sold in bakeries and is often made from leftover bread dough.

Preparation time: 15 minutes
Cooking time: 20 minutes
Oven temperature: 180°C/350°F, Gas Mark 4
To serve: 4

Metric/Imperial
0.5 kg/1 lb bread dough, or shortcrust pastry
3 tablespoons olive oil
1 large onion, peeled and sliced into rings
2 cloves garlic, peeled and chopped
1 red or green pepper, cored, seeded and sliced
0.5 kg/1 lb tomatoes, skinned and chopped or equivalent amount canned tomatoes
0.5 kg/1 lb fresh or frozen spinach or Swiss chard, cooked and chopped
salt
freshly ground black pepper
1 tablespoon chopped fresh oregano, fennel or parsley (or some of each)
a few stoned olives

American
1 lb bread dough or pie pastry
3 tablespoons olive oil
1 large onion, peeled and sliced into rings
2 cloves garlic, peeled and chopped
1 red or green pepper, cored, seeded and sliced
1 lb tomatoes, skinned and chopped, or equivalent amount canned tomatoes
1 lb fresh or frozen spinach or Swiss chard, cooked and chopped
salt
freshly ground black pepper
1 tablespoon chopped fresh oregano, fennel or parsley (or some of each)
a few pitted olives

Roll out the dough or pastry and put on to a large well-oiled baking sheet.

Heat 2 tablespoons of the oil in a frying pan (skillet), add the onion, garlic and pepper and fry gently until they start to soften. Add the tomatoes and spinach or chard and mix thoroughly. Season to taste and cook for about 5 minutes, stirring often. Spread this mix-

ture over the dough or pastry and sprinkle with the herbs and olives. Finally sprinkle with the remaining olive oil. Put into the oven and bake for about 20 minutes. Cut into squares and serve hot or cold.

Pizza Napolitana

Neapolitan Pizza

Naples is the home town of the pizza and there, in the numerous *pizzerie*, you eat it straight from the brick oven. Commercial pizza is made on a plain bread dough base which toughens as it cools. For home use it is more convenient to make a richer dough that can be reheated or frozen. The recipe below

Balearic Pizza

combines the classic Neapolitan topping with the special enriched dough.

Preparation time: about 40 minutes, (plus 2 to 3 hours for rising)
Cooking time: 25 to 30 minutes
Oven temperature: 220°C/425°F, Gas Mark 7, reduced to 180°C/350°F, Gas Mark 4
To serve: makes 2 pizzas, each serving 3 to 4 portions

Metric/Imperial
Enriched bread dough:
1 teaspoon sugar
4 tablespoons warm water
1 teaspoon dried yeast
225 g/8 oz plain flour
1 teaspoon salt
65 g/2½ oz butter at room temperature
1 egg, beaten

Topping:
4 tablespoons olive oil
0.5 kg/1 lb ripe tomatoes, skinned,
    seeded and sliced, or 1 x 400 g/14 oz
    can peeled tomatoes, well drained and
    chopped
freshly ground black pepper
1 teaspoon dried oregano or basil
175 g/6 oz mozzarella or *Primula* cheese,
    sliced
6 anchovy fillets, halved lengthways

Pizza Napolitana

American
Enriched bread dough:
1 teaspoon sugar
¼ cup warm water
1 teaspoon active dry yeast
2 cups all-purpose flour
1 teaspoon salt
5 tablespoons butter at room
    temperature
1 egg, beaten

Topping:
¼ cup olive oil
1 lb ripe tomatoes, skinned, seeded and
    sliced, or 1 x 14 oz can peeled
    tomatoes, well drained and chopped
freshly ground black pepper
1 teaspoon dried oregano or basil
6 oz mozzarella or *Primula* cheese, sliced
6 anchovy fillets, halved lengthwise

To make the dough, dissolve the sugar in the warm water and sprinkle the dried yeast on top. Leave for 10 minutes or until frothy.

Sift the flour and salt into a warm bowl and rub in the butter with your fingertips. Make a well in the centre and drop in the egg and the yeast mixture. Mix to a firm but pliable dough, adding a little more water if necessary. When the dough comes cleanly away from the sides of the bowl, turn it on to a lightly floured surface and knead thoroughly for 10 minutes or until the dough is smooth and silky. Gather into a ball, put in an oiled bowl, cover and leave in a warm place to rise until it has doubled in volume; this takes about 2 to 3 hours at room temperature.

When the dough has doubled in volume turn it on to a floured surface and divide in half. Knead each piece lightly, then place one in each of two oiled 20 to 23 cm/8 to 9 inch pie plates (pans). With floured knuckles press it out to cover the bottom and reach 1 cm/½ inch up the sides. Brush with half the oil and cover with the tomatoes to within 1 cm/½ inch of the edge. Season with pepper and sprinkle with herbs. Lay the cheese slices on top, criss-cross the anchovies over the cheese and sprinkle liberally with the remaining oil. Leave in a warm place for 30 minutes to rise.

Bake the pizzas in the hottest part of the oven for 20 minutes, then reduce the heat and bake for another 5 or 10 minutes, until cooked through. Eat while still warm.

VARIATIONS:
Sicilian topping: omit the cheese and sprinkle the tomatoes liberally with stoned (pitted) and chopped black and green olives and sliced mushrooms. Drizzle oil over all before baking.
Roman topping: omit the tomatoes, increase the Mozzarella and sprinkle the pizza liberally with grated Parmesan, oil and chopped fresh basil.
Seafood topping: omit the cheese and anchovies. Bake the pizza with the tomato base only. When cooked cover the surface with warm, freshly cooked clams and mussels and sprinkle with salt, pepper and chopped parsley.

Spinach and Cheese Pie

Spanakopitta

This recipe is one of many variations of spinach pie. On Crete a similar mixture appears in the form of individual square pies, their tops glazed with egg and sprinkled with sesame seeds. In Samos the filling is rolled in pastry like a Swiss (jelly) roll and then bent round into a circle. Yet another version contains rice and currants but omits the cheese. The pastry is sometimes brushed with melted butter instead of olive oil, resulting in a rather rich pie.

Preparation time: 35 minutes
Cooking time: about 45 minutes
Oven temperature: 180°C/350°F, Gas Mark 4
To serve: 6

Metric/Imperial
1 kg/2 lb fresh spinach leaves
9 to 11 tablespoons olive oil
100 g/4 oz onion, peeled and chopped (this should include some of the green tops of spring onions when possible)
3 tablespoons chopped fresh dill or 1½ tablespoons dried dill weed
225 g/8 oz Feta or curd cheese
2 eggs, beaten
freshly ground black pepper
salt if necessary
about 275 g/10 oz (about 14 sheets) phyllo pastry (see note on page 148)

American
2 lb fresh spinach leaves
9 to 11 tablespoons olive oil
1 cup peeled and chopped onion (this should include some of the green tops of scallions when possible)
3 tablespoons chopped fresh dill or 1½ tablespoons dried dill weed
1 cup crumbled Feta or small curd cottage cheese
2 eggs, beaten
freshly ground black pepper
salt if necessary
about 10 oz (about 14 sheets) phyllo pastry (see note on page 148)

Wash and drain the spinach thoroughly. Discard all stems and thinly slice the leaves. Heat 3 tablespoons of the oil in a large saucepan and fry the onion gently for about 5 minutes, until beginning to soften. Stir in the spinach, cover and cook over moderate heat for 5 minutes. Add the dill and cook, uncovered, stirring frequently, until most of the liquid has evaporated and the spinach is fairly dry. Remove from the heat and allow to cool to room temperature. Stir in the crumbled cheese, then little by little beat in the eggs. Taste and season as necessary.

Heat the oven. Oil a 25 cm/10 inch round baking pan, that is 5 cm/2 inches deep. Line the pan with a sheet of phyllo pastry, pressing the pastry well into the bottom and up the sides of the pan. Brush the whole surface of the pastry thoroughly with oil. Repeat with six more sheets of pastry, brushing each one with oil.

Put the filling into the pan on top of the last layer of phyllo and spread it evenly around the edge. Cover completely with a sheet of phyllo, brush with oil and repeat with five more pastry sheets. Trim excess pastry from the top of the pan.

Bake in the hottest part of the oven for about 45 minutes, until the pastry is crisp and lightly browned. Cut into portions and serve hot, warm or cold.

Above: Spinach and Cheese Pie. Below: Potato Patties

Potato Patties

Patatokeftethes

These tasty, green-flecked potato cakes are excellent to serve with any grilled (broiled) meat, fish or poultry. In Greece they are often served on their own with some boiled sliced beetroot (beets) and the Garlic Sauce on page 56.

Preparation time: 30 minutes
Cooking time: 25 minutes
To serve: makes 8 cakes

Metric/Imperial
675 g/1½ lb potatoes, peeled
salt
1 large egg, beaten
75 g/3 oz cheese, finely grated
2 tablespoons finely chopped fresh parsley
2 tablespoons finely chopped green

spring onion tops or *chives*
freshly ground black pepper
flour for coating
oil for frying

American

1½ *lb potatoes, peeled*
salt
1 *large egg, beaten*
¾ *cup finely grated cheese*
2 *tablespoons finely chopped fresh parsley*
2 *tablespoons finely chopped green scallion tops* or *chives*
freshly ground black pepper
flour for coating
oil for frying

Cook the potatoes in boiling salted water until tender. Drain, shake over the heat to dry thoroughly and then mash finely.

Add the egg, cheese, parsley, onion (scallion) or chives and salt and pepper to taste, to the potatoes and mix well. Divide the mixture into eight and with floured hands shape each portion into a ball. Flatten to 1 cm/½ inch thickness with a knife and coat each cake with flour. When all the patties are shaped, cover and chill until firm.

When ready to cook, heat enough oil to film generously the bottom of a large frying pan (skillet). When hot, fry the patties in batches over medium heat, turning once, until golden on both sides. Drain and keep hot until all are ready to serve.

Eggplant, Cheese and Tomato Casserole

Melanzane alla Parmigiana

This Calabrian version of *Parmigiani* contains hard-boiled eggs and chopped salami in addition to the fried aubergine (eggplant) slices, tomato sauce and cheese. Served on its own it is substantial enough for a main course or supper. It takes time to prepare but can be made ahead for baking later the same day.

Preparation time: 1½ hours
Cooking time: about 30 minutes
Oven temperature: 200°C/400°F, Gas Mark 6
To serve: 6

Metric/Imperial

1 *kg/2 lb aubergines, peeled and thinly sliced*
salt
flour
about 150 ml/¼ pint olive oil
600 *ml/1 pint tomato sauce (see page 135)*
175 *g/6 oz mozzarella* or *Bel Paese cheese, thinly sliced*
3 *hard-boiled eggs, sliced*
4 *slices salami, rinded and chopped*
50 *g/2 oz Parmesan cheese, grated*
2 *tablespoons dry white breadcrumbs*

American

2 *lb eggplants, peeled and thinly sliced*
salt
flour
about ⅔ cup olive oil
2½ *cups tomato sauce (see page 135)*
6 *oz mozzarella* or *Bel Paese cheese, thinly sliced*
3 *hard-cooked eggs, sliced*
4 *slices of salami, rinded and chopped*
½ *cup grated Parmesan cheese*
2 *tablespoons dry white breadcrumbs*

Eggplant, Cheese and Tomato Casserole

Put the aubergine (eggplant) slices into a colander with a generous sprinkling of salt between the layers and leave for 1 hour to allow the bitter juices to drain away. Rinse and pat dry with paper towels, then dust lightly with flour.

Heat 4 tablespoons of the oil in a large frying pan (skillet) and fry a single layer of aubergine (eggplant) slices fairly briskly until lightly browned, turning once. Drain on paper towels. Repeat until all the slices are fried, adding more oil to the pan as required.

Oil a large 5 cm/2 inch deep oven-to-table dish of about 1.75 litres/3 pints capacity. In it arrange the ingredients in layers, first half the tomato sauce, then half the aubergine (eggplant) slices, cheese, eggs, salami and grated cheese. Repeat the layers, finishing with the breadcrumbs mixed with the rest of the grated cheese.

Bake for about 30 minutes or until golden brown and bubbling. Serve hot.

Stuffed Provençal Vegetables

Les Legumes Farcis

Shallow trays of stuffed vegetables being carried to the baker's oven are a colourful sight on Sunday mornings in Provençal villages. They are eaten warm or cold, as an appetizer, main course or side dish, and also look particularly attractive on a buffet table. Use one or several vegetables, but include some aubergine (eggplant) to give body to the stuffing.

Preparation time: 1 hour
Cooking time: 30 to 40 minutes
Oven temperature: 200°C, 400°F, Gas Mark 6
To serve: 6

Metric/Imperial/American
12 to 18 young vegetables – small aubergines (eggplants), courgettes (zucchini), large onions, peppers, large tomatoes
4 tablespoons (¼ cup) olive oil
2 onions, peeled and chopped
3 cloves garlic, peeled and finely chopped
225 g/8 oz (or more) salt pork or bacon, finely diced, or mixture of salt pork or bacon and cooked meat, beef, lamb, chicken or ham
salt
freshly ground black pepper
2 teaspoons chopped fresh thyme
100 g/4 oz (¾ cup) cooked rice
1 tablespoon finely chopped fresh parsley
2 eggs, lightly beaten (optional)
50 g/2 oz (⅝ cup) fine dry breadcrumbs
50 g/2 oz (½ cup) finely grated cheese (optional)

Prepare the vegetables as follows, putting all the scooped-out flesh, roughly chopped if necessary, into a bowl.
Aubergines (eggplants): cut in half lengthways, sprinkle the cut surfaces with a little oil and bake in the oven for 20 minutes. Scoop out the flesh, leaving a shell about 1 cm/½ in thick.
Courgettes (zucchini): blanch whole in boiling salted water for 5 minutes, then drain cut in half lengthways and scoop out the centre, leaving a quite thick shell.
Onions: peel and blanch whole in boiling salted water for 10 minutes. Drain, then cut in half crossways and take out the centres, leaving a shell of 2 to 3 layers only. Chop centres with other two onions.

Peppers: cut in half lengthways, remove the core and rinse with cold water to remove all seeds. Leave very small peppers whole, slicing off the tops and scooping out the core and seeds.
Tomatoes: cut in half crossways, sprinkle with salt and leave upside down to drain for 10 minutes, then scoop out the pulp.

Heat 1 tablespoon of the oil in a frying pan (skillet), add the chopped onions and garlic and fry until softened. Add the salt pork or bacon and fry until transparent. Add the cooked meat, if used, and heat through. Stir in the mixed vegetable pulp and cook gently together for 10 minutes. Raise the heat and boil to evaporate excess moisture if necessary. Season and add the thyme, then stir in the rice and the parsley. Stir well and adjust the seasoning. If the mixture seems very moist, stir in the eggs to thicken.

Arrange the vegetable shells closely together in oiled roasting pans. Fill each one loosely with stuffing, then sprinkle on the breadcrumbs and cheese, if used. Dribble a little of the remaining olive oil on each and cook in the oven for 30 to 40 minutes, or until the vegetable shells are quite tender and the tops golden brown.

Above and right: Stuffed Provençal Vegetables
Left: Stuffed Artichokes

Stuffed Artichokes

Les Artichauts Barigoule

Use the small purple-tinged leaf artichokes of Provence for this delicate first course or light luncheon dish. The artichokes must be very young, so that the leaves are tender, and the chokes have barely developed.

Preparation time: 30 minutes
Cooking time: 1 hour
To serve: 6

Metric/Imperial
6 or 12 leaf artichokes
5 tablespoons olive oil
2 large onions, peeled and finely
  chopped
1 clove garlic, peeled and finely chopped
100 g/4 oz ham, bacon or salt pork,
  finely diced
salt
freshly ground black pepper
1 tablespoon finely chopped fresh
  parsley
1 teaspoon dried thyme
1 carrot, peeled and finely chopped
1 sprig of fresh thyme
1 bay leaf
150 ml/¼ pint white wine
150 ml/¼ pint water
1 tablespoon lemon juice

American
6 or 12 leaf artichokes
5 tablespoons olive oil
2 large onions, peeled and finely
  chopped
1 clove garlic, peeled and finely chopped
½ cup finely diced ham, bacon or salt
  pork
salt
freshly ground black pepper
1 tablespoon finely chopped fresh
  parsley
1 teaspoon dried thyme
1 carrot, peeled and finely chopped
1 sprig of fresh thyme
1 bay leaf
⅔ cup white wine
⅔ cup water
1 tablespoon lemon juice

Cut the stems off the artichokes close to the base and pull off the outer leaves. Using kitchen scissors, trim the leaves about two-thirds of the way down, leaving not more than 2.5 cm/1 inch of leaves. Cook in boiling salted water for 10 minutes. Leave to cool and drain upside down. When cool enough to handle, squeeze out excess water, open out the leaves gently and remove any choke with a teaspoon.

Heat 2 tablespoons of the oil in a frying pan (skillet), add one of the onions and the garlic and fry until softened. Add the ham, bacon or salt pork and cook gently until everything is tender. Season to taste and add the parsley and dried thyme. Allow to cool.

Press this stuffing into the centres of the artichokes and between the leaves, pushing it down as far as possible.

Heat the remaining oil in a large flameproof casserole. Add the remaining onion and the carrot and fry until softened. Set the stuffed artichokes on top, add the sprig of thyme and bay leaf and cook over a moderate heat until the artichokes begin to turn brown. Add the wine, water, lemon juice and seasoning to taste. The artichokes should be just covered, so add more water if necessary. Bring to the boil, then simmer for 30 to 40 minutes, half covered, until the artichokes are very tender.

Remove the artichokes to a serving dish and keep hot. Bring the liquid back to the boil and boil for a few minutes to thicken. Taste for seasoning. Strain over the artichokes and serve.

Stuffed Peppers

Piperies Yemistres

Rows of baking dishes filled with colourful stuffed vegetables are a familiar sight in any Greek taverna. The stuffing may consist of all meat or all rice, but the favourite is a well-flavoured mixture of the two. The proportion of meat to rice, as well as the flavourings, differs from cook to cook, but chopped fresh mint, spices, pine nuts and currants or raisins are all popular additions.

The same mixture can be used to stuff hollowed-out tomatoes, parboiled courgettes (zucchini) or aubergines (eggplants), also vine leaves.

Preparation time: 40 minutes
Cooking time: about 1 hour
Oven temperature: 180°C/350°F, Gas Mark 4
To serve: 4 to 6, depending on whether main or first course

Metric/Imperial
3 tablespoons oil
1 large onion, peeled and finely chopped
1 large clove garlic, peeled and crushed
50 g/2 oz long-grain rice
450 g/1 lb finely minced lamb or beef
1 x 400 g/14 oz can peeled tomatoes
½ teaspoon ground cinnamon or grated nutmeg
2 tablespoons chopped fresh parsley
salt
freshly ground black pepper
4 large or 6 medium peppers
25 g/1 oz butter
2 tablespoons dry white breadcrumbs

American
3 tablespoons oil
1 large onion, peeled and finely chopped
1 large clove garlic, peeled and crushed
¼ cup long-grain rice
1 lb finely ground lamb or beef
1 x 14 oz can peeled tomatoes
½ teaspoon ground cinnamon or grated nutmeg
2 tablespoons chopped fresh parsley
salt
freshly ground black pepper
4 large or 6 medium peppers
2 tablespoons butter
2 tablespoons dry white breadcrumbs

Heat the oil in a saucepan, add the onion and fry until soft and golden, about 10 minutes. Add the garlic and rice and stir and cook for 1 to 2 minutes. Add the meat and stir until it changes colour. Drain the canned tomatoes over a measuring jug and add to the meat, reserving the juice. Stir in the spice, parsley and generous seasonings of salt and pepper. Cover and simmer very gently for 10 minutes, then leave to cool.

Heat the oven. Oil a baking dish just large enough to hold the peppers.

Drop the peppers into a deep pan of boiling water, simmer for 5 to 6 minutes, then drain. When cool enough to handle cut out the stems. Slice off the tops and reserve, and scoop out and discard the seeds and pith. Stand the peppers upright in the oiled baking dish.

Check the stuffing for seasoning, then spoon into the peppers and cover with the reserved tops. Melt the butter and mix in the breadcrumbs. Scatter over the tops of the peppers. Make up the reserved tomato juice to 150 ml/¼ pint (⅔ cup), season and pour around the peppers. Bake in the centre of the oven for 45 to 60 minutes, or until the peppers are tender.

Tomato Pilaf

Domato Pilafo

Tomato is a favourite flavouring for many Greek dishes and housewives preserve quantities of tomatoes in summer to enrich their winter meals. This popular tomato pilaf is usually made from fresh tomatoes which have been skinned and seeded, or from a homemade tomato sauce. Butter is used when available, otherwise olive oil.

Preparation time: 20 minutes
Cooking time: 30 minutes
To serve: 4

Metric/Imperial
50 g/2 oz butter or 3 tablespoons olive
   oil
1 medium onion, peeled and finely
   chopped
225 g/8 oz firm ripe tomatoes, skinned,
   seeded and chopped
450 ml/¾ pint chicken or meat stock
2 teaspoons tomato purée
1 teaspoon sugar
salt
freshly ground black pepper
225 g/8 oz long- or medium-grain rice

American
¼ cup butter or 3 tablespoons olive oil
1 medium onion, peeled and finely
   chopped
½ lb firm ripe tomatoes, skinned, seeded
   and chopped
1 pint chicken or meat stock
2 teaspoons tomato paste
1 teaspoon sugar
salt
freshly ground black pepper
1 cup long- or medium-grain rice

Melt the butter or heat the oil in a medium heavy based pan with a tight fitting lid. Add the onion and fry very gently until soft and golden. Add the tomatoes and simmer, uncovered, for 10 minutes, until pulped and sauce-like. Add the stock, tomato purée (paste), sugar and salt and pepper to taste and bring to the boil.

Add the rice, and when the liquid regains boiling point stir well, cover the pan tightly and reduce the heat. Cook over low heat, without stirring again, for 17 to 20 minutes, until all the liquid has been absorbed and the rice is just tender.

Remove the pan from the heat and take off the lid. Place a clean folded tea (dish) towel over the rice and leave for 5 minutes or so to absorb the steam. Toss the rice with a fork before serving.

Left: Stuffed Peppers
Right: Tomato Pilaf

Spinach with Black-Eyed Beans

Salq bi Loubia

Delightful for its contrasts of colour, texture and taste, this nourishing dish from the Middle East can be served hot as a vegetable, cold as a salad. Olive oil gives it a distinctive taste but light vegetable oil may be used instead.

Preparation time: about 20 minutes
Cooking time: 20 minutes
To serve: 6 to 8

Metric/Imperial
250 g/9 oz black-eyed beans, soaked for
  1 hour
salt
5 tablespoons olive oil
1 large onion, peeled and finely chopped
1 kg/2 lb fresh spinach, chopped or
  0.5 kg/1 lb frozen chopped spinach,
  thawed
freshly ground black pepper

American
1⅓ cups black-eyed beans, soaked for
  1 hour
salt
5 tablespoons olive oil
1 large onion, peeled and finely chopped
2 lb fresh spinach, chopped, or 1 lb
  frozen chopped spinach, thawed
freshly ground black pepper

Put the black-eyed beans in a saucepan, cover with water and bring to the boil. Simmer for about 20 minutes or until tender, adding salt towards the end of the cooking time. Do not overcook or the beans will become mushy.

Meanwhile, heat the oil in a frying pan (skillet), add the onion and fry until soft and transparent. Add the spinach and continue to fry, stirring constantly, until well cooked. Add salt and pepper to taste, then stir the drained beans and warm through.

Brown Lentils with Noodles

Rishta bi Ads

Arab folklore has branded this much loved dish as Esau's and it is even featured in an ancient 'Book of Misers'. The reason is that lentils are plentiful and cheap throughout the Middle East. A good vegetarian main dish, it also makes an excellent side dish.

Preparation time: 15 minutes
Cooking time: 30 minutes
To serve: 6

Metric/Imperial
225 g/8 oz large brown lentils, soaked
  for a few hours and drained
salt
50 g/2 oz butter, or more to taste
1 large onion, peeled and chopped
2 cloves garlic, peeled and crushed
1 teaspoon ground cumin
1 teaspoon ground coriander
freshly ground black pepper
225 g/8 oz noodles

American
1 cup large brown lentils, soaked for a
  few hours and drained
salt
¼ cup butter, or more to taste
1 large onion, peeled and chopped
2 cloves garlic, peeled and crushed
1 teaspoon ground cumin
1 teaspoon ground coriander
freshly ground black pepper
½ lb noodles

Cover the lentils with fresh water in a saucepan, bring to the boil and simmer for about 30 minutes or until tender, adding salt towards the end of the cooking time.

Meanwhile, melt the butter in a frying pan (skillet), add the onion and fry until golden. Add the garlic and stir until it changes colour. Add spices and salt and pepper to taste.

Cook the noodles in plenty of boiling salted water until slightly underdone. Drain quickly and drain the lentils. Mix everything together in one of the larger pans and heat through. You might like to add a little more butter.

Rice with Vermicelli

Roz bel Shaghria

Virtually the staple food of the Middle East, rice is present at most meals as a side dish, often to be smothered by a sauce or stew. This is an elegant and unusual though simple way of making it. Serve it as you would plain rice.

Preparation time: about 10 minutes
Cooking time: about 20 minutes
To serve: 6

Metric/Imperial
75 g/3 oz butter
a drop of oil
175 g/6 oz vermicelli, broken
0.5 kg/1 lb long-grain rice
1 litre/1¾ pints water
2 teaspoons salt, or to taste

American
6 tablespoons butter
a drop of oil
6 oz vermicelli, broken
2⅓ cups long-grain rice
1 quart water
2 teaspoons salt, or to taste

Melt the butter in a saucepan with the oil to prevent it burning. Crush the vermicelli with your hand into the pan and fry, stirring constantly, until it is golden. Add the rice and stir to coat each grain with butter. Add the water and salt and stir well. Bring to the boil, then lower the heat as much as possible and simmer gently, covered, for about 20 minutes, or until the rice is tender but not mushy. Add a little more water, if necessary, if it has all been absorbed before the rice is cooked.

Above right: Spinach with Black-Eyed Beans
Above left: Brown Lentils with Noodles
Below: Rice with Vermicelli

Spinach with Pine Kernels

Les Epinards aux Pignons

Pine kernels are gathered in the woods behind Nice, and are a characteristic feature of Niçois cooking. This classic combination of pine kernels with spinach goes well with most meat and fish dishes.

Preparation time: 5 minutes
Cooking time: 5 to 10 minutes
To serve: 4

Metric/Imperial/American
1 kg/2 lb fresh spinach or *Swiss chard,*
or 0.5 kg/1 lb frozen spinach
salt
1 tablespoon olive oil
50 g/2 oz (½ cup) pine kernels
freshly ground black pepper
½ tablespoon orange-flower water
(optional)

Plunge the spinach or chard into plenty of boiling salted water and cook until it wilts. (Cook frozen spinach according to the instructions on the packet.) Drain, then chop very finely.

Heat the oil in a clean saucepan and add the spinach or chard. Heat through, raising the heat if necessary to evaporate excess moisture. Add the pine kernels, season to taste, and sprinkle on the orange-flower water, if using. Stir well before serving.

Courgettes (Zucchini) with Herbs

Courgettes aux Fines Herbes

This dish from Provence is made with fresh herbs, which bring out the delicate flavour of the courgettes (zucchini).

Preparation time: 10 minutes (plus 1 hour draining the courgettes/zucchini)
Cooking time: 10 to 15 minutes
To serve: 4 to 6

Metric/Imperial/American
1 kg/2 lb courgettes (zucchini), coarsely grated
salt
3 tablespoons olive oil
good (large) squeeze of lemon juice
1 tablespoon finely chopped fresh basil and parsley
freshly ground black pepper

Spread out the courgettes (zucchini) on a clean towel. Sprinkle with salt, then leave to drain in the towel in a colander for 1 hour. Squeeze out all the moisture through the towel.

Heat the oil in a frying pan (skillet), add the courgettes (zucchini) and cook over a medium heat until they are tender, stirring from time to time. Sprinkle with lemon juice and herbs, season to taste and toss gently before serving.

Left: Spinach with Pine Kernels. Right: Courgettes (Zucchini) with Herbs

Left: Braised Potatoes with Almonds. Right: Ratatouille

Braised Potatoes with Almonds

Pommes de Terre Basque

Goose fat is used a great deal in the cooking of the Languedoc, a by-product of the geese which are originally fattened for their *foie gras*, and then made into *confit d'oie*, the famous local speciality. The addition of almonds is due to the influence of the Basque country which borders on the Languedoc. Serve with lamb or poultry.

Preparation time: 10 minutes
Cooking time: 1 hour
To serve: 6

Metric/Imperial
50 g/2 oz goose fat
1 kg/2 lb small new potatoes, peeled, scraped or very well scrubbed
salt
freshly ground black pepper
50 g/2 oz blanched almonds, roughly chopped

American
¼ cup goose fat
2 lb small new potatoes, peeled, scraped or very well scrubbed
salt
freshly ground black pepper
½ cup roughly chopped blanched almonds

Melt the fat in a heavy flameproof casserole, wide enough to allow the potatoes to lie in one layer on the bottom. Add the potatoes and roll them around so that they become evenly covered in fat. Season. Cover and cook over a low heat for about 50 minutes, turning them over at least once during the cooking time. They should form a crisp golden brown crust, but not be allowed to burn.

When the potatoes are nearly cooked, add the almonds to the casserole and cook for a further 10 minutes, so that the almonds can brown, but not burn.

Ratatouille

Provençal Vegetable Ragoût

A speciality of Provence, ratatouille can be found, with local variations, all around the Mediterranean coast. It can be eaten hot or cold, on its own as an hors d'oeuvre or as a vegetable side dish, and goes equally well with fish or meat.

Preparation time: 30 minutes (plus 1 hour draining the vegetables)
Cooking time: 1 hour
To serve: 6 to 8

Metric/Imperial/American
0.5 kg/1 lb aubergines (eggplants), sliced
0.5 kg/1 lb courgettes (zucchini), sliced
salt
150 ml/¼ pint (⅔ cup) olive oil
3 large onions, peeled and sliced
2 cloves garlic, peeled and finely chopped
3 peppers (1 red, 1 yellow and 1 green, if possible), cored, seeded and cut into strips
0.5 kg/1 lb tomatoes, skinned and seeded
salt
freshly ground black pepper
½ teaspoon sugar
2 tablespoons finely chopped fresh parsley or basil and parsley

Sprinkle the aubergines (eggplants) and the courgettes (zucchini) liberally with salt and leave in separate colanders to drain for 1 hour. When they are ready, rinse, squeeze out excess moisture and pat dry.

Heat the oil in a flameproof casserole, add the onions and garlic and fry until softened. Add the aubergines (eggplants) and cook, stirring well, until they become soft and yellow.

Add the courgettes (zucchini) and peppers, cover and cook gently for 30 minutes. Stir in the tomatoes, seasoning and sugar, and cook, uncovered, for a further 30 minutes. The vegetables should be soft and well mixed but not have lost their separate identities, and most of the liquid should be evaporated. Stir in the parsley and basil before serving.

Jerusalem Artichokes with Tomatoes

Topinambours à la Provençale

Preparation time: 10 minutes
Cooking time: 20 to 30 minutes
To serve: 4 to 6

Metric/Imperial/American
0.75 kg/1½ lb Jerusalem artichokes,
*   peeled*
salt
1 tablespoon olive oil
1 large onion, peeled and roughly
*   chopped*
1 clove garlic, peeled and finely chopped
4 tomatoes, skinned and roughly
*   chopped*
freshly ground black pepper
1 tablespoon finely chopped fresh
*   parsley*

Simmer the artichokes in salted water
until nearly tender (10 to 15 minutes).
Drain. Heat the oil in a deep frying pan
(skillet) or shallow flameproof casserole,
add the onion and garlic and fry until
softened. Add the artichokes and the
tomatoes and fry together, without a lid,
until the artichokes are tender and most
of the liquid from the tomatoes has
evaporated. Season to taste and sprinkle
with parsley before serving.

Roast Eggplants

Aubergines en Gigot

Simple and surprisingly good, this recipe
from the Languedoc can be served alone
as a light main course, or separately,
after the meat.

Preparation time: 15 minutes
Cooking time: 1 hour
Oven temperature: 190°C, 375°F, Gas
    Mark 5
To serve: 6

Metric/Imperial/American
6 aubergines (eggplants)
salt
freshly ground black pepper
1 tablespoon finely chopped fresh
*   parsley, or parsley and marjoram*
100 g/4 oz (¼ cup) diced bacon or salt
*   pork*
3 cloves garlic, peeled and cut into thin
*   slivers*
1 tablespoon olive oil

Leave small aubergines (eggplants)
whole, but cut longer ones in half
lengthways.
    Mix the salt, pepper and herbs
together, and roll the pieces of bacon or
salt pork and the slivers of garlic in the
mixture. Make 4 or 6 lines of incisions
down the length of each aubergine (eggplant) and insert alternately a piece of
bacon or salt pork or a sliver of garlic.
Place in an oiled baking dish, cut side
down if the aubergines (eggplants) have
been halved, dribble on the oil and a
little more seasoning, cover and roast for
1 hour.

Baked Eggplants

Aubergines au Gratin

This may be served as a first course or
as a vegetable side dish, after meat or
fish. For a more substantial family
supper dish, finely diced leftovers of
meat can be added to the aubergines
(eggplants) before baking.

Preparation time: 15 minutes (plus 1
    hour draining the aubergines/egg-
    plants)
Cooking time: 40 to 45 minutes
Oven temperature: 220°C, 425°F, Gas
    Mark 7
To serve: 4 to 6 (see above)

Metric/Imperial/American
1 kg/2 lb aubergines (eggplants), diced
salt

4 tablespoons (¼ cup) olive oil
0.5 kg/1 lb tomatoes, skinned and
  roughly chopped
2 tablespoons finely chopped fresh
  parsley
1 clove garlic, peeled and finely chopped
freshly ground black pepper
pinch of sugar
50 g/2 oz (⅔ cup) dry breadcrumbs

Sprinkle the aubergines (eggplants) with
salt and leave in a colander to drain for
1 hour. Rinse and squeeze out excess
moisture, then dry well. Heat 1 tablespoon of the olive oil in a frying pan
(skillet), add the tomatoes, parsley and
garlic, season with salt, pepper and
sugar, and cook over a moderate heat
until the moisture has evaporated and
the tomatoes have cooked down to a
thick purée.

Heat all but a little of the remaining
oil in another heavy frying pan (skillet)
and fry the aubergine (eggplant) over a
moderate heat until it turns golden
brown and soft. Transfer to an ovenproof dish. Spread the tomato purée
over the top and cover with the breadcrumbs. Sprinkle on the remaining oil,
and bake for 20 minutes, or until the top
has browned.

Stuffed Tomatoes

Tomates à la Provençale

These are especially good served with
fish or chicken. Use sun-ripened
Mediterranean (beefsteak) tomatoes, if
possible.

Preparation time: 10 minutes (plus 15
  minutes draining the tomatoes)
Cooking time: 15 to 20 minutes
Oven temperature: 240°C, 475°F, Gas
  Mark 9, or use grill (broiler)
To serve: 6

Metric/Imperial/American
1 kg/2 lb large ripe tomatoes
salt
2 onions, peeled and finely chopped
2 cloves garlic, peeled and finely
  chopped
2 tablespoons finely chopped fresh
  parsley
2 tablespoons fine dry breadcrumbs
freshly ground black pepper
2 tablespoons olive oil

Cut the tomatoes in half and score a
criss-cross of lines across the cut surface
of each half. Sprinkle with a little salt
and leave upside down on a plate to
drain for 15 minutes.

Mix together the onions, garlic,
parsley and breadcrumbs and season the
mixture generously.

Arrange the tomato halves, cut sides
up, side by side in a lightly oiled shallow
ovenproof dish. Spread a spoonful of the
breadcrumb mixture over each one and
press in well. Dribble a little oil on each.
Bake in the oven, or cook under a very
hot grill (broiler), for 15 to 20 minutes,
or until the tomatoes are soft and very
slightly burnt at the edges.

Left to right: Jerusalem Artichokes
with Tomatoes; Roast Eggplants;
Baked Eggplants; Stuffed Tomatoes

129

Braised Fennel

Fenouil Braisé

These anise-flavoured vegetables are excellent for winter salads, or, braised as below, they go particularly well with fish or lamb.

Preparation time: 5 minutes
Cooking time: 35 to 40 minutes
Oven temperature: 190°C, 375°F, Gas Mark 5
To serve: 6 (allow one fennel bulb per person)

Metric/Imperial
6 fennel bulbs
1 bouquet garni
1 tablespoon olive oil
salt
freshly ground black pepper
1 tablespoon grated Parmesan cheese

American
6 Florence fennel bulbs
1 bouquet garni
1 tablespoon olive oil
salt
freshly ground black pepper
1 tablespoon grated Parmesan cheese

Cut the stalks off the fennel bulbs and reserve any leaves. Remove any tough outer stalks. Plunge into boiling water to which you have added the bouquet garni, and boil for 15 to 20 minutes, or until they are tender but still quite firm. Drain and leave to cool a little.

When cool enough to handle cut the bulbs into halves or quarters lengthways and squeeze out any excess water. Lay them, cut sides down, in a buttered shallow ovenproof dish. Sprinkle on the oil, salt, pepper and cheese and bake for 10 to 15 minutes, until lightly browned.

Sprinkle with the finely chopped fennel leaves before serving.

Potatoes Baked with Herbs and Oil

Pommes de Terre Gratinées aux Herbes

A lovely golden potato dish from Provence, this is particularly good with fish or lamb.

Preparation time: 20 minutes
Cooking time: 1 to 1½ hours
Oven temperature: 200°C, 400°F, Gas Mark 6
To serve: 6

Metric/Imperial
1 kg/2 lb potatoes, peeled and very thinly sliced
½ clove garlic, peeled and halved
3 tablespoons olive oil
salt
freshly ground black pepper
2 teaspoons finely chopped fresh rosemary
2 teaspoons chopped fresh thyme
300 ml/½ pint boiling stock

American
2 lb potatoes, peeled and very thinly sliced
½ clove garlic, peeled and halved
3 tablespoons olive oil
salt
freshly ground black pepper
2 teaspoons finely chopped fresh rosemary
2 teaspoons chopped fresh thyme
1¼ cups boiling stock

Soak the potatoes in cold water for 10 minutes to remove starch, then drain and dry very well.

Rub the cut surface of garlic over a shallow ovenproof gratin dish, and oil it generously. Make an even layer of potatoes in the bottom of the dish, sprinkle with salt, pepper and herbs and dribble on a little olive oil. Repeat until all the potatoes are used up.

Pour the boiling stock over the potatoes, dribble on a little more olive oil and bake for 1 to 1½ hours.

Antipasto of Peppers and Tomatoes

Peperonata

A most delicious Italian dish to make ahead and enjoy cold as a colourful appetizer, this can also be served as a hot vegetable, either freshly made or reheated, with grilled (broiled) meat or a roast chicken, or as a topping for steaks. Providing the peppers predominate, the quantities of the other vegetables can be varied, but be careful not to overcook the peppers which should be tender but firm.

Preparation time: 20 minutes
Cooking time: about 45 minutes
To serve: 6 to 8

Metric/Imperial
6 tablespoons olive oil
225 g/8 oz onions, peeled and thinly sliced
2 bay leaves
8 large fleshy peppers — red, green, yellow or mixed — cored, seeded and

Left: Braised Fennel. Right: Potatoes Baked with Herbs and Oil

cut into 1 cm/½ inch wide strips
2 large cloves garlic, peeled and crushed
0.5 kg/1¼ lb ripe tomatoes, skinned,
    seeded and sliced
salt
freshly ground black pepper

American
6 tablespoons olive oil
½ lb onions, peeled and thinly sliced
2 bay leaves
8 large fleshy peppers — red, green,
    yellow or mixed — cored, seeded and
    cut into ½ inch wide strips
2 large cloves garlic, peeled and crushed
1¼ lb ripe tomatoes, skinned, seeded and
    sliced
salt
freshly ground black pepper

Heat the oil in a wide saucepan, add the onions and bay leaves and fry over low heat until beginning to turn golden, about 10 minutes. Add the peppers and garlic and stir well, then cover and cook gently for 15 minutes, stirring occasionally.

Add the tomatoes and a little salt and pepper and cook uncovered, stirring frequently, until most of the liquid has evaporated, about 20 minutes. Remove the bay leaves, check the seasoning and turn into a serving dish.

Stuffed Mushrooms

Funghi Imbottiti

Stuffed mushrooms are an attractive way of using small quantities of cooked ham, chicken, sweetbreads or other meats. Alone they make excellent appetizers, or they can be served with grilled (broiled) dishes. Italians stuff various kinds of edible fungi, but large caps of cultivated mushrooms are very suitable.

Preparation time: 20 minutes
Cooking time: 25 to 30 minutes
Oven temperature: 190°C/375°F, Gas
    Mark 5
To serve: 4 to 6

Metric/Imperial
12 large cup-shaped mushrooms
olive oil
100 g/4 oz onion, peeled and finely
    chopped
1 clove garlic, peeled and crushed
50 g/2 oz cooked ham or bacon, finely
    chopped or minced
100 g/4 oz chicken or sweetbreads, finely
    chopped or minced
2 to 3 tablespoons chicken sauce or

Left: Antipasto of Peppers and Tomatoes. Right: Stuffed Mushrooms

    stock
salt
freshly ground black pepper
2 tablespoons fine dry breadcrumbs
2 tablespoons grated Parmesan cheese
1 tablespoon finely chopped fresh
    marjoram or parsley

American
12 large cup-shaped mushrooms
olive oil
1 cup peeled and finely chopped onion
1 clove garlic, peeled and crushed
¼ cup finely chopped or ground cooked
    ham or bacon
½ cup finely chopped or ground chicken
    or sweetbreads
2 to 3 tablespoons chicken sauce or
    stock
salt
freshly ground black pepper
2 tablespoons fine dry breadcrumbs
2 tablespoons grated Parmesan cheese
1 tablespoon finely chopped fresh
    marjoram or parsley

Remove and chop the mushroom stalks. Brush the cups on both sides with olive oil and arrange side by side, hollow side upwards, in a shallow ovenproof dish.

Heat 2 tablespoons of oil in a small saucepan, add the onion and fry gently for 5 minutes until soft and golden. Add the chopped mushroom stalks and the garlic and fry for another minute.

Add the ham or bacon and chicken or sweetbreads to the onion mixture with enough sauce or stock to moisten, then season well with salt and pepper. Divide the filling between the mushroom cups and sprinkle with the breadcrumbs mixed with the Parmesan. Drizzle a teaspoon of oil over each mushroom. Bake for 20 minutes or until golden, sprinkling with a little more oil if the mushrooms show signs of becoming dry. Sprinkle with the chopped herbs and serve hot.

Hot Pepper and Garlic Sauce

Rouille

The word *rouille,* meaning rust, describes the colour and perhaps also the coruscating fierceness of this sauce. It is usually served, in small quantities, with Provençal fish soups and stews, but it can also be served with crudités (see page 13) or as a relish with cold meat.

Preparation time: 15 minutes
Cooking time: nil
To serve: 6

Metric/Imperial/American
1 red pepper, cored and seeded
1 red chilli (chili pepper), seeded, or ½ tablespoon cayenne pepper
2 slices of French bread
4 cloves garlic, peeled
5 tablespoons olive oil
salt
freshly ground black pepper

Blanch the pepper and chilli (chili pepper), if using, for 2 minutes in boiling water. Drain. Soak the bread briefly in cold water, then squeeze out well. Put the pepper, chilli (chili pepper) or cayenne, bread and garlic into a blender or mortar and blend or pound to a smooth paste. Add the oil drop by drop, until you have a smooth thick sauce, of the consistency of mayonnaise. Add salt and pepper to taste.

Hot Red Sauce

Romescu

Another classic sauce from Catalonia, *romescu* traditionally needs special small, hot peppers grown in the region. The small dried chillis (chili peppers) available in most places are the best substitute. Serve with all kinds of fish.

Preparation time: 20 minutes
Cooking time: nil
To serve: 4

Metric/Imperial/American
2 tomatoes, skinned
2 dried chillis, seeded, or 1 teaspoon cayenne
3 cloves garlic, peeled
12 hazelnuts, shelled and toasted
12 almonds, blanched, peeled and toasted
a few pine nuts, if available, lightly toasted
300 ml/½ pint (1¼ cups) olive oil
4 tablespoons (¼ cup) vinegar
salt

120 ml/4 fl oz (½ cup) dry sherry (optional)

Put everything but the oil, vinegar, salt and sherry into a mortar, or an electric blender. Grind or blend until smooth, then add the oil gradually, as for mayonnaise, alternating with the vinegar. When the sauce has thickened, add salt to taste and the sherry, if used. This is a very hot sauce and should be treated with caution. The addition of sherry smooths it a little.

Green Sauce

Salsa Verde

A good Spanish sauce for serving with fish or cold cooked vegetables, such as haricot (navy) bean salad, *salsa verde* uses parsley as a basic herb, but others such as fennel could be added to vary the flavour.

Preparation time: about 15 minutes
Cooking time: nil
To serve: 4

Metric/Imperial/American
1 small slice of white bread, crusts removed
½ tablespoon lemon juice
1 tablespoon vinegar

3 tablespoons finely chopped or minced
fresh parsley
1 celery stalk, finely chopped or minced
1 tablespoon finely chopped fresh chives
or small spring onions (scallions)
1 clove garlic, peeled and crushed
½ teaspoon salt
200 ml/⅓ pint (⅞ cup) olive oil

Sprinkle the bread with the lemon juice
and vinegar and leave to soak for a few
minutes. Put all the ingredients except
the oil into a bowl or electric blender.
Mix or blend together, then gradually
work in the oil. When you have a
smooth, fairly thick consistency the
sauce is ready.

Garlic Mayonnaise

All-I-Oli

This well-known sauce originated in the
province of Tarragona, in Catalonia, but
it is very popular all down the eastern
coast of Spain. The name all-i-oli is
derived from the Latin words for garlic
and oil, from which this sauce is made.
It is extremely pungent and only for the
lovers of garlic. Often served in conjunc-
tion with hot romescu sauce, it is a good
complement to fish or other bland
dishes. The classic version contains no

egg yolk, but a more generally used
recipe is as follows:

Preparation time: about 20 minutes
Cooking time: nil
To serve: 4

Metric/Imperial/American
4 cloves garlic, peeled
salt
2 egg yolks, beaten (at room
temperature)
300 ml/½ pint (1¼ cups) olive oil (room
temperature)
2 tablespoons vinegar
squeeze of lemon juice

The best way to make this is in a mortar; otherwise use a heavy bowl and a
well-rounded wooden spoon. Pound the
garlic to a pulp with a little salt, then
gradually blend in the egg yolks. Add
the olive oil drop by drop to start with,
as for mayonnaise, gradually increasing
to a thin stream, stirring all the time.
When the sauce has amalgamated it will
thicken, at which point add the vinegar
a little at a time, alternating with more
oil until it is all used up. Add the lemon
juice. Adjust the salt to taste.

Left to right: Hot Pepper and Garlic Sauce;
Hot Red Sauce; Green Sauce; Garlic
Mayonnaise; Montpelier Butter

Montpelier Butter

Beurre de Montpelier

A lovely accompaniment to any poached
or grilled (broiled) fish, Montpelier butter is also good on chops or steaks, and
for stuffed eggs.

Preparation time: 10 minutes
Cooking time: nil
To serve: 6 to 8

Metric/Imperial/American
100 g/4 oz fresh spinach, or 50 g/2 oz
frozen spinach
bunch of watercress
small bunch of fresh parsley
2 sprigs of fresh tarragon
2 tablespoons capers
6 anchovy fillets
3 hard-boiled (hard-cooked) egg yolks
100 g/4 oz (½ cup) butter
1 tablespoon olive oil
good squeeze of lemon juice
freshly ground black pepper (optional)

Blanch the spinach, watercress and herbs
together in boiling water for 1 minute. If
you are using frozen spinach, you need
only thaw it. Drain well, squeezing out
as much moisture as possible, then put
in a mortar or blender with the capers,
anchovies and egg yolks. Pound or blend
to a fine paste. If you are using a mortar,
you may need to push the mixture
through a nylon sieve.
  Blend in the butter and then the oil,
drop by drop, as for making mayonnaise. Add the lemon juice and test for
seasoning – this is very unlikely to need
salt, but may be improved by a little
freshly ground black pepper.

Meat Sauce

Sugo di Carne

Meat sauce is universal in Italy and variations are legion. This version is typically southern, where they like to keep the sauce fairly liquid so that the gravy can penetrate all the crevices of the pasta shapes or the shortcut tubular pasta they love to serve it with. If a thicker sauce is required reduce it by rapid boiling towards the end of cooking. This is a most useful sauce to keep handy in the freezer.

When serving with pasta or rice finely grated cheese is always handed separately.

Preparation time: 15 minutes
Cooking time: 1 hour
Makes a generous 600 ml/1 pint (2½ cups) of sauce, enough for 6 to 8 servings of pasta

Metric/Imperial

3 tablespoons olive oil
175 g/6 oz onion, peeled and coarsely grated
1 medium carrot, peeled and coarsely grated
1 stick celery, finely chopped
1 tablespoon finely chopped fresh parsley
1 large clove garlic, peeled and crushed
450 g/1 lb finely minced lean beef
2 tablespoons flour
4 tablespoons white or red wine (optional)
1 x 400 g/14 oz can peeled tomatoes
300 ml/½ pint meat stock
2 cloves (optional)
salt
freshly ground black pepper

American

3 tablespoons olive oil
1½ cups peeled and coarsely grated onion
1 medium carrot, peeled and coarsely grated
1 stalk celery, finely chopped
1 tablespoon finely chopped fresh parsley
1 large clove garlic, peeled and crushed
1 lb finely ground lean beef
2 tablespoons flour
¼ cup white or red wine (optional)
1 x 14 oz can peeled tomatoes
1¼ cups meat stock
2 cloves (optional)
salt
freshly ground black pepper

Heat the oil in a heavy-based saucepan, add the onion, carrot and celery and fry for 5 minutes until beginning to soften and take colour. Add the parsley and garlic and fry for another minute. Add the meat, increase the heat and cook, stirring frequently, until it browns. Sprinkle in the flour and cook, stirring, for 1 to 2 minutes. Stir in the wine (if used) and allow to bubble briskly until almost absorbed, then add the tomatoes and their juice, the stock, cloves, if used, and seasonings of salt and pepper. Bring to the boil and simmer very gently, stirring occasionally, for about 1 hour. During this time the sauce should reduce to the desired consistency.

Basil, Cheese and Nut Sauce

Pesto alla Genovese

Pesto is a spicy green sauce, the essential flavouring of which is fresh basil. The sauce is a great speciality of the Genoese who claim that the basil of the Ligurian hillsides is superior to any grown elsewhere. A little fresh parsley can be mixed with the basil, but dried herbs cannot be used. The sauce is diluted with hot water and served with ribbon pasta, and when added to other dishes it qualifies them for the description *alla Genovese*.

Preparation time: 20 minutes
Cooking time: nil
To serve: 4

Metric/Imperial

75 g/3 oz fresh basil leaves, roughly chopped
25 g/1 oz pine nuts, roughly chopped
3 cloves garlic, peeled and chopped
¼ teaspoon salt
5 to 6 tablespoons olive oil
50 g/2 oz Pecorino Sardo or Parmesan cheese, finely grated

American

3¼ cups roughly chopped fresh basil leaves
¼ cup roughly chopped pine nuts
3 cloves garlic, peeled and chopped
¼ teaspoon salt
5 to 6 tablespoons olive oil
½ cup finely grated Pecorino Sardo or Parmesan cheese

Put the basil, pine nuts, garlic and salt into a mortar and pound together until reduced to a thick paste. Stir in the oil a few drops at a time until a soft purée is formed. Stir in the cheese and pack the sauce into a pot. Keep covered and use while fresh.

Note: If an electric blender is available the sauce is quickly made by blending together at low speed the first four

ingredients with 2 tablespoons of the oil, and then adding the remaining oil gradually until a soft purée is formed. Finish as before.

Tomato Sauce

Salsa di Pomodori

Homemade tomato sauce is such a feature of the Italian Mediterranean coast that it is worth making it in double quantities and freezing the surplus for another dish. Sauces made with canned tomatoes are improved with longer cooking.

Preparation time: 15 minutes
Cooking time: at least 30 minutes
Makes about 600 ml/1 pint (2½ cups)

Metric/Imperial
1 kg/2 lb ripe tomatoes, roughly chopped, or 2 x 400 g/14 oz cans peeled tomatoes
1 large onion, peeled and chopped
2 cloves garlic, peeled and sliced
1 medium carrot, peeled and sliced
2 sticks celery, sliced
1 tablespoon tomato purée
2 teaspoons sugar
salt
freshly ground black pepper

1 tablespoon chopped fresh basil, or 1 teaspoon dried basil

American
2 lb ripe tomatoes, roughly chopped, or 2 x 14 oz cans peeled tomatoes
1 large onion, peeled and chopped
2 cloves garlic, peeled and sliced
1 medium carrot, peeled and sliced
2 stalks celery, sliced
1 tablespoon tomato paste
2 teaspoons sugar
salt
freshly ground black pepper
1 tablespoon chopped fresh basil, or 1 teaspoon dried basil

Put all the ingredients except the basil into a large saucepan with a little salt and pepper. (If using canned tomatoes include the liquid). Bring to the boil, partially cover with the lid and simmer for at least 30 minutes, or until the tomatoes are pulped and well reduced. Press through a strainer. If the sauce is too liquid return it to the saucepan and boil rapidly, uncovered, until reduced to a sauce consistency. Check the seasoning and stir in the basil. Use as required.

Left to right: Meat Sauce; Basil, Cheese and Nut Sauce; Tomato Sauce; Chicken Liver Sauce

Chicken Liver Sauce

Salsa di Fegatini di Pollo

This is a uniquely Italian sauce which combines particularly well with green or cream noodles or with boiled rice.

Preparation time: 15 minutes
Cooking time: 45 minutes
To serve: 4

Metric/Imperial
65 g/2½ oz butter
50 g/2 oz onion, peeled and finely chopped
75 g/3 oz rashers unsmoked streaky bacon, rinded and finely chopped
50 g/2 oz mushrooms, finely chopped
225 g/8 oz chicken livers, trimmed and finely chopped
1 tablespoon flour
2 tablespoons Marsala
1 tablespoon tomato purée
300 ml/½ pint chicken stock
salt
freshly ground black pepper

American
5 tablespoons butter
½ cup peeled and finely chopped onion
3 oz slices bacon, finely chopped
½ cup finely chopped mushrooms
½ lb chicken livers, trimmed and finely chopped
1 tablespoon flour
2 tablespoons Marsala
1 tablespoon tomato paste
1¼ cups chicken stock
salt
freshly ground black pepper

Melt 40 g/1½ oz (3 tablespoons) of the butter in a saucepan, add the onion, bacon and mushrooms and fry over low heat for 10 minutes, stirring now and then. Add the livers and stir for a minute, then stir in the flour. Increase the heat and cook for 1 to 2 minutes, stirring. Stir in the wine and let it bubble until absorbed, then stir in the tomato purée (paste), stock and seasoning to taste. Bring to the boil, cover and simmer very gently for about 30 minutes.

Stir in the remaining butter, check the seasoning and serve hot.

Desserts

Fruit Compôte

Compôte de Fruits

A *corbeille de fruits* is the standard end to most French meals, and nowhere more so than in Provence, where the sun ripens a profusion of fruit – apricots, peaches, cherries, figs, melons, plums and even oranges and lemons – to aromatic perfection. Sometimes, however, thcy may be combined in a compôte – stewed together with great care so that each fruit retains its own shape and flavour. Such a compôte should be eaten chilled, and with no further additions, but may be accompanied by one of the sweet dessert wines of the region, such as a Frontignan or Beaume de Venise.

The following is a particularly good combination of fruits, but may be varied according to what is available.

Preparation time: 5 to 10 minutes (plus chilling)
Cooking time: 20 to 30 minutes
To serve: 6 to 8

Metric/Imperial
1 litre/1¾ pints water
1 vanilla pod

Fruit Compôte

about 175 g/6 oz sugar
1 orange
1 lemon
6 to 8 small peaches, peeled (optional), halved and stoned
0.5 kg/1 lb apricots, halved and stoned
0.5 kg/1 lb dessert plums, halved and stoned

American
1 quart water
1 vanilla bean
about ¾ cup sugar
1 orange
1 lemon
6 to 8 small peaches, peeled (optional), halved and pitted
1 lb apricots, halved and pitted
1 lb dessert plums, halved and pitted

Bring the water to the boil with the vanilla pod (bean), sugar, and two strips each of orange and lemon rind. Boil vigorously for 5 minutes. Lay the other fruit carefully in a wide saucepan, putting whichever is the hardest at the bottom. Strain on the hot syrup and simmer for anything from 2 to 10 minutes, depending on the ripeness of the fruit. Do not allow the fruit to disintegrate. As soon as it is tender, remove from the pan with a slotted spoon and place in a serving dish.

When all the fruit has been removed, bring the syrup to the boil again and boil for 10 minutes or more, until it thickens. Leave to cool a little, then add the juice of the whole orange and half the lemon, taste for sweetness and pour over the fruit. Chill before serving.

Mont Blanc

Fresh Chestnut Dessert

This is a very simple but filling dessert, to be made from fresh chestnuts.

Preparation time: 15 minutes
Cooking time: 1 hour
To serve: 6

Metric/Imperial
0.5 kg/1 lb chestnuts, peeled
150 ml/¼ pint milk
150 ml/¼ pint water
150 g/5 oz granulated sugar
1 vanilla pod or ½ teaspoon vanilla essence
50 g/2 oz caster sugar
300 ml/½ pint very lightly sweetened whipped cream

1 lb chestnuts, peeled
⅔ cup milk
⅔ cup water
1 cup less 2 tablespoons sugar
1 vanilla bean or ½ teaspoon vanilla
extract
1¼ cups very lightly sweetened whipped
cream

Put the peeled chestnuts into a saucepan with the milk, water, 150 g/5 oz (⅔ cup) of the sugar and the vanilla pod (bean) or essence (extract). Bring slowly to the boil, stirring until the sugar has dissolved, then simmer for 50 to 60 minutes, or until all the liquid has evaporated, and the chestnuts are quite tender. Add a little more water if necessary.

Push the chestnuts through a coarse nylon sieve, or pass through the finest disc of a *mouli-légume* or mincer (grinder), or work in a blender. Pile up very lightly into a mound on a serving dish and sprinkle with the caster (remaining) sugar. Pipe on the whipped cream or smooth over very gently with a palette knife.

Chestnut Charlotte

Charlotte St Clément

Inland, in the Languedoc, is the richest chestnut-growing area of France, centred on the little town of Privas, made famous by M. Clément Faugier, who set up its *marrons glacés* industry. This light but rich dessert must have been named after him or after his name saint.

Preparation time: 30 minutes (plus overnight chilling)
Cooking time: nil
To serve: 6 to 8

Metric/Imperial/American
100 g/4 oz (½ cup) unsalted butter
1 x 440 g/15½ oz can unsweetened
chestnut purée
225 g/8 oz (1 cup) sugar
5 tablespoons water
3 tablespoons rum
18 Boudoir biscuits (ladyfingers)
Decoration:
300 ml/½ pint (1¼ cups) sweetened
whipped cream
1 tablespoon rum
a few marrons glacés (optional)
chocolate flakes (optional)

Beat the butter and chestnut purée together until light and fluffy. Bring 175 g/6 oz (¾ cup) of the sugar and 4 tablespoons of the water gently to the

boil in a saucepan, stirring well until the sugar has dissolved. Boil until the syrup thickens, but do not allow it to change colour. Slowly beat into the chestnut mixture, then add the rum.

Put the remaining sugar and water into the saucepan, bring to the boil, stirring to dissolve the sugar, and allow to caramelize to a light golden brown. Remove from the heat and dip in the sides of the boudoir biscuits (ladyfingers), one at a time. Stand each one upright to line the sides of a 900 ml/1½ pint (2 pint) charlotte mould, in such a way that the caramel will bind them

Above: Mont Blanc. Below: Chestnut Charlotte

together, but does not touch the side of the mould. Cover the bottom of the mould with the remaining biscuits (ladyfingers) or the trimmings, after the biscuits (ladyfingers) have been trimmed to fit the top of the mould, and dribble any remaining caramel over them. Carefully spoon the chestnut purée mixture into the mould. Cover and refrigerate for several hours, preferably overnight.

Turn out of the mould to serve. Flavour the whipped cream with the rum and use to decorate the charlotte with some marrons glacés or chocolate flakes, if you like, Serve any remaining cream separately.

Baked Fresh Peaches

Melacotones al Horno

This is a simple and delicious dessert and is very popular with Spanish children.

Preparation time: 10 minutes
Cooking time: 5 to 10 minutes
Oven temperature: 200°C/400°F, Gas Mark 6
To serve: 4

Metric/Imperial/American
4 large ripe peaches or nectarines, halved and stoned (pitted)
4 egg whites
2 tablespoons castor sugar
a little brandy or anise

This is best made in individual earthenware dishes, though you could use one large one. Put two peach halves in each dish. Beat the egg whites until stiff, then fold in most of the sugar and a few drops of brandy or anise. Spoon the mixture over the peaches and sprinkle with the remaining sugar. Bake for about 7 minutes, or until the egg white is well browned. Pour a little warmed brandy or anise into the hot dishes and set alight.
　　Serve with cream, if you like.

Dried Fruit Salad

Khoshaf

Made in large quantities in the Middle East for the Muslim faithful to break their daily fast during the month of Ramadan, this salad improves as the days go by. Its special character is derived from the fruits being simply macerated rather than cooked. Purists use only apricots and raisins with nuts, but many others prefer to balance the sharpness of apricots with the sweetness of prunes, and some put in all the dried fruits and nuts which grow in the area.
　　Prepare it one or, better still, two days in advance.

Preparation time: 7 minutes (plus 1 or 2 days soaking)
Cooking time: nil
To serve: 8

Metric/Imperial
0.5 kg/1 lb dried apricots
225 g/8 oz prunes (preferably stoned)
225 g/8 oz seedless raisins or sultanas
100 g/4 oz blanched almonds, halved

50 g/2 oz pistachio nuts, halved or pine nuts (if available)
about 175 g/6 oz sugar
2 tablespoons rosewater or orange flower water

American
1 lb dried apricots
1½ cups prunes (preferably pitted)
1⅓ cups seedless white raisins
1 cup halved blanched almonds
½ cup halved pistachio nuts or pine nuts (if available)
about ¾ cup sugar
2 tablespoons rosewater or orange flower water

Wash and dry the fruit if necessary. Put all the ingredients in a large bowl. Cover with water, stir and leave in the refrigerator for 1 or 2 days. Serve chilled.

Apricot Cream

Mishmisheya

The apricot is one of the favourite fruits of the Middle East. It features in poems and love songs where it is likened to the loved one. During the winter months it is used dried as in this very simple and lovely recipe. Use a sharper variety rather than a sweet one.

Preparation time: 15 minutes (plus chilling)
Cooking time: 20 minutes
To serve: 8

Metric/Imperial
0.5 kg/1 lb dried apricots
100 g/4 oz sugar (optional)
100 g/4 oz blanched almonds, halved
50 g/2 oz blanched almonds, finely chopped to decorate
Cream:
150 ml/¼ pint single cream
150 ml/¼ pint double cream
2 tablespoons caster sugar
1 tablespoon orange flower water or rosewater

American
1 lb dried apricots
½ cup sugar (optional)
1 cup halved blanched almonds
½ cup finely chopped blanched almonds to decorate
Cream:
⅔ cup light cream
⅔ cup heavy cream
2 tablespoons sugar
1 tablespoon orange flower water or rosewater

Put the apricots in a saucepan and cover with water. Bring to the boil, then simmer for about 20 minutes. Though most people like this dessert sharp, you may like to add sugar to taste. Work to a purée in an electric blender. Stir in the halved almonds. Chill.
　　Make the perfumed cream by whipping the creams together until stiff. Beat in the sugar and flower water.
　　Top each portion of apricot purée with a dollop of the perfumed cream and sprinkle with chopped almonds.

Caramel Custard

Flan de Leche

By far the most popular dessert throughout Spain, *Flan de Leche* may be flavoured with orange, rum, coconut, or what you will, but this is the basic recipe.

Preparation time: 30 minutes (plus chilling)
Cooking time: 40 minutes
Oven temperature: 180°C/350°F, Gas Mark 4
To serve: 4

Metric/Imperial/American
200 g/8 oz (1 cup) sugar
1 vanilla pod (bean), or a few drops of vanilla essence (extract)
600 ml/1 pint (2½ cups) milk
4 eggs, well beaten

Half of the sugar may be flavoured with vanilla by storing it in a jar with a vanilla pod (bean), or you can put a vanilla pod (bean) into the warm milk and leave for 30 minutes. Alternatively, simply use a few drops of vanilla essence (extract).
　　Heat the milk and half of the sugar together, stirring until the sugar dissolves. Remove the vanilla pod (bean) if used, wash and keep for another day. Pour the milk on to the beaten eggs, beating well together.
　　To make the caramel, dissolve the remaining sugar in a little water and boil until it turns brown. Cool, then pour a little into each of four dampened moulds. Strain the egg custard mixture into the moulds and arrange them in a *bain-marie* (or roasting pan) with the water coming about half-way up the moulds. Bake for about 40 minutes. Chill, and turn out just before serving.

Above left: Dried Fruit Salad
Above right: Baked Fresh Peaches
Below left: Apricot Cream
Below right: Caramel Custard

Macaroons

Les Macorons

The little macaroons of France are light and slightly bitter, because a few apricot kernels are often added to the almonds. If this is not possible, you can achieve a similar effect by using at least half unblanched almonds.

Preparation time: 10 minutes
Cooking time: 15 to 20 minutes
Oven temperature: 190°C, 375°F, Gas Mark 5
To serve: 8 or more

Left: Macaroons. Right: Apricot Tart

Metric/Imperial
225 g/8 oz almonds (see above), finely ground
400 g/15 oz caster sugar
½ teaspoon ground rice or cornflour
4 egg whites
split blanched almonds or halved glacé cherries to decorate (optional)

American
2 cups finely ground almonds
2 cups less 2 tablespoons sugar
½ teaspoon ground rice or cornstarch
4 egg whites
split blanched almonds or halved candied cherries to decorate (optional)

Mix together the almonds, sugar and ground rice or cornflour (cornstarch) in a bowl. Add the egg whites and combine thoroughly with a wooden spoon. Leave for a few minutes, then beat again briefly. Spread sheets of rice paper on baking sheets, rough side down. Using a teaspoon, make little mounds of the almond mixture on the sheets, leaving plenty of space between each one, to allow room for the macaroons to spread.

Press a split almond or half a glacé (candied) cherry in the centre of each one, if you like. Bake for 15 to 20 minutes. Do not overcook, as the macaroons should be light and dry on the outside, but slightly tacky in the centre.

Remove from the oven, break off each macaroon from the sheets of paper and leave to cool on a wire rack. Crumble off any surplus rice paper around the edges before serving.

142

Apricot Tart

Tarte aux Abricots (ou aux Pêches)

This tart is equally delicious made with either peaches or apricots.

Preparation time: 20 minutes (plus 1 hour resting the dough)
Cooking time: 30 to 40 minutes
Oven temperature: 190°C, 375°F, Gas Mark 5
To serve: 4 to 6

Metric/Imperial
Pastry:
75 g/3 oz plain white flour
pinch of salt
1 tablespoon icing sugar
50 g/2 oz unsalted butter
½ tablespoon iced water
Filling:
100 g/4 oz sugar
0.5 kg/1 lb apricots or peaches, halved and stoned
15 g/½ oz unsalted butter

American
Pastry:
¾ cup all-purpose flour
pinch of salt
1 tablespoon confectioners' sugar
¼ cup unsalted butter
1 tablespoon iced water
Filling:
½ cup sugar
1 lb apricots or peaches, halved and pitted
1 tablespoon unsalted butter

Make the pastry by sifting the flour, salt and sugar onto a pastry board. Cut the butter in with a palette knife, then crumble together with your fingertips until the mixture resembles fine bread-crumbs. Sprinkle with the water and gather together into a ball. Sprinkle the board with a little more flour, then quickly spread the dough away from you with the heel of the hand, to ensure that the butter is evenly distributed. Gather the dough into a ball again and allow to rest in the refrigerator for about 1 hour.

Roll out the dough very lightly, from the centre outwards, and use to line a buttered 20 to 25 cm/8 to 10 in flan case (tart pan). Sprinkle with half the sugar. Lay the apricots or peaches on top, domed sides up and as close together as possible. Sprinkle with the remaining sugar and dot with a little of the butter.

Bake for 30 to 40 minutes, by which time the fruit should be cooked and a rich, thick syrup will have formed.

Serve warm.

Chocolate Macaroon Dessert

Chocolate Macaroon Dessert

St Emilion au Chocolat

A very rich dessert, this is for special occasions.

Preparation time: 30 minutes (plus overnight chilling)
Cooking time: nil
To serve: 8 to 10

Metric/Imperial
100 g/4 oz unsalted butter
100 g/4 oz caster sugar
150 ml/¼ pint milk
1 egg yolk
200 g/7 oz bitter or plain eating chocolate
1 batch macaroons (see page 142)
3 tablespoons brandy or Armagnac
Decoration (optional):
150 ml/¼ pint whipped cream
chocolate shavings

American
½ cup unsalted butter
½ cup sugar
⅔ cup milk
1 egg yolk
7 squares (7 oz) semisweet chocolate
1 batch macaroons (see page 142)
3 tablespoons brandy or Armagnac
Decoration (optional):
⅔ cup whipped cream
chocolate shavings

Cream the butter and sugar together until very light and fluffy. Scald the milk, then mix a little of it into the egg yolk, to form a smooth cream. Break up the chocolate and add to the milk remaining in the saucepan. Return to a low heat and stir until the chocolate has completely melted and the mixture is absolutely smooth. Add the egg and stir until smooth. Slowly beat this chocolate cream into the butter and sugar mixture, and beat until the mixture is very light and smooth.

Arrange a layer of macaroons in the bottom of a glass or soufflé dish. Sprinkle with a little brandy or Armagnac. Smooth on a layer of the chocolate cream. Repeat until everything has been used up, ending with macaroons. Leave in the refrigerator overnight to mature. Decorate, if you like, with a layer of whipped cream, sprinkled with chocolate shavings, before serving.

Island Cheese and Honey Pie

Melópitta Nissiótiki

The cheese used in the Greek islands for this pie is Mizithra, an unsalted soft cheese made from ewe's milk, but curd or cottage cheese can be used instead. When baked the filling puffs up, but settles into a more cheesecake-like texture when cold. It makes an unusual and delicious dessert.

Preparation time: 30 minutes
Cooking time: 1 hour in all
Oven temperature: 200°C/400°F, Gas Mark 6, reducing to 180°C/350°F, Gas Mark 4
To serve: 6 to 8

Metric/Imperial
Pastry crust:
150 g/5 oz plain flour
75 g/3 oz butter, in small cubes
1 tablespoon caster sugar
2 to 3 tablespoons cold water
Filling:
225 g/8 oz curd or cottage cheese
75 g/3 oz caster sugar
2 eggs
1½ tablespoons honey
finely grated rind of ½ lemon
¾ teaspoon ground cinnamon

American
Pie crust:
1¼ cups all-purpose flour
6 tablespoons butter, in small cubes
1 tablespoon sugar
about ¼ cup cold water

Filling:
1 cup cottage cheese
6 tablespoons sugar
2 eggs
1½ tablespoons honey
finely grated rind of ½ lemon
¾ teaspoon ground cinnamon

To make the pastry put the flour, butter and sugar into a mixing bowl and rub in with your fingertips until crumbly. Pressing the crumbs together with your hands, add enough cold water to form a firm but pliable dough. Wrap the ball of dough in cling film (plastic wrap) or foil and chill for 30 minutes.

Heat the oven to 200°C/400°F, Gas Mark 6. Roll out the dough on a lightly floured board and use to line a 20 cm/8 inch diameter flan ring (tart pan). Prick the bottom with a fork. Line the pastry case with kitchen foil, pressing it well into the sides, and bake for 10 minutes. Remove the foil carefully and leave the case to cool a little. Reduce the oven temperature to 180°C/350°F, Gas Mark 4.

To make the filling put all the ingredients into a mixing bowl and beat until smoothly combined. Pour the filling into the partially cooked pastry case and bake for 35 to 40 minutes until firm to the touch and slightly puffed up. Serve hot or cold.

Walnut Cake

Kárythopitta

Sweet tooths will adore this nutty, rough-textured cake from Greece, made sticky and gooey with a lemon-flavoured syrup. Serve it with tea or coffee, or as a dessert, and provide pastry forks for eating it.

Preparation time: 30 minutes
Cooking time: 40 to 45 minutes
Oven temperature: 180°C/350°F, Gas Mark 4.
To serve: cuts into 16 pieces

Metric/Imperial
175 g/6 oz plain flour
1½ teaspoons baking powder
100 g/4 oz butter
75 g/3 oz caster sugar
finely grated rind of ½ orange
2 eggs, lightly beaten
75 ml/2½ fl oz milk
50 g/2 oz walnuts, coarsely ground
Syrup:
175 g/6 oz sugar
120 ml/4 fl oz water
2 tablespoons lemon juice

American
1½ cups all-purpose flour
1½ teaspoons baking powder

½ cup butter
6 tablespoons sugar
finely grated rind of ½ orange
2 eggs, lightly beaten
5 tablespoons milk
½ cup coarsely ground walnuts
Syrup:
¾ cup sugar
½ cup water
2 tablespoons lemon juice

Heat the oven. Well grease a 20 x 20 cm/8 x 8 inch baking pan, that is 5 cm/ 2 inches deep.

Sift the flour and baking powder together. Put the butter, sugar and orange rind into a warmed mixing bowl and cream very thoroughly until light and fluffy. Little by little beat in the eggs. With a metal spoon fold in the flour alternately with the milk, adding the walnuts with the last of the flour. Transfer to the prepared pan and spread out evenly. Bake in the centre of the oven for 40 to 45 minutes until firm to the touch.

Meanwhile put the syrup ingredients into a saucepan. Heat gently until the sugar has dissolved, then boil for 5 minutes.

As soon as the cake comes out of the oven spoon the hot syrup evenly over the surface. Leave in the tin until quite cold. Cut into squares or diamonds.

Rice Dessert

Rizóghalo

Forget about the stodgy rice puddings of childhood and enjoy this golden, creamy pudding which the Greeks eat at any hour of the day as well as after meals. Serve it hot or cold in pretty individual dishes. It is especially delicious cold or chilled.

Preparation time: 10 minutes
Cooking time: 1 hour
To serve: 6

Metric/Imperial
300 ml/½ pint water, plus 4 tablespoons
4 tablespoons round-grain rice
900 ml/1½ pints milk, plus 4 tablespoons
1½ tablespoons cornflour
100 g/4 oz sugar
2 egg yolks
1 teaspoon finely grated lemon rind
a little ground cinnamon

American
1½ cups water
¼ cup short-grain rice
2 pints milk
1½ tablespoons cornstarch

Left: Island Cheese and Honey Pie
Centre: Walnut Cake
Right: Rice Dessert

½ cup sugar
2 egg yolks
1 teaspoon finely grated lemon rind
a little ground cinnamon

Bring 300 ml/½ pint (1¼ cups) of the water to the boil in a heavy-based saucepan. Shower in the rice and simmer, covered, for 15 minutes. Add 900 ml/1½ pints (3¾ cups) of the milk, bring back to simmering point and simmer, covered, for 25 minutes longer, stirring occasionally.

Mix the cornflour (cornstarch) smoothly with the remaining water. Stir this and the sugar into the rice and simmer for a further 15 minutes.

Mix the egg yolks with the remaining milk, and off the heat stir into the pudding with the lemon rind. Return to the heat and cook for 2 minutes, stirring continuously. Pour into individual custard cups or small dishes and dust the surface liberally with cinnamon.

145

Above: Walnut and Honey Fudge Tart. Below: Spinach, Apple and Pine Kernel Tart

Walnut and Honey Fudge Tart

Tourte aux Noix et au Miel

Made with the rosemary- and lavender-scented honey of Provence, and the fresh, juicy walnuts of the area, this is a rich but delicately-flavoured dessert. Leave overnight to set.

Preparation time: 1¼ hours
Cooking time: 30 to 40 minutes
Oven temperature: 200°C, 400°F, Gas Mark 6
To serve: 6 to 8

Metric/Imperial
Pastry:
175 g/6 oz plain white flour
pinch of salt
1 tablespoon icing sugar
100 g/4 oz unsalted butter
1 tablespoon iced water

Filling:
275 g/10 oz sugar
150 ml/¼ pint water
225 g/8 oz freshly shelled walnuts
  (about 0.5 kg/1 lb before shelling)
100 g/4 oz unsalted butter
150 ml/¼ pint milk
2 heaped tablespoons honey

American
Pastry:
1½ cups all-purpose flour
pinch of salt
1 tablespoon confectioners' sugar
½ cup unsalted butter
2 to 3 tablespoons iced water
Filling:
1¼ cups sugar
⅔ cup water
½ lb freshly shelled walnuts (about 1 lb
  before shelling)
½ cup unsalted butter
⅔ cup milk
2 heaping tablespoons honey

Make the pastry dough as for the apricot tart (see page 143), but with double the quantity. Prepare the filling while the dough is resting.

Bring the sugar and water to the boil, stirring until the sugar has dissolved. Boil rapidly until the mixture begins to thicken and starts to change colour. As soon as it turns the palest brown, remove from the heat and add the walnuts and butter. Stir well, then add the milk and return to a low heat. Simmer gently for 15 to 20 minutes, or until the mixture becomes quite thick. Remove from the heat and stir in the honey. Leave to cool a little.

Roll out two-thirds of the dough and use to line a 20 cm/8 in flan tin (tart pan). Prick the bottom with a fork. Pour in the filling and spread out evenly. Cover with the remaining dough, seal the edges well and make a pattern of vents in the top. Bake for 30 to 40 minutes, or until the top is lightly browned. Allow to cool a little, then turn out of the pan and leave to cool on a wire rack.

146

Spinach, Apple and Pine Kernel Tart

Tourte de Blettes

A traditional dessert, this *tourte* is always served on feast days in Nice. Odd though the combination may seem, the use of spinach with sweet ingredients has a long and honourable history, and in fact they blend extremely well. If you quail at the use of a savoury cheese, substitute curd (cottage) cheese, at least for the first time of making.

Preparation time: 1¼ hours
Cooking time: 30 to 40 minutes
Oven temperature: 200°C, 400°F, Gas
 Mark 6
To serve: 6 to 8

Metric/Imperial
Pastry:
175 g/6 oz plain white flour
pinch of salt
1 tablespoon icing sugar
100 g/4 oz unsalted butter
1 tablespoon iced water
Filling:
100 g/4 oz raisins
2 tablespoons rum
1 kg/2 lb fresh spinach or Swiss chard or
 0.5 kg/1 lb frozen spinach, cooked,
 thoroughly drained and finely
 chopped
50 g/2 oz pine kernels
75 g/3 oz icing sugar
4 eating apples, peeled and diced
2 tablespoons diced Cheddar or Gouda
 cheese, or curd cheese (see above)
grated rind of 1 lemon
good squeeze of lemon juice
2 eggs, lightly beaten
1 tablespoon icing sugar to decorate

American
Pastry:
1½ cups all-purpose flour
pinch of salt
1 tablespoon confectioners' sugar
½ cup unsalted butter
2 to 3 tablespoons iced water
Filling:
⅔ cup raisins
2 tablespoons rum
2 lb fresh spinach or Swiss chard, or 1 lb
 frozen spinach, cooked, thoroughly
 drained and finely chopped
½ cup pine kernels
¾ cup confectioners' sugar
4 eating apples, peeled and diced
2 tablespoons diced Cheddar or Gouda
 cheese, or cottage cheese (see above)
grated rind of 1 lemon
large squeeze of lemon juice

2 eggs, lightly beaten
1 tablespoon confectioners' sugar to
 decorate

Make the pastry dough as for the apricot tart (see page 143), but with double the quantity. Prepare the filling while the dough is resting.

Leave the raisins to soak in the rum for 10 minutes, then bring gently to the boil and simmer until the liquid has been absorbed.

Drain the spinach again thoroughly after chopping. Put the spinach in a

Palafrugell Market in Gerona, Spain

bowl and blend in all the other filling ingredients.

Roll out two-thirds of the dough and use to line a 25 cm/10 in flan tin (tart pan). Prick the bottom with a fork. Spread in the filling and cover with the remaining dough. Seal the edges well and make a pattern of vents in the top. Bake for 30 to 40 minutes, or until the top is lightly browned. Allow to cool a little, then turn out of the pan and leave to cool on a wire rack.

Serve warm or cold, dredged with icing (confectioners') sugar.

Nut Stuffed Pastry Rolls

Nut Stuffed Pastry Rolls

Plákoundes

Typically Greek, these luscious, nutty, syrup-drenched pastries are not at all difficult to make using ready-made phyllo pastry (see note below). Serve them for dessert, or when friends drop in for coffee. They are sticky so remember to provide pastry forks.

Preparation time: about 40 minutes plus cooling time; (even better made the day before required)
Cooking time: about 25 minutes
Oven temperature: 180°C/350°F, Gas Mark 4
To serve: makes about 18 rolls

Metric/Imperial
about 100 g/4 oz unsalted butter
225 g/8 oz phyllo pastry (about 12 sheets)
Syrup:
100 g/4 oz sugar
150 ml/¼ pint water
1 tablespoon mild honey
1 tablespoon lemon juice
strip of thinly pared lemon rind
Filling:
225 g/8 oz almonds, coarsely ground
2 medium egg yolks, lightly beaten
50 g/2 oz caster sugar
2 teaspoons ground cinnamon
½ teaspoon grated nutmeg

American
about ½ cup unsalted butter
½ lb phyllo pastry (about 12 sheets)
Syrup:
½ cup sugar
⅔ cup water
1 tablespoon mild honey
1 tablespoon lemon juice
strip of thinly pared lemon rind
Filling:
2 cups coarsely ground almonds
2 egg yolks, lightly beaten
¼ cup sugar
2 teaspoons ground cinnamon
½ teaspoon grated nutmeg

Prepare the syrup in advance so that it has time to become cold before using. Simply put all the syrup ingredients into a small saucepan, heat gently until the sugar dissolves, then boil rapidly for 5 minutes. Remove from the heat and leave to become cold and syrupy. Remove the strip of lemon rind when cold.

Prepare the filling by putting all the ingredients into a bowl and mixing together thoroughly.

Heat the oven. Melt the butter and thoroughly grease a shallow baking sheet with some of it.

Lay the phyllo sheets flat, one on top of the other, on a work surface. With a sharp knife cut the longest side into three, making 36 strips roughly 30 x 13 to 5 cm/12 x 5 to 6 inches. Taking two strips at a time, brush them evenly with melted butter and place one strip on top of the other. Put 1 tablespoon of the filling on one end of the doubled strip, fold in the sides to contain the filling and roll the strip down to the other end. Place the roll, join underneath, on the greased baking sheet. Fill and roll all the strips in the same manner and arrange them closely, side by side, on the baking sheet.

Brush the tops with the remaining melted butter and bake in the hottest part of the oven for 25 minutes until crisp and golden. As soon as the pastry rolls are removed from the oven, spoon the cold syrup over them. Leave, covered, on the baking sheet with the syrup until quite cold and ready to serve.

Phyllo Pastry

(Also called *fila*, *yufka*, *brik* and *malsouka* in various parts of the Middle East.)

This pastry is usually bought ready made in Greek stores or pastry shops and consists of paper thin sheets of pastry stacked one on top of another. It is sold in long polythene (plastic) packs containing 225 g/8 oz or 0.5 kg/1 lb of pastry. The number and size of the sheets vary a little from one producer to another, but a 0.5 kg/1 lb pack will contain from 18 to 24 large sheets measuring roughly 30 x 36 to 50 cm/12 x 14 to 20 inches. Fresh phyllo in an unopened polythene (plastic) pack should keep for 5 days in a refrigerator or for several months in a freezer. Before using frozen phyllo thaw it slowly and completely in its wrap, otherwise the delicate sheets will break up. Once removed from its pack, phyllo should be used quickly to prevent the pastry becoming dry and brittle. Promptly rewrap any unused portion in cling film or polythene (plastic wrap).

Sugared Fried Bread Squares

Torrijas or *Picatostes*

These are a popular dessert in Spain and may be flavoured with rum, sherry, or lemon, and made in a variety of ways.

Preparation time: 20 minutes
Cooking time: 10 minutes
To serve: 4

Metric/Imperial/American
*8 thick slices of stale bread, crusts
    removed (not pre-sliced)*
3 eggs, well beaten
2 tablespoons rum or sherry

oil for frying
2 tablespoons sugar

Cut the bread slices in half lengthways. Mix together the beaten eggs and rum or sherry, add the bread and soak for about 10 minutes.

Heat the oil in a frying pan (skillet) and fry the bread squares a few at a time, until crisp and golden on both sides. Drain on paper towels, sprinkle with sugar and serve at once.

Almond Cake

Pastel de Almendras

The Spanish use a lot of eggs in their cakes and desserts, and often use ground almonds to add richness and flavour, a legacy from the Moorish occupation of Spain.

Preparation time: 20 minutes
Cooking time: 45 minutes
Oven temperature: 180°C/350°F, Gas
    Mark 4
To serve: 4

Metric/Imperial
100 g/4 oz butter
200 g/8 oz sugar

3 eggs, beaten
100 g/4 oz flour, sifted
100 g/4 oz blanched almonds, ground
1 tablespoon anise or brandy
Decoration:
whipped cream
a few toasted split blanched almonds

American
½ cup butter
1 cup sugar
3 eggs, beaten
1 cup flour, sifted
1 cup ground blanched almonds
1 tablespoon anise or brandy
Decoration:
whipped cream
a few toasted split blanched almonds

Cream the butter and sugar together until light and fluffy, then gradually add the eggs, beating well between each addition. Fold in the flour and ground almonds and add the anise or brandy. Turn the mixture into a greased and floured deep 20 cm/8 inch cake pan. Put into the oven and bake for about 45 minutes or until a skewer inserted in the centre comes out clean. Turn out on to a rack to cool.

Decorate the top with whipped cream scattered with toasted almonds. This could be served either as a dessert, or for afternoon tea or *merienda*.

Left: Almond Cake. Right: Sugared Fried Bread Squares

Apple Tart

Tarta de Manzana

The best apples in Spain are grown in the northern province of Asturias, from where they are transported to all parts of the country. Choose hard eating apples for this recipe.

Preparation time: 20 minutes (plus 30 minutes chilling dough)
Cooking time: 40 minutes
Oven temperature: 190°C/375°F, Gas Mark 5
To serve: 4

Metric/Imperial
Pastry:
pinch of salt
200 g/8 oz plain flour
50 g/2 oz lard
50 g/2 oz butter
3 to 4 tablespoons chilled water
Filling:
1 kg/2 lb apples, peeled, cored and thinly sliced
100 g/4 oz raisins, soaked in a little sherry
75 g/3 oz sugar
2 teaspoons ground cinnamon
1 teaspoon ground allspice
1 teaspoon ground coriander
knob of butter

American
Pastry:
pinch of salt
2 cups all-purpose flour
¼ cup lard
¼ cup butter
4 to 6 tablespoons chilled water
Filling:
2 lb apples, peeled, cored and thinly sliced
⅔ cup raisins, soaked in a little sherry
6 tablespoons sugar
2 teaspoons ground cinnamon
1 teaspoon ground allspice
1 teaspoon ground coriander
pat of butter

Add the salt to the flour and sift into a bowl and cut the fat into it with a knife until each piece is the size of a small pea. Add the cold water a little at a time and, still using the knife, work into a dough. Bring the dough together very lightly with the fingertips and form into a ball. Wrap in greaseproof (wax) paper and chill for about 30 minutes.

Roll out the dough and use to line a 25 cm/10 inch tart pan. Arrange the slices of apple in a decorative pattern in the pastry case. Scatter with the raisins and a little of the soaking sherry, sprinkle with the sugar and spices and dot with butter. Bake for about 40 minutes or until the pastry is golden. Serve hot or cold.

Gipsy's Arm

Brazo de Gitano

This is a classic cake from Andalucia made in the form of a cream-filled roll, often elaborately decorated with butter icing and sugar flowers.

The filling is usually cream, either real or mock, but you could use a flavoured custard.

Preparation time: about 20 minutes
Cooking time: 15 minutes
Oven temperature: 190°C, 375°F, Gas Mark 5
To serve: 4

Metric/Imperial
4 eggs
150 g/6 oz castor sugar
50 g/2 oz self-raising flour
pinch salt
Filling:
¼ litre/½ pint sweetened whipped cream
Decoration:
75 g/3 oz butter
150 g/6 oz icing sugar, sieved
a few drops fruit flavouring
sugar flowers

American
4 eggs
¾ cup sugar
½ cup all-purpose flour sifted with ½ teaspoon baking powder
pinch salt
Filling:
1¼ cups sweetened whipped cream
Decoration:
⅓ cup butter
1½ cups sifted confectioners' sugar
a few drops fruit flavoring
sugar flowers

Select an oblong baking tin of suitable size and rub it over with butter paper. Dust with flour and tip off surplus.

Thoroughly whisk the eggs and sugar together until light and frothy. Sift flour and salt together, then fold into the eggs and pour this mixture into the prepared tin. Put into the pre-heated hot oven for about 15 minutes.

Turn out on to a sheet of greaseproof paper sprinkled with sugar, cover with another piece of paper and roll up whilst still warm. Allow to cool, then unroll; it should keep its shape reasonably well, which makes it easier to fill.

Spanish confectioners often manage to make the roll into a hollow tube filled with cream, but for home cooking it is easier to spread the filling on to the sponge before rolling it up.

To make the butter icing, cream the butter and icing (confectioners') sugar until well blended. Beat in the flavouring (flavoring) very gradually as required. Use this and the sugar flowers to decorate the cake. Let your imagination run riot!

Rich Chocolate Mousse

Crema de Chocolate Valenciana

This delightful sweet combines dark bitter chocolate with the flavour of Valencian oranges.

Preparation time: about 15 minutes, excluding chilling
Cooking time: 10 minutes
To serve: 4

Metric/Imperial/American
4 eggs, separated
50 g/2 oz (¼ cup) sugar
1 tablespoon flour
4 tablespoons milk
50 g/2 oz (¼ cup) butter, lightly salted
200 g/8 oz (1 cup) dark (semisweet) chocolate pieces
a few drops vanilla essence (extract)
grated rind of one orange (preferably Valencian) plus a little juice
Decoration:
whipped cream
toasted chopped hazelnuts

Put the egg yolks, sugar and sifted flour into a medium-sized saucepan. Blend them together and add the milk. Heat very gently, stirring all the time until the mixture is smooth. Add a little piece of the butter, stirring after each addition.

Remove the saucepan from the heat and add the chocolate, the vanilla essence (extract) and the orange juice and rind. Stir until the chocolate has melted. Whisk the egg whites until light and stiff and fold them into the chocolate mixture, which will have cooled by now. Pour into four glass dishes and chill thoroughly.

Decorate with whipped cream and sprinkle with hazelnuts.

Above right: Apple Tart
Centre: Rich Chocolate Mousse
Below: Gipsy's Arm

Crêpes Suzette

Pancakes (Crêpes) in Liqueur Sauce

Though now a world-famous dessert, this was actually born – by accident, like many of the best inventions – in the Café de Paris, in Monte Carlo. Legend has it that the Prince of Wales came in with a party of friends, and the chef, in his nervousness, set fire to the sauce. This made it especially delicious, and the dish was named after the little girl in the Prince's party.

Preparation time: 20 minutes (plus 2 hours chilling the batter)
Cooking time: 30 minutes
To serve: 6 to 8

Metric/Imperial
Crêpes:
150 g/5 oz plain flour
1 tablespoon icing sugar
2 eggs, beaten
150 ml/¼ pint milk
150 ml/¼ pint water
50 g/2 oz butter, melted
1 tablespoon brandy
oil for frying
Sauce:
4 lumps sugar
3 oranges
juice of 1 lemon
65 g/2½ oz caster sugar
100 g/4 oz butter
2 tablespoons Grand Marnier or orange Curaçao
2 tablespoons brandy

American
Crêpes:
1¼ cups all-purpose flour
1 tablespoon confectioners' sugar
2 eggs, beaten
⅔ cup milk
⅔ cup water
¼ cup butter, melted
1 tablespoon brandy
oil for frying
Sauce:
4 lumps sugar
3 oranges
juice of 1 lemon
5 tablespoons sugar
½ cup butter
2 tablespoons Grand Marnier or orange Curaçao
2 tablespoons brandy

To make the crêpes, sift the flour and sugar together into a bowl, make a well in the centre and add the eggs. Work the flour into the eggs, then slowly stir in the milk and water. Beat until the batter is smooth. Add the melted butter and the brandy, beat well once again, then chill for at least 2 hours.

Make the sauce by rubbing the sugar lumps over 2 of the oranges until they are completely impregnated with the oil from the skins. Peel the rind off the third orange very thinly, and cut it into very fine strips. Put the juice of all the oranges and of the lemon, together with the strips of orange rind, the impregnated sugar lumps, 50 g/2 oz (¼ cup) of the sugar, the butter and orange liqueur into a deep frying pan (skillet) or chafing dish. Bring slowly to the boil, stirring well, and allow to bubble for 1 minute. Keep warm.

Make small crêpes, 20 cm/8 in in diameter, as thin as possible. Dip each one into the sauce on both sides, fold over twice and arrange in a heated serving dish, or on the side of the chafing dish.

Bring the remaining sauce quickly to the boil again and pour over the crêpes, or arrange the crêpes in the centre of the chafing dish. Sprinkle with the remaining sugar. Heat the brandy, pour it over the crêpes and set it alight. Bring the dish flaming to table.

Orange-flower Water Ice Cream

Glace à Fleurs d'Oranges

An exquisitely delicate ice cream, this is flavoured with one of the characteristic scents of Provence.

Preparation time: 10 minutes (plus freezing)
Cooking time: 15 minutes
To serve: 6

Metric/Imperial
6 egg yolks
100 g/4 oz sugar
600 ml/1 pint milk, or mixed milk and single cream
1 vanilla pod
2 to 3 tablespoons orange-flower water
bitter chocolate gratings to decorate

American
6 egg yolks
½ cup sugar
2½ cups milk, or mixed milk and light cream
1 vanilla bean
2 to 3 tablespoons orange-flower water
bitter chocolate gratings to decorate

Beat the egg yolks and sugar together until thick and creamy. Bring the milk, or milk and cream, to the boil with the vanilla pod (bean), remove from the heat and leave to infuse for 5 minutes.

Remove the pod (bean) and bring the milk back to just below boiling point, then pour slowly on to the egg mixture, beating well. Return the custard to the pan and stir over a very low heat (or use a double saucepan) until the mixture begins to thicken and just coats the back of the spoon. Do not allow to boil. Leave to cool. When the custard is quite cold, add the orange-flower water. Taste and add more if necessary (some flavour is lost in freezing). Pour into ice-trays and freeze until firm around the edges. Turn into chilled bowl and beat until smooth. Return to ice trays or ice-cream mould and freeze. Remove the ice cream from the freezer 30 minutes before serving and leave in the refrigerator. Decorate with gratings of bitter chocolate.

Niçois Sabayon

Le Sabayon Niçois

The Niçois have their own version of the Italian *zabaglione*. While the Italians always make theirs with Marsala, the Niçois allow free rein to their imagination, sometimes using the sweet muscatel wines of the Languedoc, sometimes port, Madeira or a mixture of dark rum and water.

Preparation time: 10 minutes
Cooking time: 10 minutes
To serve: 6

Metric/Imperial/American
6 egg yolks
100 g/4 oz (½ cup) sugar
juice and grated rind of 1 lemon
150 ml/¼ pint (⅔ cup) sweet wine or liquor, see above

Beat the egg yolks and sugar together in a heatproof bowl until pale and fluffy. Beat in the lemon rind and juice, then slowly beat in the wine.

Set the bowl over a pan of simmering water, or pour the mixture into a very heavy saucepan (preferably copper), and continue to beat steadily over a moderate heat, until the mixture thickens and becomes creamy. Do not allow to come to the boil or it will curdle.

Pour into individual cups or glasses and serve at room temperature.

Above: Niçois Sabayon
Centre: Orange-flower Water Ice Cream
Below: Crêpes Suzette

Hazelnut Ice Cream

Left: Hazelnut Ice Cream
Centre: Orange Sorbet (Sherbet)
Right: Chilled Zabaione

Gelato alla Nocciola

A creamy custard flavoured with hazelnuts makes one of the simplest and best of homemade ice creams. This one can be made without an ice-cream churn as it needs no whipping during freezing. For family use freeze in individual containers and simply sprinkle with chopped nuts before serving. For special occasions freeze in a 1 litre/1¾ pint (1 quart) mould that can be turned out and decorated with whipped cream, toasted nuts and fresh raspberries.

Preparation time: 20 minutes (plus cooling and freezing)
Cooking time: 20 minutes
Oven temperature: 180°C/350°F, Gas Mark 4
To serve: 6

Metric/Imperial
100 g/4 oz shelled hazelnuts
450 ml/¾ pint milk
5 large egg yolks
100 g/4 oz caster sugar
300 ml/½ pint double cream

American
1 cup shelled hazelnuts
1 pint milk
5 large egg yolks
½ cup sugar
1¼ cups heavy cream

Spread the hazelnuts on a baking sheet and bake for 10 to 12 minutes or until the skins split. Turn the nuts into a rough towel and rub off the loose skins. Pick out the nuts, reserve a few whole for decorating and grind the rest to a powder.

Pour the milk into a saucepan and heat almost to boiling point. Put the egg yolks and sugar into a bowl and beat thoroughly until pale and creamy. Gradually stir in the hot milk followed by the ground nuts. Return the mixture to the cleaned saucepan and heat very gently, stirring constantly, until the custard thickens enough to mask thickly the back of a spoon. Take care not to let the mixture reach boiling point. Remove from the heat, place the covered saucepan in cold water, and leave until cold, stirring the custard now and then.

When the custard is cold whip the cream until thick but not stiff and fold lightly into the custard. Turn into individual containers, cover and freeze until firm.

Before serving transfer the ice cream from the freezer to the refrigerator and allow time for it to soften and mellow, about 1 hour for individual sizes, or 2 hours for a large mould. Roughly chop the reserved nuts and sprinkle a few on each portion before serving.

Orange Sorbet (Sherbet)

Sorbette di Arancia

Orange and lemon groves abound along the coast of Italy, and the vibrant colour and refreshing flavour of these fruits enhance so many savoury and sweet dishes. It is difficult to imagine a prettier sight than hollowed out oranges, filled with sorbet (sherbet), nestling among green grapes on a dish decorated with sprigs of shiny green leaves.

Preparation time: 20 minutes (plus 2 to 3 hours freezing)
Cooking time: 5 minutes
To serve: 6

Metric/Imperial/American
300 ml/½ pint less 3 tablespoons water (1 cup water)
175 g/6 oz (¾ cup) granulated sugar
thinly pared rind of 1 orange
6 large juicy oranges
3 tablespoons lemon juice
2 egg whites
Decoration:
bunches of green grapes
sprigs of small shiny green leaves

Put the water and sugar into a small saucepan and heat gently, stirring until the sugar has dissolved. Add the orange rind and boil for 3 minutes. Set aside until cold.

Meanwhile, cut off the top of each orange and reserve. Scoop out the flesh, taking care not to pierce the skin 'case'. Put the cases in the refrigerator to chill. Squeeze the flesh to extract the juice. Add the orange and lemon juice to the cold syrup and mix well. Strain into a shallow ice tray, cover with foil and freeze.

Make the final preparations when the ice is lightly frozen but not solid. Have everything ready so that you can work quickly. Beat the egg whites until firm but not dry. Turn the ice into another bowl and beat for a minute or so until a semi-frozen mush. With a metal spoon gently but thoroughly fold in the egg whites, then immediately spoon the mixture into the chilled orange cases. Replace the tops and quickly return to the freezer. Freeze until frozen solid. If not required the same day slip the oranges into a freezer bag for freezer storage.

Remove the oranges to the refrigerator about 1 hour before required, to allow the ice to soften and mellow. Serve on individual plates, or arrange as suggested in the introduction.

Chilled Zabaione

Biscuit allo Zabaione

The luxurious foam which results from beating egg yolks, sugar and Marsala over hot water is often served warm and straight from the stove, but this iced version of the famous Italian sweet is much simpler for the cook-hostess because it can be prepared ahead and refrigerated. Serve with light sponge finger biscuits (ladyfingers).

Preparation time: 10 minutes (plus 2 to 3 hours cooling and chilling)
Cooking time: 5 to 8 minutes
To serve: 4 to 6

Metric/Imperial
3 egg yolks
75 g/3 oz caster sugar
6 tablespoons Marsala
1 egg white
200 ml/⅓ pint whipping cream
a little grated plain chocolate to decorate

American
3 egg yolks
6 tablespoons sugar
6 tablespoons Marsala
1 egg white
1 cup whipping cream
a little grated semisweet chocolate to decorate

Beat the egg yolks and sugar together in a large heatproof mixing bowl, then beat in the Marsala. Rest the bowl over a saucepan of near boiling water, taking care that the bowl does not touch the water. Beat continuously and vigorously until the mixture increases in volume and becomes thick enough to hold soft peaks. This will take from 5 to 8 minutes. When this stage is reached, immediately remove the bowl from the heat and continue beating intermittently until the mixture is quite cold.

Beat the egg white to a firm foam. In a separate bowl, whip the cream until thick but not stiff. Very gently and lightly fold first the cream and then the egg white into the cold Marsala custard. When evenly blended spoon into tall glasses or custard cups and chill in the refrigerator for 1 to 2 hours or longer. Sprinkle the tops with a little coarsely grated chocolate just before serving.

Index

Almond
  Almond Cake 149
  Braised Potatoes with Almonds 127
  Chicken in Almond Sauce 102
  Cold Almond and Grape Soup 32
  Toasted Almonds 20
Anchovies
  Anchovy and Potato Salad 39
  Anchovy Spread 14
  Chicken in Anchovy and Olive
    Sauce 95
  Lamb with Anchovy and Garlic 76
  Neapolitan Cheese and Anchovy
    Toasts 16
  Onion, Anchovy and Olive Tart 115
  Tuna, Egg and Anchovy Salad 37
Andalucian Dishes
  Eggs Flamenca 110
  Gazpacho 32
  Kidneys in Sherry Sauce 69
  Melon and Ham 20
Antipasto of Peppers and Tomatoes 130
Appetizers
  Chicken Croquettes 18
  Cracked Wheat Salad 41
  Crudités, Les, 13
  Cucumber in Yogurt 25
  Egg Nests 20
  Fried Whitebait 18
  Eggs with Tuna Fish Mayonnaise 16
  Jumbo Shrimp Fries 18
  Lemon Mushroom Hors d'Oeuvre 13
  Melon and Ham 20
  Miniature Meat Balls 24
  Mussels Taranto-Style 28
  Neapolitan Cauliflower Salad 38
  Neapolitan Cheese and Anchovy
    Toasts 16
  Piquant Artichokes 12
  Poached Eggs with Yogurt 26
  Pork Terrine 17
  Ragoût of Peppers and Tomatoes 112
  Stuffed Tomato Salad 38
  Stuffed Vine Leaves 34
  Taramosalata 27
  Tuna, Egg and Anchovy Salad 37
Apples
  Apple Tart 150
  Spinach, Apple and Pine Kernel
    Tart 147
Apricots
  Apricot Cream 140
  Apricot Tart 143
Arcadian Baked Fish 56
Artichokes
  Jerusalem Artichokes with
    Tomatoes 128
  Piquant Artichokes 12
  Stuffed Artichokes 121
Aubergine (Eggplant), Cheese and
  Tomato Casserole 119 *see also*

Eggplant
Avocado Purée 22

Balearic Pizza 116
  Basil, Cheese and Nut Sauce 134
  Bass, Stuffed 44
  Beans, Casserole of, with Pork and
    Lamb 76

Beef
  Baked Vegetables with Beef 113
  Beef Baked with Capers 71
  Beef and Potato Casserole 64
  Boeuf en Daube Niçoise 62
  Boeuf en Daube Provençale 62
  Boiled Beef with Lamb and
    Vegetables 72
  Braised Beef with Pomegranate 68
  Casserole of Beef with Wine and
    Herbs 62
  Marinated Beef with Wine and
    Olives 62
  Pot-au-feu Provençal 72
  Winter Casserole 64
Black Eyed Beans, Spinach with, 124
  Bouillabaisse 46
  Bream, Baked Mediterranean, 50

Cakes
  Almond Cake 149
  Gipsy's Arm 150
  Walnut Cake 144
Capers
  Beef Baked with Capers 71
  Caper and Olive Dip 14
  Pork with Sage and Capers 80
Caramel Custard 140
Casseroles
  Beef and Potato Casserole 64
  Boeuf en Daube Niçoise 62
  Boeuf en Daube Provençale 62
  Casserole of Beans with Pork and
    Lamb 76
  Casserole of Beef with Wine and
    Herbs 62
  Casserole of Fresh Sardines 50
  Daube D'Avignon 70
  Eggplant, Cheese and Tomato
    Casserole 119
  Lamb and Vegetable Casserole 70
  Marinated Beef with Wine and
    Olives 62
  Veal Casserole 66
  Winter Casserole 64
Cassoulet de Toulouse 76
  Catalan Vegetable Soup 30
  Cauliflower Salad, Neapolitan, 38
  Caviare, Countryman's, 14
  Celery, Pork with, 78
Cheese Dishes
  Basil, Cheese and Nut Sauce 134
  Cheese Triangles 24
  Eggplant, Cheese and Tomato
    Casserole 119
  Neapolitan Cheese and Anchovy
    Toasts 16
  Spinach and Cheese Pie 118

Chestnuts
  Chestnut Charlotte 139
  Fresh Chestnut Dessert 138
  Mont Blanc 138
  Chick Peas, Chicken with, 99; *see
    also* Falafel, Humus
Chicken Dishes
  Braised Chicken Pieces with
    Peppers 104
  Chicken in Almond Sauce 102
  Chicken in Anchovy and Olive
    Sauce 95
  Chicken Served in Bread 101
  Chicken with Chick Peas 99
  Chicken Croquettes 18
  Chicken Cooked with Dried Fruit 100
  Chicken Grilled Over Charcoal 98
  Chicken Liver Sauce 135
  Chicken with Peppers, Tomatoes and
    Olives 94
  Chicken Pie 100
  Chicken in Tomato with Noodles 96
  Chicken with Yogurt 96
  Circassian Chicken 98
  Garlic Chicken 94
  Paella 52
  'Ragged Egg' Chicken Soup 29
Chocolate
  Chocolate Macaroon Dessert 143
  Rich Chocolate Mousse 150
  Circassian Chicken 98
  Cod, Salt, with Garlic Sauce 56
  Compôte, Fruit, 138
Courgettes (Zucchini)
  Courgette Soup 28
  Courgettes with Herbs 126
  Couscous with a Lamb Stew 88
Cracked Wheat
  Cracked Wheat Baked with Meat 90
  Cracked Wheat Salad 41
  Crêpes Suzette 152
  Crudités, Les, 13
  Cucumber in Yogurt 25

Desserts
  Almond Cake 149
  Apple Tart 150
  Apricot Cream 140
  Apricot 143
  Baked Fresh Peaches 140
  Caramel Custard 140
  Chestnut Charlotte 139
  Chilled Zabaione 155
  Chocolate Macaroon Dessert 143
  Crêpes Suzette 152
  Dried Fried Salad 140
  Fresh Chestnut Dessert 138
  Fruit Compôte 138
  Gipsy's Arm 150
  Hazelnut Ice Cream 154
  Island Cheese and Honey Pie 144
  Macaroons 142
  Mont Blanc 138
  Niçois Sabayon 152
  Nut Stuffed Pastry Rolls 148
  Orange Sorbet 154
  Orange-flower Water Ice Cream 152

Rice Dessert 145
Rich Chocolate Mousse 150
Sherbet 154
Sugared Fried Bread Squares 149
Walnut and Honey Fudge Tart 146
Dolmathes 34
Duck with Olives 106

Eggplants *see also* **Aubergines**
Baked Eggplants 128
Eggplant, Cheese and Tomato
Casserole 119
Roast Eggplants 128
Eggs
Eggs Flamenca 110
Egg and Lemon Soup 26
Egg Nests 20
Eggs with Tuna Fish Mayonnaise 17
Meat Balls with Egg and Lemon
Sauce 78
Poached Eggs With Yogurt 26
Tuna, Egg and Anchovy Salad 37

Falafel 23
Fennel
Braised Fennel 130
Fennel, Orange and Walnut Salad 36
Fennel Salad 39
Fish with Fennel 44
Roast Pork with Fennel 81
Fettuccine *see* Noodles
Fish Dishes *see also* **Anchovies** *etc*
Anchovy and Potato Salad 39
Anchovy Spread 14
Arcadian Baked Fish 56
Baked Fish with Ratatouille 44
Baked Mediterranean Bream 50
Bouillabaisse 46
Casserole of Fresh Sardines 50
Eggs with Tuna Fish Mayonnaise 17
Fish with Fennel 44
Fish with Rice 54
Fish Salad 54
Fish Sticks 55
Fried Whitebait 18
Hake with Spinach 58
Jumbo Shrimp Fries 18
Lobster, Fish and Vegetable Salad 59
Mackerel in Paper Cases 58
Mallorcan Fish Soup 30
Mediterranean Fish Stew 46
Mussels Taranto-Style 28
Octopus, Stewed, 49
Paella 52
Red Mullet 50
Salt Cod with Garlic Sauce 56
Seafood Pizza 117
Vermicelli with Clams and
Mussels 53
Zarzuela de Pescados 48
French Dishes *see also* **Niçois** *and*
Provençal Dishes
Apricot Tart 143
Baked Eggplants (Aubergines) 128
Bouillabaisse 46
Braised Fennel 130
Braised Potatoes with Almonds 127

Casserole of Beans with Pork and
Lamb 76
Chestnut Charlotte 139
Chocolate Macaroon Dessert 143
Crêpes Suzette 152
Fennel, Orange and Walnut Salad 36
Fish with Fennel 44
Fresh Chestnut Dessert 138
Macaroons 142
Mediterranean Fish Stew 46
Mont Blanc 138
Montpelier Butter 133
Pork with Sage and Capers 80
Pork Terrine 17
Ragoût of Peppers and Tomatoes 112
Roast Eggplants (Aubergines) 128
Salad with Croûtons and Walnut
Oil 36
Tomato Salad 37
Fruit *see also* **Apples** *etc*
Chicken Cooked with Dried Fruit 100
Dried Fruit Salad 140
Fruit Compôte 138

Garlic
Fried Lamb with Garlic 72
Garlic Chicken 94
Garlic Mayonnaise 133
Garlic Sauce 56
Garlic Soup 33
Hot Pepper and Garlic Sauce 132
Lamb with Anchovy and Garlic 76
Salt Cod with Garlic Sauce 56
Gazpacho 32
Genoese Dishes
Basil, Cheese and Nut Sauce 134
Lobster, Fish and Vegetable Salad 59
Grapes
Cold Almond and Grape Soup 32
Greek Dishes
Beef and Potato Casserole 64
Cheese Triangles 24
Chicken in Tomato with Noodles 96
Chicken with Yogurt 96
Cucumber in Yogurt 25
Dolmathes 34
Egg and Lemon Soup 27
Garlic Sauce 56
Greek Summer Salad 35
Island Cheese and Honey Pie 144
Lamb on Skewers 75
Meat Balls with Egg and Lemon
Sauce 78
Miniature Meat Balls 24
Mousaka 74
Nut Stuffed Pastry Rolls 148
Pork with Celery 78
Potato Patties 118
Rice Dessert 145
Roast Stuffed Turkey 102
Salt Cod with Garlic Sauce 56
Spinach and Cheese Pie 118
Stuffed Peppers 122
Stuffed Vine Leaves 34
Taramosalata 27
Tomato Pilaf 123
Walnut Cake 144

Winter Casserole 64
Greek Summer Salad 35
Green Sauce 132
Gipsy's Arm 150

Hake with Spinach 58
Ham, Melon and, 20
Hazelnut Ice Cream 154
Herbs *see* **Basil** *etc*
Honey
Island Cheese and Honey Pie 144
Hot Red Sauce 132
Humus bi Tahina 22

Italian Dishes *see also* **Neapolitan** *and*
Genoese Dishes
Anchovy and Potato Salad 39
Antipasto of Peppers and
Tomatoes 130
Braised Chicken Pieces with
Peppers 104
Casserole of Veal 66
Chicken Liver Sauce 135
Chilled Zabaione 155
Courgette (Zucchini) Soup 28
Duck with Olives 106
Eggs with Tuna Fish Mayonnaise 17
Eggplant, Cheese and Tomato
Casserole 119
Family Style Meat Loaf 82
Fennel Salad 39
Fried Lamb Chops with Piquant
Dressing 66
Hazelnut Ice Cream 154
Macaroni with Meat Sauce 114
Mackerel in Paper Cases 58
Meat Sauce 114, 134
Mussels Taranto-Style 28
Onion, Anchovy and Olive Tart 115
Orange Sorbet (Sherbet) 154
Potato and Salami Pie 84
Rabbit Stewed in Roman Style 107
'Ragged Egg' Chicken Soup 29
Ribbon Noodles Capri Style 107
Roman Pizza 117
Seafood Pizza 117
Sicilian Pizza 117
Stuffed Meat Roll 83
Stuffed Mushrooms 131
Stuffed Rice Balls 85
Stuffed Tomato Salad 38
Stuffed Veal Rolls with Peas 82
Tomato Sauce 135
Tunisian Meat Pie 86
Turkey Breasts with Marsala 104
Wild Pigeons Braised with
Vegetables 106

Jerusalem Artichokes with Tomatoes 128

Kebabs, Ground Meat, 87
Kidneys in Sherry Sauce 69

Lamb
Boiled Beef with Lamb and
Vegetables 72
Casserole of Beans with Pork and

Lamb 76
Couscous with a Lamb Stew 88
Fried Lamb with Garlic 72
Fried Lamb Chops with Piquant
    Dressing 66
Lamb with Anchovy and Garlic 76
Lamb Pilaf 89
Lamb and Rice Patties 86
Lamb on Skewers 75
Lamb and Vegetable Casserole 70
Lemon
Egg and Lemon Soup 26
Lemon Mushroom Hors d'Oeuvre 13
Meat Balls with Egg and Lemon
    Sauce 78
Lentils
Brown Lentils with Noodles 124
Lentil Soup with Vermicelli 33
Lobster, Fish and Vegetable Salad 59

Macaroni with Meat Sauce 114
Macaroons 142
Chocolate Macaroon Dessert 143
Mackerel in Paper Cases 58
Mallorcan Fish Soup 30
Mayonnaise, Garlic, 133
Meat Dishes *see also* **Beef** *etc*
Family Style Meat Loaf 82
Meat Balls with Egg and Lemon
    Sauce 78
Meat Balls, Miniature, 24
Meat Omelette 112
Meat Sauce 134
Mousaka 74
Rice with Meat and Nuts 91
Stuffed Meat Roll 83
Tunisian Meat Pie 86
Mediterranean Fish Stew 46
Melon and Ham 20
Middle Eastern Dishes
Apricot Cream 140
Avocado Purée 22
Brown Lentils with Noodles 124
Chicken Served in Bread 101
Chicken with Chick Peas 99
Chicken Cooked with Dried Fruit 100
Chicken Grilled over Charcoal 98
Chicken Pie 100
Circassian Chicken 98
Couscous with a Lamb Stew 88
Cracked Wheat Baked with Meat 90
Cracked Wheat Salad 41
Falafel 23
Fish with Rice 54
Fish Salad 54
Fish Sticks 55
Ground Meat Kebabs 87
Humus bi Tahina 22
Lamb Pilaf 89
Lamb and Rice Patties 86
Lentil Soup with Vermicelli 33
Orange Salad 40
Poached Eggs with Yogurt 26
Rice with Meat and Nuts 91
Rice with Vermicelli 124
Spinach with Black-Eyed Beans 124
Sweet and Sour Salad 40

Tomato and Pepper Salad 40
Yogurt Cream Cheese 26
Mont Blanc 138
Montpelier Butter 133
Mousaka 74
Mullet, Red, 50
Mushrooms
Lemon Mushroom Hors d'Oeuvre 13
Stuffed Mushrooms 131
Mussels
Mussels Taranto-style 28
Vermicelli with Clams and
    Mussels 53

Neapolitan Dishes
Neapolitan Cauliflower Salad 38
Neapolitan Cheese and Anchovy
    Toasts 17
Neapolitan Pizza 116
Vermicelli with Clams and
    Mussels 53
Niçois Dishes
Beef Baked with Capers 71
Boeuf en Daube Niçoise 62
Chicken with Peppers, Tomatoes and
    Olives 94
Lemon Mushroom Hors d'Oeuvre 13
Marinated Beef with Wine and
    Olives 62
Niçois Sabayon 152
Spinach, Apple and Pine Kernel
    Tart 147
Spinach with Pine Kernels 126
Stuffed Bass 44
Tuna, Egg and Anchovy Salad 37
Noodles, Capri Style, Ribbon, 84
Nuts *see also* **Almonds** *etc*
Almond Cake 149
Basil, Cheese and Nut Sauce 134
Braised Potatoes with Almonds 127
Chestnut Charlotte 139
Chicken in Almond Sauce 102
Cold Almond and Grape Soup 32
Fennel, Orange and Walnut Salad 36
Fresh Chestnut Dessert 138
Hazelnut Ice Cream 154
Mont Blanc 138
Nut Stuffed Pastry Rolls 148
Rice with Meat and Nuts 91
Toasted Almonds 20
Walnut Cake 144
Walnut and Honey Fudge Tart 146

Octopus, Stewed, 49
Offal *see* **Kidneys** *etc*
Omelettes
Meat Omelette 112
Spanish Potato Omelette 110
Olives
Caper and Olive Dip 14
Chicken in Anchovy and Olive
    Sauce 95
Chicken with Peppers, Tomatoes and
    Olives 94
Duck with Olives 106
Marinated Beef with Wine and
    Olives 62

Onion, Anchovy and Olive Tart 115
Orange
Fennel, Orange and Walnut Salad 36
Orange Salad 40
Orange Sorbet 154
Orange-flower Water Ice Cream 152

Paella 52
Pancakes *see* **Crêpes**
Party Snacks
Anchovy Spread 14
Avocado Purée 22
Caper and Olive Dip 14
Cheese Triangles 24
Countryman's Caviare 14
Falafel 23
Humus bi Tahina 22
Neapolitan Cheese and Anchovy
    Toasts 16
Provençal Sandwich 14
Toasted Almonds 20
Yogurt Cream Cheese 26
Pasta *see also* **Macaroni** *etc*
Brown Lentils with Noodles 96
Chicken in Tomato with Noodles 96
Lentil Soup with Vermicelli 33
Macaroni with Meat Sauce 114
Ribbon Noodles Capri Style 84
Rice with Vermicelli 124
Vermicelli with Clams and
    Mussels 53
Peaches, Baked Fresh, 140
Peppers
Antipasto of Peppers and
    Tomatoes 130
Braised Chicken Pieces with
    Peppers 104
Chicken with Peppers, Tomatoes and
    Olives 94
Hot Pepper and Garlic Sauce 132
Ragoût of Peppers and Tomatoes 112
Stuffed Peppers 122
Tomato and Pepper Salad 40
Pies
Chicken Pie 100
Island Cheese and Honey Pie 144
Minced Meat and Vegetable Pie 74
Potato and Salami Pie 84
Spinach and Cheese Pie 118
Tunisian Meat Pie 86
Pigeons, Wild, Braised with
    Vegetables 106
Pine Kernels
Spinach, Apple and Pine Kernel
    Tart 147
Spinach with Pine Kernels 126
Pipérade 112
Pizzas 116
Pomegranate, Braised Beef with, 68
Pork
Casserole of Beans with Pork and
    Lamb 76
Cassoulet de Toulouse 76
Pork with Celery 78
Pork with Eggplants (Aubergines) 79
Pork with Sage and Capers 80
Pork Terrine 17

Provençal Roast Pork 81
Roast Pork with Fennel 81
Potatoes
Anchovy and Potato Salad 39
Beef and Potato Casserole 64
Braised Potatoes with Almonds 127
Potatoes Baked with Herbs and
Oil 130
Potato Patties 118
Potato and Salami Pie 84
Pot-au-feu Provençal 72
Provençal Dishes
Baked Fish with Ratatouille 44
Boeuf en Daube Provençale 62
Caper and Olive Dip 14
Casserole of Beef with Wine and
Herbs 62
Chicken in Anchovy and Olive
Sauce 95
Countryman's Caviare 14
Courgettes (Zucchini) with
Herbs 126
Fruit Compôte 138
Garlic Chicken 94
Hot Pepper and Garlic Sauce 132
Jerusalem Artichokes with
Tomatoes 128
Lamb with Anchovy and Garlic 76
Lamb with Orange and Olives 70
Lamb and Vegetable Casserole 70
Orange-flower Water Ice Cream 152
Piquant Artichokes 12
Potatoes Baked with Herbs and
Oil 130
Pot-au-Feu Provençal 72
Provençal Gratin 114
Provençal Roast Pork 81
Provençal Sandwich 14
Ratatouille 127
Roast Pork with Fennel 81
Stuffed Artichokes 121
Stuffed Provençal Vegetables 120
Stuffed Tomatoes 129
Walnut and Honey Fudge Tart 146
Prawns see Jumbo Shrimp Fries 18

Quails, Roast, 105

Rabbit Stewed in Roman Style 107
'Ragged Egg' Chicken Soup 29
Ragoût of Peppers and Tomatoes 112
Ratatouille 44, 127
Red Sauce, Hot, 132
Rice Dishes
Fish with Rice 54
Paella 52
Rice Dessert 145
Rice with Meat and Nuts 91
Rice with Vermicelli 124
Stuffed Rice Balls 85
Stuffed Tomato Salad 38
Stuffed Vine Leaves 34
Tomato Pilaf 123
Roman Pizza 117

Sage
Pork with Sage and Capers 80

Salads
Anchovy and Potato Salad 39
Cracked Wheat Salad 41
Crudités, Les, 13
Fennel Salad 39
Fennel, Orange and Walnut Salad 36
Fish Salad 54
Greek Summer Salad 35
Lobster, Fish and Vegetable Salad 59
Neapolitan Cauliflower Salad 38
Niçoise Salad 37
Orange Salad 40
Salad with Croûtons and Walnut
Oil 36
Stuffed Tomato Salad 38
Sweet and Sour Salad 40
Tomato Salad 37
Tomato and Pepper Salad 40
Tuna, Egg and Anchovy Salad 37
Salami
Potato and Salami Pie 84
Salt Cod with Garlic Sauce 56
Sardines, Casserole of Fresh 50
Sauces
Basil, Cheese and Nut Sauce 134
Chicken Liver Sauce 135
Egg and Lemon Sauce 78
Garlic Mayonnaise 133
Garlic Sauce 56
Green Sauce 132
Hot Pepper and Garlic Sauce 132
Hot Red Sauce 132
Meat Sauce 114, 134
Sherry Sauce 69
Tomato Sauce 135
Seafood Pizza 117
Shrimp Fries, Jumbo, 18
Sherbet 154
Sicilian pizza 117
Sorbet, Orange, 154
Soups
Bouillabaisse 46
Catalan Vegetable Soup 30
Cold Almond and Grape Soup 32
Courgette (Zucchini) Soup 28
Egg and Lemon Soup 26
Garlic Soup 33
Gazpacho 32
Lentil Soup with Vermicelli 33
Mallorcan Fish Soup 30
'Ragged Egg' Chicken Soup 29
Spanish Dishes see also **Andalucian
Dishes**
Almond Cake 149
Apple Tart 150
Baked Fresh Peaches 140
Baked Mediterranean Bream 50
Baked Vegetables with Beef 113
Balearic Pizza 116
Braised Beef with Pomegranate 68
Caramel Custard 140
Casserole of Fresh Sardines 50
Catalan Vegetable Soup 30
Chicken in Almond Sauce 102
Chicken Croquettes 18
Cold Almond and Grape Soup 32
Egg Nests 20

Eggplant, Cheese and Tomato
Casserole 119
Fried Lamb with Garlic 72
Fried Whitebait 18
Garlic Mayonnaise 133
Garlic Soup 33
Green Sauce 132
Gipsy's Arm 150
Hake with Spinach 58
Hot Red Sauce 132
Jumbo Shrimp Fries 18
Mallorcan Fish Soup 30
Meat Omelette 112
Pork with Eggplants (Aubergines) 79
Paella 52
Quails, Roast, 105
Rich Chocolate Mousse 150
Spanish Potato Omelette 110
Stewed Octopus 49
Sugared Fried Bread Squares 149
Sweetbreads with Marsala and
Sage 67
Toasted Almonds 20
Tongue with Sauce 68
Zarzuela de Pescados 48
Spinach
Hake with Spinach 58
Spinach, Apple and Pine Kernel
Tart 147
Spinach with Black-Eyed Beans 124
Spinach and Cheese Pie 118
Spinach and Pine Kernels 126
Sugared Fried Bread Squares 149
Sweet and Sour Salad 40
Sweetbreads with Marsala and
Sage 67

Taramosalata 27
Tarts
Apple Tart 150
Apricot Tart 143
Onion, Anchovy and Olive Tart 115
Spinach, Apple and Pine Kernel
Tart 147
Walnut and Honey Fudge Tart 146
Terrine, Pork 16
Tomato
Chicken with Peppers, Tomatoes and
Olives 94
Chicken in Tomato with Noodles 96
Eggplant, Cheese and Tomato
Casserole 119
Jerusalem Artichokes with
Tomatoes 128
Ragoût of Peppers and
Tomatoes 112
Stuffed Tomatoes 129
Stuffed Tomato Salad 38
Tomato and Pepper Salad 40
Tomato Pilaf 123
Tomato Salad 37
Tomato Sauce 135
Tongue with Sauce 68
Tuna
Eggs with Tuna Fish Mayonnaise 17
Tuna, Egg and Anchovy Salad 37
Tunisian Meat Pie 86

Turkey
Roast Stuffed Turkey 102
Turkey Breasts with Marsala 104

Veal
Casserole of Veal 66
Stuffed Veal Rolls with Peas 82
Winter Casserole 64

Vegetable Dishes
Antipasto of Peppers and
Tomatoes 130
Baked Eggplants (Aubergines) 128
Braised Fennel 130
Braised Potatoes with Almonds 127
Courgettes (Zucchini) with
Herbs 126
Crudités, Les, 13
Eggplant, Cheese and Tomato
Casserole 119
Jerusalem Artichokes with
Tomatoes 128
Piquant Artichokes 12
Potatoes Baked with Herbs and
Oil 130
Potato Patties 118
Provençal Gratin 114
Ragoût of Peppers and Tomatoes 112
Ratatouille 44, 127
Roast Eggplants (Aubergines) 128
Spinach with Black-Eyed Beans 124
Spinach with Pine Kernels 126
Stuffed Artichokes 121
Stuffed Mushrooms 131
Stuffed Peppers 122
Stuffed Tomatoes 129
Stuffed Tomato Salad 38
Stuffed Vegetables Provençal 120
Tomato Pilaf 123

Vermicelli
Lentil Soup with Vermicelli 33
Rice with Vermicelli 124
Vermicelli with Clams and
Mussels 53
Vine Leaves, Stuffed, 34

Walnuts
Fennel, Orange and Walnut Salad 36
Walnut Cake 144
Walnut and Honey Fudge Tart 146

Wine
Casserole of Beef with Wine and
Herbs 62
Marinated Beef with Wine and
Olives 62
Whitebait, Fried 18
Winter Casserole 64

Yogurt
Chicken with Yogurt 96
Cucumber in Yogurt 25
Poached Eggs with Yogurt 26
Yogurt Cream Cheese 26

Zabaione, Chilled 155
Zarzuela de Pescados 48
Zucchini *see* Courgettes

Acknowledgments

All photography by PAUL KEMP except for:

12-13, 77, 120-121, 126-127, 146, 153
Robert Golden; endpapers, 18, 70
(below) Robert Estall; 9, 64, 110, 160
Stephanie Colasanti; 53 (right) Zefa
(K. Heydemann Müller); 96, 147
Picturepoint; 14 Peter Montagnon; 34
(right) Witold Kay-Korzeniewicz

*The publishers would like to thank the
following companies for the loan of
accessories for photography:*
Craftsmen Potters Association;
Elizabeth David Ltd; Imports from
Tuscany; Leon Jaeggi & Sons Ltd.

Designed by Wensley Bown, Chesham